THE INTIMATE UNIVERSITY

DUKE UNIVERSITY PRESS DURHAM & LONDON 2009

THE INTIMATE UNIVERSITY

KOREAN AMERICAN STUDENTS *and the* PROBLEMS *of* SEGREGATION

Nancy Abelmann

© 2009

Duke University Press

All rights reserved

Printed in the United States of America

on acid-free paper ∞

Designed by Katy Clove

Typeset in Scala by Keystone Typesetting, Inc.

Library of Congress Cataloging-in-Publication

Data appear on the last printed page of this book.

For my sister Ruth
And in memory of Tamie Murakami

CONTENTS

ACKNOWLEDGMENTS

Thanks to my remarkable writing partner and friend Catherine Prendergast, this book is my shortest. Cathy, how did I ever write without you?

But I have been helped along the way by far too many people for these acknowledgments to be short.

My deepest gratitude goes to those of you who appear as pseudonyms in this book, and to many of you who shared your experiences but did not make it into these pages. You made time in college to talk to me, a harried professor; you were generous, open, and interesting and brought (sometimes weekly) accounts of revelation and transformation. You introduced me to your parents, relatives, and friends. To Mary, Owen, and Tony in particular, thank you. Matt Malooly, Audrey Suh, and Na-Young Kim, you really got me started—many thanks.

What can I say to the many who gave me the gift of research assistance? Thank you so much Steve Gump, Hye-young Jo, Jiyeon Kang, Grace Kim, Hyunhee Kim, Shanshan Lan, Roswell Quinn, Steven Vaughan, and Katharine L. Wiegele. Hyunhee, Shanshan, and Steve, you made important contributions to this book's arguments, analysis, and reference material; Katie, you are deservedly named in this book for the contributions you made to chapter 2; and Jiyeon, you were there to help in the final stretch. Coryn Shiflet, many thanks for the map and kinship chart and Jan Williams for the index. Hyunhee Kim, Hye-young Jo, Judi Smith, and Nancy Sarabi, your painstaking transcriptions are at the heart of this book.

In addition to Cathy, a handful of you read this book in full. What generosity. Thank you, Steve Gump, Shanshan Lan, Keith Osajima, and Eun Hui (Emily) Ryo. Eun Hui, you have gone through every book of mine and the grant application that began this project as well! Others of you were kind enough to read a piece. Thank you, Bill Kelleher, Hyunhee Kim, Noriko Muraki, Kent Ono, Andrew Orta, So Jin Park, Junaid Rana, and Sumie Okazaki.

This book, long in coming, inspired and grew up with another project, the Ethnography of the University Initiative (EUI). The EUIers made a profound impact on the ways I have come to see the university. My heartfelt thanks to all of you: Mark Aber, Timothy R. Cain, Bill Kelleher, Gina Hunter, David McDonald, Tim McDonough, Peter L. Mortensen, Catherine Prendergast, Teresa Ramos, and Gardner Rogers. The book has a second sibling project with Sumie Okazaki on Korean American teens and parents in the Chicago area (and a related survey and interviews with college students). Thank you, Sumie and our wonderful research teams, Grace Chung, Jin-Heon Jung, Noriel E. Lim, Hyeyoung Kang, Euna Oh, Chu Kim-Prieto, and Angela Wiley. Yet another project took root in the final days of this one and has helped me to think about important changes in Korean America; thank you, Soo Ah Kwon, Adrienne Lo, and Sumie Okazaki for our discussions about the so-called early study abroad of South Korean young people.

Many other colleagues at the university continue to inspire and help me. Thank you, Edward Bruner, Clark Cunningham, Ramona Curry, David Goodman, Karen Kelsky, Jungwon Kim, Viveka Kudaligama, Sharon S. Lee, Steven Leigh, Alejandro Lugo, Martin Manalansan, Peggy Miller, Ellen Moody, Andrew Orta, and Ronald Toby. Clark, your early contributions to this book are well remembered. My students (some former) simply make my life better and more interesting and inspire me to keep at it. Thank you, Marsha Brofka, Seun Ju Chae, John Cho, Hee Jung Choi, Thomas Denberg, Ida Fadzillah, Richard Freeman, Hye-young Jo, Jinheon Jung, Yoonjung Kang, Chung-kang Kim, Hyunhee Kim, Kyungsook Kim, C. Richard King, Shanshan Lan, Soo Jung Lee, Sangsook Lee-Chung, Wei Li, Soo Kyung Lim, Noriko Muraki, So Jin Park, Teresa Ramos, Jesook Song, Josie Sohn, and Han-Sun Yang.

This book has been touched by many (I was stunned to review just *how* many) kind and critical audiences at Columbia University, Illinois Wesleyan University, Indiana University, the Korea Society, McCormack Seminary, Oxford University, Princeton University, Purdue University, Stanford University, Syracuse University, University of California at Berkeley, University of Iowa, University of Maryland, University of Texas, University of Toronto, University of Washington, Wellesley College, and Yale University. At each venue many people prodded me and gave me ideas. To name only a small number of these folks: thank you, Sealing Cheng, JaHyun Kim Haboush, Sally A. Hasting, Seung-kyung Kim, Robert Oppenheim, Linda-Anne Rebhun, Michael Robinson, Gi-Wook Shin, Jesook Song, and Clark W. Sorenson. I must also extend my gratitude to the many University of Illinois audiences, including those in the Departments of Educational Psychology, Sociology, the Division of Clinical and Community Psychology, and the Program in Asian American Studies, who kindly sat in as I read parts of the book.

I am grateful for this book's happy landing at Duke University Press. Thank you, Courtney Berger, Tim Elfenbein, Judith Hoover, and Ken Wissoker for a pleasurable publication process and my anonymous reviewers for your enormous contributions to this book. And thank you, Michael Aronson, for directing this book their way.

Foundation and university support have provided the greatest research gift: time. I am deeply grateful to the Spencer Foundation (with particular thanks to Catherine Lacey) for the postdoctoral fellowship and small research grant that seeded and propelled this project. At the University of Illinois, the Departments of Anthropology and East Asian Languages and Cultures, and with them the College of Liberal Arts and Sciences, have been amazingly generous to me. From 2005–2008, the Center for East Asian and Pacific Studies housed me as I served as its director. Without the enormous help of Sandy S. Burklund, Tysza Gandha, Tanya Lee, Emily Lewis, Anne Prescott, Eric T. Tate, and Lucretia Williams this book could never have been completed.

Many, yes, many amazing people have helped care for my children over the years of this book, and all of them now are good friends: Kelly Beaulin, Jenna Corban, Jenny Coulter, Stephanie Harris, Jill Kurtz, Christy Simon, Sarah Stalzer, Krissy Tracey, and Caitlin Vitosky, you amaze. Jenny, Kelly, and Krissy, what years!

And then there are even more friends without whom none of this would matter nor could ever have taken shape. I love you all: Cho Han Haejoang, Tina Choi, Nicole Constable, Tysza Gandha, Gina Hunter, Hye-Seung Kang, Bill Kelleher, Sun Joo Kim, Craig Koslofsky, Jack Lee, Miho Matsugu, Noboru Murakami, Rika Murakami, Laura Nelson, Sang-gyu Park, Dana Rabin, Patricia Sandler, Suketu Sanghvi, Keiko Sakamoto, Ann Saphir, Cara Seiderman, Jeanie Taylor, Alex Winter-Nelson, and Karen Winter-Nelson. I am lucky to be a lifetime member of one of those amazing women's reading groups. You are great, Marilyn

Booth, Sharon Irish, Frances Jacobson, Jo Kibbee, Bea Nettles, Carol Spindel, and Karen Winter-Nelson.

The most monumental support of all is that of my family. My octogenarian parents' unfailing love, understanding, and kindness remind me daily that parenting is for the long haul. Rena and Walter Abelmann, you are awesome! And what siblings and siblings-in-law, and what a next generation! Thank you, Ruth, Michael, Graham, Molly, and Katie; Charlie, Emiliana, Tobias, and Emilio; Arthur, Kristen, and Amanda; Karen, Stephen, and Zack; Letty, Mark, Beverley, and Gregory; Susan and Kumar; and Dan and Nanette. Even further along the kinship trails I have the good fortune of much support: in gratitude, Tim, Maret, Emma, and Carola; Ronald and Jeryl; Michael, Wendy, Charlotte, and Holden; David, Julia, and Danielle; Jetta and Kathy; Teddy, Bachir, Azzizza, and Ramsey; Marie-Hélène; and Julie and Henry.

What can you say to the people who are nearest and from whom you sneak away (mostly when they're asleep) to work on things so much less important than they are? Andy Gewirth, you are simply the best. Carmen, Simone, and Isaac, how I love you!

I learned from teaching that nobody ever grows up in a group.
People grow up, if at all, one at a time in spite of the group.
Richard Peck, *Fair Weather*

College is a big investment, of time and money, of course, and
most powerfully of dreams. For its aspirants it looms on the
horizon for years. Long before classes begin college comes to
life as ideas, ideals, and images. It is this university imaginary,
quite apart from any university reality, that drives many of the
college-related decisions young people make.[1] It is no surprise
that college can disappoint, for the imaginary investment is so
great. For the Korean Americans featured in this book, first-
or second-generation immigrants of color, both the investments and the disappointments are often enormous. I argue
that Korean Americans reveal, with perhaps greater intensity
than other students, a general story of the contemporary American university, albeit with a racial twist.

Korean Americans represent a racialized American college
population grappling with liberal college dreams (namely, notions of ideal personal development), their own segregation in
college, and their worries about their future. While many of
the dilemmas they face in college are decidedly American, it is
their particularity that is at the heart of this book, for they
are students of a particular color managing their complex college dreams in an age that celebrates diversity even as it is
largely silent on race, and in a moment that paradoxically both
downplays and asserts Asian American difference.[2] First- and
second-generation Asian Americans offer a compelling case
because they have been posited in the popular imagination as
ideal college subjects and because of their immigrant embrace
of the American dream. What is more, as Asian Americans

these students are expected to add color to the college landscape. But this calculus is fraught: Asian Americans offer, by many counts, the one color that does not count. Even as Asian American students experience often troubling segregation, U.S. racial politics teach them that they are somehow different from other college students of color and thus undeserving of race-based programs and policies. The university we meet in this book is rife with contradictions about both its education and diversity missions, and the Korean American students we meet are beacons of our historical moment as they experience these contradictions.

University imaginaries are dated, reflecting their time and place: here, the end of the twentieth century in the United States. In that not so distant past, college disappointed, or at least confounded, in patterned and meaningful ways that reveal the particular tensions and contradictions of our times. This book focuses on one of these tensions: that between what I dub "liberal ideals," ideals about a universal humanity in which people can become fully human regardless of the contingencies of the likes of race, nation, and religion, and the life of particularities: family, race, and community. This is an intimate tension. Both the liberal ideals for which college students strive "one at a time" (as Richard Peck writes of growing up) and the particularities of family, race, and community are experienced as deeply personal. However, the apparent contradiction blurs a bit when we remember that today's liberal embrace of universal humanity is steeped in an almost counterintuitive way in the celebration of diversity (of precisely family, race, and community, that is, multiculturalism)![3] In other words, to be fully human, a person must have experience and comfort with difference. Not surprisingly this tension can confuse students during their time at college.

It was ethnic segregation in college that most troubled the Korean American students in this book. The "intimate university" thus refers foremost to the struggle students have as they reconcile ideas of highly individualized (liberal) human development, ethnic and racial segregation, and multicultural ideals. This segregation, often assumed to be the mark of excessive ethnic or familial affiliation and attachment, threatens many students' ideas about personal growth. It runs against the grain of the liberal ideals that were so important to many of the Korean Americans in this book. Thus the students here struggled to be fully human against the realities of both racial and ethnic segregation at college, as well as persistent ethnic and racial stereotypes. For first- and second-generation Americans of color, *their* race and segregation can mire college ideals. Further, as immigrants whose families nurtured particular American dreams, their college hopes and investments are often colossal, making college disappointments particularly poignant.

Most of the Korean Americans featured here attended the University of Illinois at Urbana-Champaign (the U of I), a large, research-extensive, relatively affordable land grant university, and as such a powerful hearth in the promise of American higher education that is at issue in this book.

At the U of I Korean Americans found themselves among many co-ethnics, reflecting both Chicagoland's concentration of Korean Americans (the third largest in the late 1990s, fifth largest today) and the university's overwhelmingly Chicagoland-centered student body (the U of I is approximately 138 miles south of Chicago). For Korean Americans this college ethnic intimacy was fraught. Korean American social circles, often nearly exclusive ones, dogged the liberal promise of college in the pinnacle of the American celebration of diversity championed by the ideology of multiculturalism. Indeed, by the college years of these students, diversity or multiculturalism had become a critical tenet of liberalism. These students' segregation is perhaps all the more profound because with its nearly forty thousand students, the U of I is hardly an intimate university. Prevailing multicultural ideologies aside, that theirs was a segregation that didn't seem to bother the university administration was a contradiction that was not lost on Jim (a pseudonym, as are all the names in this book), whom I introduce below, or on many of the students in this book.

When I was just beginning to write this book I was contacted by a freelance journalist working on an article on self-segregation for *Time* magazine. In a relentless interview she tried hard to get me to say that the students I was studying were "self-segregating," that is, that they were moved by their own choices and actions rather than any particular racialized circumstances. The reporter fished for students' choice in the matter, wanting thus to downplay race, to suggest that segregation was merely a matter of cultural comfort.

I hung up the phone frazzled and exhausted and fearful that despite my best efforts her tactics might have worked. This is what I think now: it makes no sense to categorically distinguish self-segregation from some sort of segregation proper. In nearly all instances in this book in which students commented on Korean American responsibility for their own segregation, moments earlier or later in the conversation they reflected on the ways their segregation was sculpted by forces far beyond their own making. Likely the journalist could have pressed U of I Korean Americans to say just what her article called for, but I venture that they too would have felt cornered, and hung up the phone muttering something like "She doesn't get it."

COMFORT ZONES

This book is the fruit of conversations with over fifty Korean American undergraduates in public higher education in Illinois from 1997 to 2000 and a handful of students since 2000. I followed many of the students throughout their college years and in some cases beyond.[4] I talked to them about college: how they found their way to college generally and to their particular college; how they managed their lives and studies in college; how they envisioned life after college; and when it mattered to them (and most often it did) how their families figured in their college lives. In the research phase of this project I took a transnational and intergenerational approach to this immigrant student group. As an anthropologist with equal interests in South Korean and Korean American realities, I was interested in how to think about what I often described at the time as "education across the border," namely, the ways education often both motivates immigration and is calibrated by looking to and from South Korea and the United States. A transnational approach can consider financial or communication links between homelands and immigrants, as well as more broadly the ways people often imagine lives elsewhere.[5] As I look back, I have come to think that with this exclusive approach I was caught up in my own abiding interests in South Korean family and class. Fieldwork is a relentless teacher, though, intervening in the researcher's often long-standing interests or biases. It is my research interlocutors who directed this book's predominant focus on race, segregation, and liberalism, concepts and tensions that surfaced in their own time and on their own terms. In my analysis of Jim in this introduction I weave together both my persistent interest in transnationalism and family and my commitment to a sustained analysis of the American university. While I have retained immigration and inter-generational interests here, in the final analysis this book offers an American college story.

The college ethnic intimacy of the Korean Americans featured here is also a resolutely local story, one animated by Chicagoland's particular ethnic geography. At the U of I there is a Chicagoland Korean American mainstream typified by normative ideas of certain suburbs, specific life trajectories, and a particular practice of Christianity. For many Korean American students, a single large ethnic Protestant church at the U of I stood most profoundly for both this mainstream and a troubling ethnic intimacy in college.

It was the phrase "comfort zone" that more than any other spoke to race, segregation, and the liberal dream and its disappointments. Some-how—and just how was the source of endless conversation—many of the Korean Americans featured here felt that they had not been able to leave their comfort zone while in college. This was a conversation that the *Time* journalist was not privy to, I surmise. Where the journalist thought to take comfort at face value—an intangible that somehow naturally compels people to congregate—I think we can ask how comfort zones speak of and to race and racism. The value placed on diversity, however, asked these students and all students to make intimate ties with diverse people, ideas, and cultures. Talk of comfort zones was one way these students were able to comfortably speak about race. As many have ar-gued, race in the United States is often discussed only obliquely, and often under the guise of class, gender, or faith.[6]

Comfort zones were a popular topic during these students' college years. The most comprehensive college student survey in the history of higher education, the National Survey on Student Engagement, synthe-sized its major findings in a pithy brochure, *College: What You Need to Know before You Go*, and proclaimed that students must exit their comfort zones.[7] Ask, they advised, "In what ways do faculty challenge [you] to leave [your] 'comfort zone' in order to excel?" Comfort zones were thus a problem, thwarting personal and academic growth and achievement.

My interlocutors spoke of the multicultural ideal to take stock of their segregation, to understand why their social circles often seemed to stretch no further than coethnic high school and church chums, or even family members.

FAMILY, LIBERALISM, AND THE MULTICULTURAL UNIVERSITY

First and foremost, college promises change: at the end of the tunnel, young adults must emerge transformed.[8] This liberal college ideal offers a universal humanity, unfettered by race, family, class, religion, and any contingency. The well-worn American myth of open education mobility claims that education beckons and develops all; it is thus blind. This myth lives most fully in public, affordable education. It is precisely universities like the U of I that opened higher education and its promise of full citizenship to large numbers of Americans. And within the liberal university it is the liberal arts that have long espoused this sort of development in which a tutored mind wrestles with universal human joys and struggles.[9]

This college ideal isn't an entirely perfect fit at the U of I, with its service-oriented land grant history and its public, practical mission.[10] Like many other public universities, the U of I touts both the elitist mantra of the liberal arts and the promise of practical employment and public service. Many have argued that these are competing strains in the American education experiment as it wrestles between elitist European roots and pretensions and its American democratic and practical strivings. The late twentieth century found the large American public university, the plurality of the American four-year college experience, struggling with the competing American college ideals of excellence and service, basic and applied research, and liberal and practical training. This identity crisis of the American public university is all the more piqued by the pressures of the neoliberalizing university, with shrinking public support but nonetheless asked to produce ever more workers for the transforming and escalating demands of late capitalism.[11] These college paradoxes are not borne by students alone; rather, they take life as institutional confusions animating the messages and practices of the American university itself.[12]

Complicating the picture is family. While college might happen one person at a time, the college imaginary is necessarily intergenerational, born in the education dreams and histories of parents. Although the immigration histories of the families of the students in this book are diverse—distinct by era, class, occupation, and legal arrangements—for the most part they are united by the liberal dream promised by both America at large and the American college or university. For immigrants, still clothed in the language and ways of the old country, it is their children who can truly become fully and universally human and at home, as the story goes, in the free and democratic world of America, a fictional ideal in its own right. The American university thus stands as the sine qua non of the fulfillment of that American dream, for it is there that the immigrant's children will enter as equals, equally poised to grow into that dream.[13] This book introduces some of the education histories of the immigrant parent generation in order to examine these immigrant intergenerational workings at the American university.

But there is another side to this intergenerational equation. The students in this book struggled with prevailing American popular images of the Asian American family that run counter to the liberal imaginary; these are stereotypes of instrumental calculations and striving that have little to do with ideals of universal human development. This image can be appreciated as the darker underbelly of the model minority myth.[14] Implicated in the image of academically successful and hardworking Asian Americans is their portrayal as narrow, maniacally focused, materialistic, and striving. In this way, foisted on Asian Americans are both inaccurate ideas that *all* Asian Americans are hardworking and successful (particularly in schooling and small entrepreneurship) and that they are commensurately instrumental and striving, a psychological attribution that claims to explain success.[15] While there is extensive literature debunking the model minority stereotype and the burden imposed by its assumptions and expectations, less scholarship takes up this equally costly psychological projection. Indeed, for many of the students I spoke with, "Korean" stood almost matter-of-factly for this portrait of instrumental striving and materialism. In the light of these psychological impositions, many students offered intermittent claims that *their* families were somehow different from the fray, somehow less Korean (i.e., in this negative sense of the word). "Enlightened" parents, I often heard, were in contrast those who were "Americanized." These assertions are somewhat distinctive in ethnic America, where historically (and recently as well) many groups have asserted the value of their own ethnic distinction in opposition to white America. For many of the students in this book, however, proclaiming their families' modernity, enlightenment, or Americanness proved a way to rescue them from pejorative stereotypes. As my discussions of the parent generation will show, these associations of enlightenment and modernity with the West are old stories in the modern history of East Asia, and particularly so for postcolonial South Korea, asserting its place in the world in the aftermath of Japanese colonialism and in relation to the imperial presence of the United States. I consider this student appeal to family distinction as a way to critically respond to racism. Jim, for instance, offers a telling instance of a student struggling with how to make sense of aspects of family that seem to run against the liberal ideals of the American university.

Beyond the stereotype of instrumental striving, in the last decade of the twentieth century ethnic family ties themselves could jostle the liberal university because, as mentioned earlier, diversity or multiculturalism had become implicit in the liberal human development promised by college. In order to grow personally, a student was to both leave the fold of friends and family and encounter diversity, namely, students from *different* families, *different* circles. And so students stressed the importance of "getting out of your comfort zone." Again, although seldom named as such, race and ethnicity were the cornerstones of that comfort zone. These demands are all the more difficult for Asian Americans who bring diversity to the table but are asked to leave their own particularity behind.

Developments over the 1990s foretold the paradox of the simultaneous American embrace of diversity and silence on race.[16] True to their times, the Korean American college students at the heart of this book came to college both shy to talk about race, fearing with many of their classmates that to talk of race was to be racist (even as race mattered in their lives), and convinced of the value of diversity. Mid-1990s resolutions that eliminated the use of race and gender in admissions, hiring, and promotion at the University of California presaged the swift exit of race from public discourse. Multiculturalism, on the other hand, was in its prime; students were to learn about and from difference, be it from new canons in the classroom or diverse roommates.[17] This retreat from race was echoed in the 1997 *Gratz v. Bollinger* and 2003 *Grutter v. Bollinger* suits, which challenged affirmative action in undergraduate and law school admissions at the University of Michigan. With their settlement diversity reigned. The defense of affirmative action in the *Grutter v. Bollinger* decision simultaneously affirmed the educational value of diversity and integration. However, the race that became acceptable in American public discourse did not refer explicitly to social justice, let alone historical redress. It was a multicultural, Benetton version of diversity that prevailed. In this context students were *not* quick to name race or racism as the problem; they seldom *explicitly* offered it as the source of the comfort zone from which there seemed to be no easy exit. This book thus interrogates how a racialized second generation meets the American university with its own ideologically invested and transforming imaginary.

Although this book examines college troubles of our times, few of the students introduced here were having significant academic trouble in college. It has been well documented, however, that Asian Americans disproportionately suffer psychologically in college, even in comparison with their racialized college peers.[18] College troubles often exceed overt measures of success, such as academic performance or college retention. Ethnography, fine-grained field research, in this case spanning entire college careers, has the luxury of being able to look beyond these most obvious (and in this case, most stereotypical) indicators of college success. Indeed, for many in this book, college did prove at least confusing, sometimes deeply troubling, and at points even paralyzing. It is challenging to study college lives ethnographically, for students often feel that theirs is a unique college path. It is the task of scholarship to ask how these college lives are patterned and historically specific, students' feelings aside. But I also aim to appreciate the often singular way people, especially young people, experience and narrate their lives.

JIM: INTIMATE STRUGGLES

With Jim I begin this book's examination of the struggles of the American college student, particularly those of the second-generation racialized student. I begin with a description of Jim's liberal college imaginary, his sense of the class and racial limits to his college dreams, and his deep-seated critique of what he believes are the real commitments of the American university. I then turn to his conflicted sense of his parents in the equation and end with his persistent and personal liberal confidence, a confidence that takes life in the shadow of his imagined Korea.

"If you're going to grow as a person . . ."
Jim embraced the liberal college dream I described earlier, and with so many of his cohort worried about whether he would be able to grow at the U of I in particular. He fretted that the university might be too

ethnically intimate, and as such too sheltered: "I don't know, personally for me, *if you're going to grow as a person* you have to know how to leave that area of security and try to live amongst people you've had no contacts with, try to make sense of new environments. Otherwise how else are you going to mature as an adult and try to cope with new situations? I thought the University of Illinois would have kind of sheltered me, in a sense."[19] Jim went on to describe how hard it was to distinguish himself at the U of I: "Everyone is doing the same thing and I just wanted to be 'Jim for Jim,' not for other people." "Jim for Jim" offers, I suggest, a liberal personhood in which an individual is unfettered by group attributes of race, religion and the like. Jim for Jim would proceed apace, developing in his own way, something that Jim figured was nearly impossible among over five hundred Korean Americans at the U of I. He elaborated on the particular conundrum for Korean Americans who conform so seamlessly that they don't even "feel" the pressure to conform: "I don't know, there were a lot of unforced pressures that you don't feel as a Korean American because everybody tends to think the same and to want to do the same things." In Jim's calculus it was difficult to break out of the ethnic fold, for one's thoughts and desires compelled one to stay comfortably ensconced.

"But sometimes for different people . . ."

It was eminently clear to Jim that the liberal, and American, college dream was not so easily realized by all students. He described these ideal college experiences as both classed and racialized; that is, liberal ideals of universal humanity aside, a person's particular background did make a difference. He contrasted the college lives of most Korean Americans with those of students who enjoy greater economic freedom and whose parents impose different (or lesser) pressures: "For most people, if they're in LAS [the College of Liberal Arts and Sciences], they're here for the *college experience*. . . . You can take your time, study what you want that's interesting to you, and enjoy it and feel the *college experience*. If it leads to a job, then fine, but if it doesn't then you always have opportunities available later for graduate school or something else. Most Korean Americans are like, 'Oh, we've got to get a job now and graduate fast and get out of here.'" On the flip side of experience for Jim was an instrumental approach to college that dogged him as the Korean college way. He elaborated on his own embrace of liberal ideals, his own desires for that sort of college experience, but admitted to not being able to make good on it.

A critical component of the experience that he imagined people having in college was, perhaps ironically, diversity. He described the importance for that liberal college dream of "experiencing different people" but mused that "different people" themselves (i.e., like Jim) "sometimes" don't share the luxury of this ideal college experience: "If I had it my way, if I had all the advantages, I would have gone through and taken anything that interested me a lot . . . just living the college life, experiencing *different people*, just taking fun classes. . . . This is how life should be. You shouldn't rush to do anything in life. I admire that mentality, *but sometimes for different people*, you don't have that luxury." Although he did not name them explicitly, it was white people who weren't "different," white people who had the luxury of "experience" and of experiencing "different" people. In his first mention of "different people," Jim expressed the multicultural ideal, while in the second instance he singled out people of color, such as himself. Thus while it is "different people" like Jim who contributed to white students' college experience, his own experience didn't measure up: it was not as much fun, not as interesting, not as luxurious.

"Have a nice day! . . . Nice talking to you"
Jim described an ethnic impulse to conform and the naked workings of class and race sculpting his college experience. He also placed responsibility for his own dashed college dreams at the feet of the university itself. In the company of many scholars and writers on higher education, Jim asserted that a diverse campus does not in and of itself achieve the mission of diversity.[20] He thus described a racialized university in a racialized country. He claimed that Korean Americans were segregated at the U of I precisely because the university refused to even acknowledge, let alone "care about," that very segregation: "I think [the university] does show what America looks like, *but people still segregate themselves*. It's hard to make any clear judgment. It's physically visible, but whether you feel it is a different story. . . . *It doesn't seem like the university cares about the segregation*. I don't think they even acknowledge that there is [segregation]. Because of that, it exists." Jim thus asserted that it is one thing to diversify the student body, but something else entirely to live that racial diversity; racial demographics are one thing, the "feeling"

something else entirely. In Jim's words we also find the tension between self-segregation and the realities of race: it is perhaps, he offers, precisely because the university doesn't seem to "care about segregation" that it exists. He went on to talk about the university's weak orientation programs and missed opportunities: "Just group potential students with students from different areas, different backgrounds, different ethnicities and have workshops based on that." When I asked him about his own orientation to the university, he described the cavalier and off-putting attitude he found there: " 'This is the U of I. This is what academic life is like. This is what our programs are offering. *Have a nice day!*' . . . Just, 'This is our campus, these are the courses we offer, these are the types of problems you might see,' but otherwise '*Nice talking to you.*' " "Have a nice day!" was Jim's inspired way of putting words to the gaping distance between college rhetoric and reality.

Jim's is the first of many critiques of the U of I offered by the students in this book. Thus caveats are in order: the U of I is but one of many predominantly white American universities; and, as I discuss in the conclusion, at the U of I there have been remarkable developments in academic and extra-academic programming related to Asian Americans and other students of color. This said, the students' critiques do warrant serious attention.

That the U of I wasn't making good on diversity did not surprise Jim, for it spoke to a larger American "collective identity" that doesn't really know what to do with the likes of Jim, with "different" people. Speaking about his parents' immigration in the 1980s as the "last big wave," he came to this matter of American identity: "In terms of immigration in general, I think it's always been encouraged to die down by the United States. It's probably premature for me to say, but I think that the U.S. has its own *collective identity*. I don't know, by accepting *more people* you kind of confuse that identity, I think." Jim is talking about race: "more people" here, like the "different people" he spoke of earlier, are nonwhites, while the "collective identity" is decidedly white.

Although Jim described an ethnic community, university, and American society that to some extent thwarted his college dream, he nonetheless held to some measure of distinction, that indeed, to some extent, he had managed to be "Jim for Jim." In his register of this distinction, family figured prominently, as it did for many students. With this account we begin to understand the enormous investment that many students have in asserting that their families do not conform to the stereotype of Asian or Korean American families. In this student narration, it was Koreanness that came to stand for all that was negative and illiberal. Nonetheless, I understand these assertions as critical responses to racism. In chapter 1 and throughout the book I argue that even as many students felt trapped by the very stuff of ethnic stereotypes, they often asserted themselves as distinct from ideas of an ethnic mainstream, what some scholars have dubbed "intraethnic othering."[21] In this vein, Jim described parents who were different, even as they too were implicated in the college path that diverted him from ideal liberal development.

"We want you to be a human being"

Jim described enlightened parents who shared his ideals about "growing as a person." Their enlightenment was to be measured against the drab landscape of Asian American instrumental, ethnic striving for material and other external measures of success. His parents had, "surprisingly," wanted to expose him to the "real world" through their small restaurant. "I needed to help them out," Jim admitted, but his parents believed that restaurant work would keep their children from being "sheltered." Recall that Jim worried about ending up at the U of I, where he would be "sheltered" (i.e., in the ethnic fold). Jim was proud of his parents, who told him, "*We want you to be a human being*, not a robot that studies." He explained, "They want me to have a strong education but they also understand you're a *human being*. You have to live life. You can't hope to understand people if you don't see and *experience* them. For you to be a good person, you have to understand everyone's situation." His parents' exhortation to "experience people" and "understand everyone's situation" recalls that necessary brush with diversity en route to a liberal universalistic humanity, and that college "experience" that Jim spoke of. But Jim also conceded that his parents, like "typical" Koreans, have professional desires for their children. He struggled to nonetheless hold on to some sense of their distinction. The (typical) imperative to make money aside, Jim told me that they cared both about *how* he makes money ("that you don't just make money but make money from a profession that is respectable") and about *how* he would spend that money: "They believe money is not something to cherish, it's something to be spent, that's all it is. . . . They believe money is a tool; it's meant to be used." With these comments Jim reached for the lofty, liberal, and experiential against the narrow, ethnic, and instrumental images that peg Asian Americans.

Central to Jim's efforts to assert his parents' difference, the ways they diverged from ugly racist stereotypes, was his understanding of their own personal histories in Korea, as well as his own early childhood memories of South Korea. This book's students show that Korea, both as it emerges in their parents' histories and in their own experiences of South Korea, figured meaningfully in their lives. For Jim, as for a number of other students in this book, it was class distinction, the ghost of more prosperous and privileged lives before the often downward occupational mobility of immigration, that was a central tenet of his parents' enlightenment.[22]

Jim nonetheless struggled over his parents' contradictions: their enlightenment, on the one hand, and the "typical" pressures they placed on their children, on the other hand. He contrasted the harsh realities of their immigrant life with what he recalled of childhood visits to his parents' distinguished houses in South Korean villages. In so doing he wrestled with their simultaneous distinction and conformity. They were distinct, he figured, because of their relatively privileged backgrounds; their village houses were bigger than any others. And they conformed to ethnic stereotypes because of the indignities of immigrant life.

On several occasions Jim described how his parents' village houses viscerally communicated their "prestigious background":

Well, whenever I would go to my mom's house, all the kids used to say, like, that's the kid that lives in that house. And it was the biggest house in that village; and it still is. . . . And, like, because of that, all that respect associated with my mom's household, she really knew the prestige and honor that's not really owed her but what's expected if you're in that position. And my dad's the same thing . . . and he was in a big house too and I remember those big houses distinctly. . . . That's what I remember distinctly whenever I'd go to my grandparents' houses. They're huge, it's just amazing how big they are. . . . And, like, yeah, they just stick out in my mind because they're bigger compared to the rest of the houses that are adjacent to them. I knew my, I already knew as a kid, like, my parents come from prestigious backgrounds.

I commented that I was impressed with his vivid recollections and Jim agreed, "Yeah I have a pretty good memory." Those houses marked his parents' distinction, even in immigrant America. Although Jim conceded that "migrations tend to mix everybody together," he said that his parents "stick out": "Because the way my parents carry themselves, they have this dignified etiquette about themselves and you can tell them apart from so many other Korean parents."

Once, after his excursus on these many houses, I asked him, "So what does all this have to do with *your* life?" I wonder now why I felt the need to ask this question; it strikes me that for Jim it was so obvious how this distinction played in his life that he didn't think to come full circle. He answered, "I understand where my parents come from when they expect something from me because that's what was expected from them, so it's, like, families try to instill the same values that they were taught, and *so I don't blame my parents for any bad policies that they tried to enforce on me but I try to understand it.*" Jim was reconciling competing images of his parents, liberal and illiberal versions. "Bad policies" refer to the conventional Korean American value placed on achievement and success, the stuff of the prevailing stereotypes. When I asked for an example, he said, "I try to understand where they're coming from, and memories of that five-year-old kid help a lot." For Jim, the meaning of those houses took particular shape in the contrasting light of his parents' immigrant realities, and hence their striving. With this genealogical (and class) specificity, Jim diverted the racial stereotype of Asian American or Korean American instrumentality; rather, in the distinctive case of *his* family, striving had its roots in former class glory.

On another occasion when Jim again turned the conversation to those houses—I grew increasingly intrigued by their play in our conversations—he had just been talking about the "tragedy" of immigration: "I don't know. I tend to view most migrations to be tragic." The tragedy for Jim, which by that point in our conversations was obvious enough that he didn't need to explicate it, was that his parents could come from those countryside houses and end up laboring as small entrepreneurs in the American city. Jim didn't mince words: "Americans try to view immigrants as this glorious thing, but the fact of the matter is people don't move unless they're forced to move. Why would you want to go to a country that doesn't speak your own language? Let's interpret this glory aspect!" He underscored both the harsh realities of immigrant life, a far cry from "glorious," and the circumstances that propel immigration. As he put it, there is nothing so glorious about "a country that doesn't speak your own language." Recall Jim's similar description of comfort zones: Why would people so easily self-segregate? To borrow Jim's idiom, "Let's interpret this segregation aspect!" This is exactly what I hope this book does.

"I find myself more Caucasian"

Jim's liberal dream had a color: white. On one occasion when he spoke of his "difference," he claimed that dream by distancing himself from the normative lives of Korean American Christians: "It's a cultural thing, to tell you the truth, because I find Korean people tend to be very fanatical in any ideology they subscribe to. There is no moderate point of view. It's either one extreme or the other extreme. . . . Keeping that in mind, when it comes to religion it is even more volatile because it's such a personal issue. . . . Because of that, I find myself, I don't mean to sound biased or anything like that, but *I find myself more Caucasian*, in a sense, in terms that I tend to accept the ideas more of other people and just try to take everything with a grain of salt." As before, Caucasians (my interlocutors seldom used the term "white," a word that seemed to make them nervous) were liberal, laid back, open to new ideas, and prone to "take everything with a grain of salt."

Jim was certain that the liberal dream would have been much further from his grasp had his family not immigrated, that he would never have developed as he had if he remained in South Korea, despite his family's large houses. This transnational calculus—"What if my family had never come?"—is one that many students made, including those born in the United States. It is certainly alive in the imaginations of the parent generation.

Jim explained, "[I have become] more of a person to myself than I would be if I was in Korea." In his words, "I wouldn't trade the whole thing." In South Korea, he figured, he would have become "a drone . . . a drone of many drones." When I questioned his evidence for this dramatic assertion, he held his ground because of his elementary school experience with Korean afterschool programs in Chicago, where the rule was "Don't question my authority, just follow what I'm telling you to do." It was on just this point that he distinguished himself: "I tend to question things more, you know, Americans tend to prize their own personal liberty." For Jim, it was just this sort of liberty that took life in his parents' interest in his "experiencing the world," even as in other ways they charted a narrower course for him.

Jim's relationship to his family was ambivalent. On the one hand, he referred to his family's distinction (beginning with those bigger houses) to mark his own distinctive approach to college; on the other hand, he was reconciled to limits (ones that made him typically ethnic) born of familial, economic, and racial circumstances or constraints.

Jim's struggles in college reflected millennial conflicts inherent in the American university between liberalism and race, liberalism and (ethnic) family, and liberalism and the realities of the economic or social insecurity that drives immigration. In this book we meet the American university with its own very particular confusions about "different people" (wanting their [white] students to experience them but not quite knowing what to do with those different people) and how that difference should really matter anyway. When Jim described the way the university welcomed his difference—"Have a nice day!"—he made a powerful claim about the university's contradictions, contradictions that sculpted his college struggles, and even disappointments.

Jim ended up transferring. His liberal dream hadn't been answered at the U of I, where he had been a pre-med student with a passion for political science, which he would have majored in, "If I could have," he said. The promise of secure and speedy employment carried him to a medical-related professional program at a city university closer to home.

OFF TO COLLEGE

Jim's story sets the stage for many students in this book who similarly navigated the contradictions of the contemporary American university. Part I introduces the Chicagoland Korean American landscape, its geography and demography, and its class, residence, race, religious, and gender contours.

Chapter 1, "Here and There in Chicagoland Korean America," examines the U of I take on the Chicagoland Korean American mainstream and margins as a window on Korean American student heterogeneity. I introduce four students to tell the story of Korean American settlement and mobility in Chicagoland. I then return to Korean American segregation at the U of I in the context of that geography. This geography goes far to introduce the horizons and constraints that students meet as they pursue their own college dreams.

Chapter 2, "The Evangelical Challenge to College and Family," looks inside Korean American student Christianity for a powerful contrast to secular college ideals and parent religiosity. I argue that Christian practice promises its own liberal project, one that can challenge both college and family culture. While for many Korean Americans at the U of I it was the church that stood for a troubling ethnic intimacy, the struggle against that intimacy happens within the ethnic church in much the same way it does beyond.

Chapter 3, "Shattered Liberal Dreams," introduces Mary, a working-class city girl who headed to the U of I with big liberal dreams bred in part in the embrace of her father's American immigration romance. Like Jim, Mary blamed the university for dashing her dreams but spoke most often about suburban Korean Americans and her palpable exclusion from their fold. Over the course of college she became deeply cynical about both her father's own dashed dreams and the American university. Her liberal ideals teetered in the racialized realities of the course of her college years. With Mary I take up the margins of the U of I's Chicagoland Korean American geography and begin this book's foray into the intergenerational coordinates of the liberal college and immigration project.

Part II introduces a single extended family, the Hans, for an elaborated examination of how family, immigration, liberalism, and the American university meet in late twentieth-century America. Chapter 4, "An (Anti–)Asian American Pre-med," introduces squarely suburban and middle-class Owen, who arrives at the U of I, like Mary, with large and liberal dreams. Although college does disappoint him, Owen offers a largely successful instance of liberal human development in college. His real disappointments, though, along with the struggles of Jim and Mary, reveal the college paradoxes of his era. For pre-med Owen, liberal college dreams took on a particular challenge, for he needed to wrest himself from the stuff of ethnic stereotypes.

Chapter 5, "Family versus Alma Mater," turns to John, Owen's brother, and Tony, Owen's paternal first cousin, for a look at ways students can challenge the liberal college ideal through their ethnic family. I argue that these two young men in different ways position the family against the university. They query the contradictions at the heart of the university itself: John wonders if college isn't a "waste," and Tony is skeptical of whether the university really aims to fashion "well-rounded" and employable students. Further, I examine how John and Tony understand the lives of the immigration-generation men in their family who represent diverse American lives. In this chapter and the previous one I examine the considerable heterogeneity of even brothers and cousins.

Chapter 6, "Intimate Traces," turns to the education and immigration history of Owen and John's father. Mr. Han's case presents a palpable South Korean and American liberal dream, a deep-seated desire to become a world citizen. Mr. Han's history and desires take life in his competing visions of the American university. Through him I learn that the college imaginary is intimately intergenerational and, for immigrants, transnational.

Chapter 7, "It's a Girl Thing," turns to three women in the Han family, an immigration-generation sister, a wife, and a daughter, to consider the gendered contours of the college imaginary. I argue that liberalism, in its South Korean postcolonial and American university forms, has particular hues for both immigrant women and American college women.

In the conclusion I return to the questions of race and college, considering how best to think about segregation in the American university today. I also return to intraethnic othering, the persistent ways in which Korean Americans draw distinctions among themselves, practices I believe are best understood in the broader context of race in America. I revisit family, an intimate piece of the American university experience. Finally I ask "What is to be done?" and consider the potential of race and ethnic studies and programming at the American university.

PART I: THE LANDSCAPE

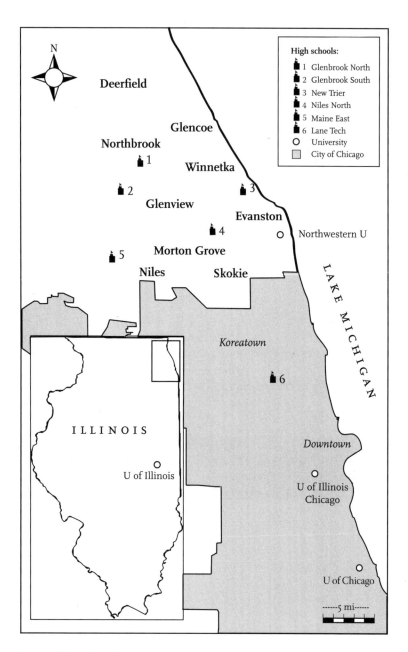

Map 1. Chicagoland Korean America

1

HERE AND THERE IN CHICAGOLAND
KOREAN AMERICA

Jim struggled with the distance between his college ideals and his own college realities. Like so many Korean Americans at the the U of I, he worried about his increasingly ethnic social circle and normative career path, fretting that they impeded the liberal promise in which he would be "Jim for Jim." Jim had a palpable sense of a Korean American mainstream, a constellation of values and behaviors that he seemed to simultaneously claim, albeit with a sense of inevitability, and eschew. The mainstream that Korean American students at the U of I identified, although not with that word, refers to an ideal and upwardly mobile trajectory.[1] While appreciating that this trajectory hardly represents a typical Korean American life or family course, I call it mainstream because so many of the students I spoke with believed that this was indeed how most Korean Americans lived and progressed. In this sense "mainstream" refers to the way in which certain life ideals operate as normative, hence calling attention to those whose lives diverge in some way. Further, this mainstream takes on particular life at the U of I, with its disproportionately suburban and middle-class Korean American population. Jim's perception of a Korean American mainstream had its own very particular geography, its "here" and "there" on the Chicagoland map. Indeed, a geographic here and there comprises a landscape of distinction from which many Korean Americans made their way to college.

Like all geographies, Chicagoland Korean America is more than a map of where people reside. Geographies are social maps detailing where people live, move, and make meaning.[2] Chicagoland Korean Americans thus share ideas about, for example, what it is to live in one or another place, to have moved away from one or another place, to cross town on Sundays to attend one or another church or to visit with relatives. These mental maps provide a way to parse other people's lives and movements and also to put oneself on the map. This chapter introduces the ethnic geography of Chicagoland Korean America at the U of I to better appreciate the powerful image and coordinates of what I introduce as a Korean American mainstream as well as the ways Korean Americans render the considerable heterogeneity of their community. For Korean Americans, ethnic intimacy at the U of I begins in the mainstream and margins of this geography.

I begin with a brief overview of the social geography of Korean America at the U of I before moving on to illustrate that geography's mainstreams and margins through the narratives of four students: Lisa, a student who considered herself to be at the heart of the northern suburban scene (I dub this "being there"); Jane, a recent suburbanite who described what it is to move into the mainstream ("moving in"); Joe, a city guy who looked in on the mainstream ("looking in"); and Min, a recently immigrated city dweller who glanced nervously at the mainstream ("from afar"). I end with the university, with the specificity of the U of I in the Illinois geography of public higher education and in the Chicagoland Korean American mainstream.

In taking students' accounts seriously, I walk a fine line. On the one hand, I appreciate important divides in the Chicagoland Korean American social geography, foremost those of class, such as the very real differences between those students who never left the city and those who come from the suburbs. These are divides that make for real social groups. On the other hand, I also pay attention to how, like Jim, most students narrate their own life courses as singular, listening in, for example, to the ways even students whose social coordinates placed them squarely in the mainstream narrate their own distinctiveness. If this chapter convinces readers of the existence only of unique individuals I will not have done this geography justice. If, on the other hand, I reduce these students to stock figures representing their geographical nodes or networks, I will have done my research interlocutors, young people carving out distinctive lives, a disservice. I aim for a balance: a serious look at differences (e.g., of class and immigration history) and an appreciation of the still very real ways that people mark their own distinctiveness.

Early on in this research I analyzed the towns and high schools of all

U of I students of Korean heritage (to the extent that I could determine this based on surnames, and in some cases first and middle names). From this I was able to discern, for example, the primary feeder schools for Korean Americans; I also compared this information with the same information for other Asian Americans and for the college population at large. All of the material in this book, however, emerges from open-ended, qualitative interviews and from some participant observation (i.e., hanging out) with families and student groups. The demographic analysis did, though, allow me to gauge aspects of students' perceptions against reality. What impressed me was how close students' subjective maps, as well as my own sense of aggregate geography on the basis of qualitative research, were to real geography. In this chapter I draw not only on the cluster of students I introduce but also on the immigration, residence, and schooling histories of over fifty Korean Americans I interviewed who I am confident represent the heterogeneity of Korean Americans at the U of I. Not represented in this book, however, is the experience of those Korean Americans hailing from downstate (i.e., not from Chicagoland). Theirs is a different experience indeed, as most of them arrive at college with very few or no ethnic colleagues from their high schools. Also not appearing in this book are the many students I interviewed from the University of Illinois at Chicago (UIC) and Oakland Community College, which serves those Chicago suburbs with the largest numbers of Korean Americans; while their demography *is* different (e.g., for UIC, more urban, working class, and recently immigrated), they share the same ideas of a Korean American mainstream or normative life from which they more easily diverge.

AT A GLANCE: KOREAN AMERICA AT THE U OF I

The vast majority of Korean Americans and Asian Americans in the United States are post-1965 immigrants; this is even more true in the Midwest, which had fewer earlier settlements of people of Asian ancestry. Thus in the post–Korean War period Asian American college students are increasingly foreign-born and first and second generation. The Korean American representation at the U of I echoes this profile; they are largely, although by no means uniformly, second-generation and early childhood immigrants, so-called 1.5ers, for being between first- and second-generation immigrants. The immigration and settlement patterns of Korean Americans in Chicagoland replicate the immigration histories of many groups; they have followed the geography of the laws that allowed their entrance, particularly occupational preferences in the immediate post-1965 period, and increasingly over time family reunification provisions (primarily parents and siblings).[3] At a glance, pre-1965 Korean immigrants were bifurcated: they were either education elites or, more often, poor, rural-origin wives of U.S. servicemen. Post-1965 immigrants were disproportionately educated, city-residing, Christian, and professional. However, as the share of those emigrating for reasons of family reunification became greater, the Korean American immigration has become increasingly class variegated, representing a larger, although by no means representative, swath of the South Korean population. Nonetheless, Korean immigrants in the United States remain more economically privileged, better educated, more urban, and more often Christian than their South Korean counterparts. They have long arrived almost exclusively from cities and settled largely in cities, and have thereafter left cities for the suburbs. Noteworthy in recent years are the immigration (although small) directly from the South Korean countryside, as well as increasing settlement directly in the American suburbs, without an initial period of urban residence. In the late 1990s U of I Korean American students' settlement geography typically included an early childhood in the city (Chicago), sometimes in neighborhoods with a concentrated Korean population; in the early immigration years some coresidence with the young families of uncles and aunts, most often with one or more grandparents present, in single apartments, adjacent apartments, or split-level houses; a move to an independent nuclear family residence, sometimes within the city but most often in the suburbs; and later one or more suburban moves, often entailing home ownership as well as class and education mobility (i.e., larger homes and better school systems).

This settlement is racialized in important ways. Typically, students' urban lives were residentially more racially diverse than their lives in the suburbs. The racial composition of their urban schools, however, varied according to their attendance at private (most often Catholic), public, or public magnet schools (mostly relevant as they headed into middle and high school). A number of the students I interviewed attended largely white Catholic schools, though they were not necessarily Catholic themselves. The racial composition of the suburban neighborhoods the families moved to varied enormously. Their own suburbanization mirrored that of many other Asian Americans, and students reported the coincident or slightly skewed (before or after) Asianization of the once largely white suburbs they moved to. Again and again I heard from students about the surprise and anguish of their parents as their once white suburban neighborhoods become increasingly Asian American over time, and in some cases particularly Korean American. They feared falling property values and worried about a transformed (less ideal) neighborhood. Thus although the general contours of the multiethnic city and the predominantly white suburbs do hold to some extent, for many students suburbanization coincided with increasing contact with Asian or Korean Americans and less contact with other racialized populations, both in their neighborhood and at school. As mentioned earlier, the mainstream course of the settlement of U of I Chicagoland Korean Americans operates as a working norm from which students can deviate (e.g., if they never lived in the suburbs, if they did not move into the northern suburbs) or inhabit in a distinctive manner.

BEING THERE

> *It seems that* we do know everyone. . . . *Well, maybe it's because of the churches. That's a big part too.*—Lisa

I dub Lisa's geography "Being There" because of the comfortable way she inhabited the U of I Korean American mainstream, easily distinguishing herself from Korean Americans who found their way to the suburbs considerably later than she had.

Lisa attended Glenbrook North High School (GBN), which during the late 1990s, the time of this research, was the U of I's largest Korean American feeder school, as well as a significant U of I feeder school generally. Lisa estimated that she had attended high school with about fifty Korean American classmates, nearly one-eighth of the high school population. Since kindergarten she had lived in Northbrook, one of the wealthy suburbs that many consider a Korean American hub. Before moving 11.5 miles to Northbrook, Lisa's highly educated family lived in Skokie, one of the suburbs that for some Korean Americans at the U of I don't quite count as suburban. Lisa matter-of-factly sketched the typical Korean American trajectory in which people "start off in the city," then "slowly move to the suburbs, the Skokie or Niles area," and finally make their way "north to Northbrook, Glenview, New Trier." Skokie and Niles, she explained, are transition areas, still cityish, while Northbrook and Glenview are squarely suburban. Interestingly, New Trier is not a suburb but the name of the high school that serves some of Chicagoland's richest suburbs, including Winnetka and Glencoe; in Lisa's litany, it stood at the pinnacle of the move to the wealthiest northern suburbs.

For Lisa, Skokie, where she lived as a young child, was a "city," not because of its built environment but because of its racial makeup. She described her occasional high school return visits this way: "It was so different—like I was going into a whole different world." She felt particularly uncomfortable at Old Orchard, the mall there. And she recalled how "loud and rowdy" it had been when her high school team played volleyball with Niles North, one of Skokie's schools. "I just got a bad impression of them. We would walk into their cafeteria and there'd be all these people on Friday afternoon and they'd be break dancing. . . . I thought these people were so weird." She went on to overtly racialize the portrait, noting that most of the kids in the cafeteria were Asian Americans, many of them Filipino Americans. For Lisa, the city suburbs were more Asian American, and they were particularly distinguished by the behavior of the Asian Americans who were not Korean American. Also implied in her comments was the African American tenor of these "weird" cultural forms, such as break dancing.

Lisa was not alone in singling out the suburbs that ringed the city. A student who moved in third grade from the city to a rental apartment in Skokie, and later to a rental home in Morton Grove and finally back to the city late in high school, described Skokie and bordering Morton Grove as "borderline Chicago." She explained that the city neighborhood she moved to in high school was in fact "no different" from the borderline suburbs. Another student who moved from a "borderline Chicago" suburb to a more northern suburb in middle school described his new town as "upper suburbia, like a higher class kinda place." Yet another student detailed her borderline suburban "ghetto school"; she rattled off a list of suburban high schools, and concluded, "[My high school] would probably be at the bottom." She described its lower academic quality, its higher incidence of violence, its greater racial diversity, and its proximity to the city: "Sports were horrible. The education was bad. The neighborhood was bad . . . and there was a drive-by shooting in eighth grade that didn't help."

Although Northbrook was at a comfortable remove from Skokie, Lisa explained that her own neighborhood and high school had become increasingly Korean American: "There were floods of Koreans moving in . . . and our whole street is Korean American." She described her father's reaction to this coethnic flood: "My dad was upset because he thought our house value was going to go down because of all these Koreans moving in." Her father's race and class anxiety aside, Lisa was confident in the quality of her high school and certain that it was wealthier and "more stuck up" than its nearby suburban neighbor Glenbrook South High School (GBS), another school with many Korean Americans.

It was against this backdrop that Lisa recalled the later wave of Korean Americans who made their way to the northern suburbs just in time for high school: "At first when you see them, they look kind of as if they're from the city or from Skokie. The have their baggy pants and Cross Colors. . . . a brand that was big back then. It's baggy clothes and all these different colors. They came out with green and purple jeans. . . . They would look kind of punkish, but after a year they got into preppy clothes." But for Lisa, it wasn't just clothes that distinguished these recent settlers. The newcomers "didn't buy into the 'everything is grades and doing well' approach to school." She went on, "[They] never cared about studying. They would just go out and party. . . . They never really got down any good study habits." She explained that in fact it didn't take the newcomers very long to adjust, that they "adapted really well" and "quickly buckled down." In this way she sketched what it meant to "buy" and "buy into" things suburban, material and otherwise.

Integral to Lisa's sketch of the town and high school as the pinnacle of the Chicagoland Korean American mainstream was the place of the Korean American Protestant church generally, and her church in particular. Interestingly, she first mentioned her church to allay any impression I might have that she had meant to suggest that she and her cohort were "the people that everyone should know." "But," she went on, as if admitting the inevitable, "*it seems that* we do know everyone. . . . *Well, maybe it's because of the churches. That's a big part too.*" She was referring to the large churches in her immediate vicinity, those with large English-language youth ministries. She quickly named the network of churches that meet for joint worship and collective revival meetings. And she added, "We know all these people." But Lisa's geography also makes for a comfort zone that can itself pose as a problem (i.e., for its ethnic intimacy), so it wasn't surprising that she balked a bit at her own place in the picture. Nonetheless, her several references to her dense ethnic social network point to this very comfort and, despite her reluctance, to her keen sense that hers is a normative or even ideal trajectory or way of inhabiting the Chicagoland Korean American geography.

MOVING IN

> *I have to admit to you . . . after four years in the suburbs, I've become more relaxed about money.*—Jane

Whereas Lisa was "there," Jane was precisely the sort of Korean American Lisa described as "moving in" with the coethnic "flood." Jane moved from the city to one of the borderline suburbs in eighth grade and one year later to the high school that Lisa described as similar but not quite on a par with her own (GBS). As we saw with Lisa, students often comfortably listed towns and high schools in parallel fashion because they stood so easily for one another and because school quality was so much a part of many suburban moves. Jane, like Lisa, described GBS as "over-populated with Koreans," but in her case it wasn't the newly arrived flood of Korean Americans that she thought to comment on but the longer term suburbanites like Lisa. It was, she said, her own city background that distinguished her from the school's "typical rich kid." Although she admitted to her own "custom-built" and "pretty nice" home, she insisted that her city past made a real difference: "When my parents wanted to give me a new car when I was sixteen, I was like 'Are you crazy?' No way am I going to drive a new car. So I drove, like, the old Taurus around." Despite these city affinities, she continued, "*But I have to admit to you . . . after four years in the suburbs, I've become more relaxed about money.*"

Jane recalled her early "shock" at the way the kids dressed in the suburban middle school that she moved to at fourteen. For her part, she "made a social statement" by dressing in a particular way: "It wasn't necessarily how I dressed in the city [i.e., when she lived there] but how I would have ended up dressing had I stayed. . . . Okay so here's my thing: it was an act of saying, 'Hey I'm different from all of you.' Most of the kids, they are all, like, J. Crew, preppy-looking, nice kids, and here's this girl coming with, like, boots and the short permed hair and leather coat and just wacked-out clothes." Jane said that her clothes most resembled those of two other recent suburban settlers, one Filipina American and the other Irish American. They swapped clothes with each other and "looked forward to seeing what each other would be wearing the next day." Regardless of these clothing differences, like Lisa, Jane distinguished herself most from the suburbanites' attitudes about life: "I thought they were stuck up and they just cared for themselves. They were looking out for number one." Moreover, she "couldn't stand" their "cliques" and "social hierarchies." She went from being a "straight-A" student in the city to a "straight C [-student]" in the suburbs, but when I probed she insisted that this had nothing to do with her academic preparation. It was, she explained, the "emotional" transition that led to her poor grades. Jane described herself as "anti-everything" in her early suburban days; she contrasted herself with her younger sister, who moved to the suburbs just in time for elementary school. Her younger sister became "totally different than me": "She's, like, an All-American Girl, like, head of the tennis team, like, student council, but I was anti-everything." Whereas her sister stayed inside the house, was "book smart," and "just grew up very nice," Jane was "street-smart." This was a contrast that many students made: between street life and camaraderie in the city and the cloistered, selfish, and bookish ways of life in suburban neighborhoods with big houses and big yards.

In much the same way that Lisa sketched a stock portrait of newly arrived city kids, Jane elaborated on suburbanites' "selfishness": "I was so shocked by it [the selfishness]. I had been thinking it will be cool to live in a new house. I was very like, 'Wow, I'm going to live in a big house for once,' and I went to school and I was like, 'Oh, this sucks.' . . . Chicago kids are a lot rougher on the edges but I think their hearts are really good. They seem to have a sense of loyalty to one another. Like there were so many times [in the city] that I would get into fights because somebody called my friend a bad name or something like that." Jane described neighborhood life that makes for this sort of loyalty and the contrast between being a "street kid" in Chicago and the suburbs, where "you don't see a lot of neighborhood kids playing outside in sprinklers or going to the playground and playing on the monkey bars and stuff." The student who spoke of Chicagoland's "upper suburbia" echoed Jane's sentiments when he described himself as caught between "Chicago dreams" to "have fun, do things," and the suburban mentality "Oh, I have to go to college." Although this student imagined himself in upper suburbia someday, he wavered: "I don't think I'll have that mentality 'cause I've, like, lived in Chicago. . . . You see, every day you see pollution, you see people dying, you see graffiti, and you see all these things left and right." In the same way that Jane described a sort of urban ethic, so did these remarks index ambivalence about the perceived normative Chicagoland Korean American trajectory: the image of the bookish, instrumental path of the ethnic striver Jim described.

Coloring Jane's transition was race. When she mentioned the predominance of Caucasians at her new suburban middle school she spoke of feeling "inferior": "I grew up with, it seemed like every color of the world. . . . Of course the suburbs have them too, but the main people you see are Caucasians. . . . Honestly, when I went there I felt very inferior." In this comment Jane mixed class and race: the less prosperous city schools with people of "every color of the world" and the predominantly white suburban middle school with its more prosperous Korean Americans.

The city-suburb dichotomy featured in Jane's account of moving in was, however, in flux by the end of her high school years. She detailed the strange ways GBS had been changing, with the emergence of *kkangp'ae,* or "gang" Korean Americans. While city transplants like herself "come by it [i.e., city ways and ethics] naturally," when it came to suburban kids, she maintained that they "are purposely trying to do it." "I don't know what they are doing. They are not studying hard—they're just goofing off way too much, getting themselves in a lot of trouble." Her purported urban style aside, Jane's was an account of becoming suburban, if with some sense of difference. By describing these city imitators, she registered her discontent: it was one thing for her to be different and urban, another entirely for kids whose real trajectory didn't warrant it (i.e., kids like Lisa who had long "been there"). This said, Jane acknowledged that not all long-term suburbanites were squarely mainstream, and she took the time to talk about Korean Americans who were not squarely middle class and lived in "not, like, great homes." Thus she reminds us that the social geography is a complex constellation of past and future trajectories and of class and racial identifications.

In Jane's account we see the mainstream at a slight remove, standing for whole ways of being and living. This is the landscape against which Jane charts her own distinction.

LOOKING IN

[The cousins] thought of us as bad Chicago-influenced kids, those Korean gangbangers.—Joe

Joe was a city Korean American who, while remaining outside of the Korean American mainstream I describe here, was able to look in at the suburbs because he had suburban relatives as well as friends he knew through his Christian networks. Joe emigrated from South Korea to Chicago at age four and attended a Chicago magnet high school, Lane Tech. In the late 1990s Lane Tech was the largest Korean American city feeder school for the U of I. In addition to his suburban cousins and suburban friends whom he met through a high school Korean Christian club, Joe had a handle on another population of Korean Americans: "FOB" (fresh off the boat, i.e., recently arrived) friends from his neighborhood who went to neighborhood high schools. Joe prided himself on being able to "mediate" among the disparate groups. His Korean American geography, like Lisa's and Jane's, took stock of this universe of distinction in which residence, high school, and age at immigration could all make a difference.

Joe was one of fourteen first cousins in their twenties. He and his full siblings (he had two half-siblings who lived in a remote suburb), however, were the only ones to have remained in the city, becoming, in a revealingly colored metaphor, the "black sheep of the family": "When we were younger and used to go over to any of the cousins' homes, there was tension between us. . . . *They thought of us as bad Chicago-influenced kids, those Korean gangbangers.*" That he and his brother used to swear a lot only fed into the cousins' naïve image of the city. He explained that while his siblings changed in college, they still remained somehow distant from the suburban cousins, four of whom also attended the U of I.

Joe recalled longing for the suburbs as a kid: "I can't really think of a time when I was really satisfied living in the city." I asked him to say more. "The crime and the people that are around, as in gangbangers and just criminals. I also had a picture in my head of the suburbs as being the nice, family-type of atmosphere. I guess I wanted that." Echoing Jane, he said that he was nevertheless proud of his city "exposure to different cultures and people." The city here stood for racial diversity, but more particularly for non–Korean American and non–Asian American racial diversity.

In high school Joe was very active in the Korean Club and the school's Korean Christian group, which he described as "one and the same." Joe's case was not atypical; a Catholic by upbringing, he was nonetheless intermittently active in high school Protestant circles precisely because the Korean American social scene was so overwhelmingly Protestant. He admitted, "Initially I didn't really go for the religion. I went just because. Later on I got a little more involved." Early in college he became involved in the large Korean American nondenominational Christian church at the U of I. Later in college, however, he returned to the white Catholic church that he had attended in high school. There were also times in college when he opted for a "non-Christian crowd."

Joe's non-Christian Korean American circles began in high school with his "cooler" friends from the neighborhood who attended neither his church nor his magnet high school; most of these friends were what he and most students called FOBS. Typically, FOBS are thought of as having emigrated late enough that they are more comfortable speaking Korean and thus don't quite register as American.[4] Joe was matter-of-fact about attending the magnet school rather than his neighborhood school; he was comfortable "hanging" with the FOBS there, he explained, on account of his fluent Korean and city upbringing. He explained that FOBS found in him an "appealing mix": he seemed so Korean but "knew American culture well." Just as Lisa and Jane made distinctions on the basis of attitude (e.g., study habits, values, selfishness), so too did Joe for these neighborhood FOBS: "Their attitudes—they're pretty proud—they're not really the studying group. They're not that motivated to go to school every day or to try to succeed through academics. From the beginning, I noticed they were party animals and just liked the social environment." He said that they simply don't believe in school as the "way to succeed," that they'd rather be "cool" than "nerdy," and that most of them "end up just working throughout the city" without having gone to college.

Just as Jane described the newly emerging Korean American suburban "gangbangers," Joe described Korean American trajectories that ran counter to the powerful image of a normative suburban trajectory, that constellation of affiliations and values that Lisa admitted to somewhat reluctantly as her own vortex.

FROM AFAR

I feel more comfortable with American friends than with the second generation.—Min

For Joe, it was suburban cousins, as well as high school and college Christian networks, who connected him, if ambivalently, to the suburbs. For Min, the suburban mainstream was a whole other world, one he spoke of with considerable disdain. Min counted himself as a FOB for having arrived in the United States as a high schooler. Although he was a citizen, his parents were only intermittently resident in the United States, and Min's family life resembled that of the so-called early study abroad students (*chogi yuhak saeng*), South Korean youth who come to study abroad before college. This is a population that continues to increase.[5] Indeed, today Korean America at the U of I is radically transformed by their presence. These South Korean citizens who have been continuously or intermittently present in the United States since their elementary, middle, or high school years introduce whole new vectors of difference against which long-standing immigrants—first-, 1.5-, or second-generation Korean Americans—calibrate themselves. It is not an understatement to say that when I was interviewing Min in the mid-1990s this demographic phenomenon had yet to be even recognized or named in South Korea or the United States.

Whereas Joe was comfortable with both FOBs and his Korean American suburban cousins, Min couldn't have been more ill at ease with, or more disdainful of, suburban Korean America and of the Korean American mainstream at the U of I. He described himself as "half/half" in every way, fluent neither in English nor in Korean, and fully at ease neither with South Koreans nor Korean Americans. He had never heard of the large Korean American high schools in the more prosperous northern suburbs, such as the ones that Lisa and Jane attended; what Lisa and Jane called the borderline suburbs, Min took to be the Korean American mainstream. His suburban imaginary included both second-generation Korean Americans and high school immigrants like himself. For Min, Korean American suburbanites were first and foremost Christian, and he considered his status as a non-Christian to be his biggest barrier to being able to socialize with the Korean American mainstream (not that he necessarily wanted to). He didn't mince words: "I'm embarrassed . . . by those nuts." He described being "attacked" by them at the U of I if he dared to comment on their faith: "It's amazing how fast they can attack." Indeed, Min described feeling "more comfortable" with his American (i.e., white) friends than with second-generation Korean Americans; this said, most of his college friends were city Korean Americans and other Asian Americans.

Min's Korean American social circle, both in his neighborhood high school and at the U of I, was narrow, a handful of recently immigrated urban non-Christian Korean Americans. He described them this way: "Well, me and my friends, we have our own *small group*. We are completely isolated from *them* [i.e., the churchgoing suburban Korean Americans]. . . . Especially with AAC [the large Korean American nondenominational Christian church at the U of I], I mean, one of my friends who graduated from here, he was in AAC, and he didn't go to small groups so he got discriminated against. And I'm not Christian. I don't want to go to AAC, and most Korean groups here are related to Christianity. It's all religion." "Small groups" is the term for the church's residentially organized cell groups of fifteen to twenty people that convene at least weekly. Whether or not Min meant to joke referring to his own "small group" of friends I am not sure, but clearly he considered himself far removed from Christianity and its suburban hearth.[6]

Min diagnosed the suburban ethnic malady: the "problem" with the suburbs, he said, was in fact Korean Americans themselves. Echoing Lisa's father, Min described suburbs that had been "ruined because of too many Koreans coming in." Like Jane, he spoke of Korean American suburbanites in gangs and in trouble. Korean American kids, he said, leave the purportedly "dangerous" city for the "in fact more dangerous" suburbs. Unlike Jane, though, who described suburban second-generation kids going wild for no "natural" reason, Min was mostly speaking of early study abroad students who resided in the suburbs without their parents; in his own case, his father was at least intermittently present, while his older brother had always been there. To this group he also added recent immigrants whose parents worked so hard that they had no time to supervise their children, who were getting into lots of trouble. Min was not alone among city Korean Americans in his view that the suburbs ironically were far more dangerous than the city.

Min said that most of his buddies at the U of I intended to return to "to their own native country [South Korea]" someday. Unlike many Korean Americans, he boldly fingered racism as what motivated their desire to return. His friends figured that they would be "limited" in the United States, that race would come to matter someday, if it hadn't already. He worked hard to convince me that one of his immigrant friends had remained "one hundred percent Korean" and would have no problem readjusting to South Korea: "I mean, American culture has *no influence whatsoever* on that guy." For his own part, he explained that returning to South Korea would be hard because of "the people and the laws and stuff," but he imagined that he would somehow "make do." That said, he was "really scared" about Seoul because he wasn't really a "downtown" guy, having grown up in a "moderate" Chicago neighborhood, not "downtown where it's, like, really crowded and there's people walking all over and cars."

Min was certain that race mattered on the job market. He even ventured that grade point average might not really matter at all. In Min's talk it was clear that language ability and American-style social skills correlated with race and difference. He claimed that he just wanted to graduate so he could leave the country: " 'Cause I don't expect to get a job anyway." He predicted that he would end up working in Japan or South Korea. According to Min, where a person goes to college doesn't matter as much as "confidence," that even excellent students from the U of I can end up jobless because "they're not confident in themselves." For Min, being confident required speaking English fluently and being part of the mainstream, be it white or ethnic.

Min thus described trajectories at a considerable remove from suburban ones, trajectories that left open the possibility of so-called return migration back to South Korea and of racism which could preclude easy participation in the American mainstream. Yet, like many of the Korean Americans in this book, Min reserved his harshest criticism not for racist whites but for snooty Korean American Christian suburbanites at the U of I. Throughout this book I argue that race is often spoken through these sorts of distinctions made among coethnics.

With Lisa, Jane, Joe, and Min, I have introduced the mainstream and margins of Chicagoland Korean America and by extension of Korean America at the U of I. While Lisa admitted, if a bit sheepishly, to being at the center of that northern suburban mainstream, Jane and Joe straddled the mainstream and margins, in Jane's case because she moved to the suburbs only late in middle school, and in Joe's because he lived in the city but maintained both kin and nonkin ethnic ties to the suburbs. Min offered the perspective of an outsider who was strongly identified against the mainstream, an identity that he carried to college as well. In the rest of this chapter and most of the rest of this book, we leave Chicagoland for the U of I, where students mobilize their dreams in another geography, a new and promising landscape. But of course geography, as the contemporary idiom has it, "comes with." Much of the Chicagoland mainstreams and margins reconfigure themselves at the U of I, complicating yet other structures of constraint and possibility that students face as they enter this new chapter of their lives.

THE U OF I: "THIS IS THE LAST PLACE I WANTED TO GO TO COLLEGE"

For Chicagoland Korean America, the U of I, imagined so easily as an extension of the northern suburbs, often figured as a problem: the problem of ethnic intimacy. Most important, there were simply "too many" Korean Americans from the Chicagoland mainstream at the U of I. This posed a problem because college "should be" about new horizons, the experience of diversity, and the chance to "get out of [one's] comfort zone." However, as the students I have just introduced would predict, mainstreams and margins looked very different depending on where you stood.

Many students spoke clearly about what the U of I was *not*: it was *not* Northwestern, *not* the University of Chicago, *not* a better Big Ten school (most often mentioned were the University of Michigan and the University of Wisconsin), *not* an elite small college, *not* an Ivy, *not* on the East

Coast, and *not* in California. Many students referred in passing to having entertained various college dreams, but it was nearby Northwestern, and a little bit farther down the road the University of Chicago, that were most often idealized as offering "higher quality" education. Northwestern (in Evanston, just beyond Skokie and en route to the popular northern suburbs) represented a prestigious private university that many Chicagoland Korean Americans were familiar with because of its proximity to the concentration of northern suburban Korean Americans. Countless students told me that they had thought about applying or had applied there or had even been accepted but were unable to attend for financial reasons. The University of Chicago, while farther away from the suburbs, has a national reputation and academic aura. Many students spoke of the experiences of a relative, friend, or acquaintance at these two schools. But on occasion I also encountered a healthy defense of the U of I as, in its own right, an excellent and highly selective university.

The U of I is the flagship campus of the University of Illinois system, priding itself on its "Research One" Carnegie Foundation classification, a mark of its academic prestige, and on its land grant history that asserts its importance to the state.[7] While its northernmost multimillion-dollar Beckman Center looks to the future with its robotics, the south campus Morrow Plots, the oldest uninterrupted experimental agricultural plots in the country, cultivate its historical legacy. These competing images tell the story of the competing values of public higher education in the United States: national excellence and personal achievement on the one hand, service and the well-being of the state on the other. Urbana and Champaign, adjacent towns combining for a population of about one hundred thousand, are surrounded by agribusinesses. The corporate character of the surrounding farming aside, what meets the eye are the interminable corn and soy fields that begin immediately to the south of the campus and three to four miles in every other direction. The U of I is decidedly downstate, outside of the Chicagoland orbit. The undergraduate population, however, is largely Chicagoland, with most hailing from the suburbs.

That the campus is disproportionately Chicagoland, suburban, and white is not lost on most students at the U of I, and certainly not lost on Korean Americans. But if there is one thing that all Korean Americans at the U of I agree on it is that they join *many* other Korean Americans there. In the late 1990s Korean American undergraduate students made up 29 percent of Asian Americans on campus and 3.7 percent of the total undergraduate population. In 1997 there were 527 Korean Americans arriving from thirty high schools, joining from one to eighty-one of their high school Korean American classmates in college. It is critical to note, however, that there were also some sixty-three students who arrived at the U of I with fewer than ten fellow Korean Americans from their high schools, and four students were the only ones from their high schools. Although Korean American students could not rattle off the figures I have just presented, I would argue that most of them had a very well-developed sense of where they fit in this particular statistical landscape, a sort of subjective statistical common sense.

It is this statistical mainstream that often breeds contempt and is the reason so many students described the U of I as the "last place" they wanted to go, not the college they chose, as a vast literature on college choice would have it, but the school that they "ended up at."[8] Yet despite this repeated disparaging talk of the U of I in the high school imaginary, many Korean Americans described "somehow" "knowing all along" that they would in fact attend the U of I. As one student explained, "One by one [my other] options were closed by my parents and I ended up here." There is no question that "ending up at" the U of I was foremost an economic matter, indexing families' financial status (as well as, of course, academic achievement). Telling for the late 1990s were the differences in the Korean American demography of the University of Illinois at Chicago. At that time, UIC drew disproportionately from the city and the transition suburbs, while the U of I drew disproportionately from the more prosperous northern suburbs. By the twenty-first century some things had changed: the city Korean American population has become smaller and older, with increasingly more immigration directly to the suburbs; the U of I is less and less of a bargain due to escalating tuition rates (reflecting in large part the rescission of state funds); and many report that the school has become more and more competitive.

It was, however, the university's ethnic intimacy that figured foremost in the often simultaneous appeal, rejection, and resignation of its Korean American students. As one student said, "It puts you in a stagnant position. You just don't grow. It's so comfortable. It's so easy. You just kind of die." Nothing could be further from the liberal ideas of growth in college than the notion of "death by comfort."

The comfort of the campus is more than just a matter of ethnic intimacy. The U of I also presented a comfortable choice because of its apparently safe rural environs; that Urbana and Champaign are racially and socioeconomically diverse communities that have many of America's contemporary urban problems is lost on many students at the U of I. One student described the U of I campus as "really cute and, like, comfortable" but "isolated": "Like, if you go to Northwestern or, like, other campuses near the city, it's much, it's like there's more hustle, bustle, there's, like, more business there, you know, and professionals and it's closer to more things, you know. But here's kind of isolated. But it's cute because there's, like, small shops and you know the neighborhood, you can't really get lost." For most Korean Americans, UIC represented the most obvious and affordable urban option. The contrast was sharp: "into the city" for UIC or "downstate" for the U of I. Many with city childhoods described the UIC option as an unwelcome return "back to" the city: "It's in the middle of the dirty city, like the dirtier part of the dirty city too." For many at the U of I, UIC conjures images of city kids as well. When I asked one of Joe's cousins at the U of I where Joe's younger brother went to college, she said, "I have no idea—UIC probably," registering the city otherness that Joe described his suburban cousins attributing to him, calling him and his brother "ghetto." These associations come to easy life as we listen in on his suburban cousin assuming that these city kids would attend UIC.

Some UIC students I spoke with were explicit about their college choice in terms of race, explaining that they had opted against comfort for racial diversity.[9] One UIC student from a suburb with few Korean Americans chose UIC against the U of I, where she knew that many of her Korean American churchmates were headed: "I wanted to stay away from the U of I and I just wanted to *experience* a *different* college life than everyone else does. You know, you go to a place and you get the feel of meeting new people, but then there's all these people you know around you." It is remarkable that even as she stayed close to home and to the church that she continued to attend each Sunday with over twenty-five of her own relatives, she could still find meaning in avoiding the U of I and its large Korean American church!

We have seen that the ethnically intimate university must be appreciated in relation to Chicagoland ethnic geography, not simply a map of ethnic concentration and distribution but a mental map of normative Korean American ways of settling, living, and being. The heterogeneity that the students in this chapter registered was very real to them, even though to outsiders their shared status as Korean American college students at the U of I might conjure homogeneity.

2 THE EVANGELICAL CHALLENGE TO
COLLEGE AND FAMILY

with Katharine L. Wiegele

If there is any single image, group, or lifestyle choice that stands for the ambivalent Korean American college comfort zone, it is the largely Korean American AAC, a nondenominational college church.[1] For many Korean American students, Korean America at the U of I, not unlike the Korean clubs in high school that Joe described, was Christian, and more specifically AAC. In the late 1990s those who attended AAC were overwhelmingly Korean American and undergraduate. Interestingly, by 2006 the church's more than eight hundred members had become self-consciously multicultural: 42 percent were non–Korean Americans, over 5 percent were non–Asian Americans, and over 25 percent were nonundergraduates.[2] Nonetheless, even today, for many Korean Americans and U of I students generally, AAC remains Korean American, although most dub it simply Korean.

It was widely appreciated that AAC was religiously resonant with large northern suburban churches, particularly with their English-language youth ministries, which are often more intensely evangelical and charismatic than their parent churches. "Charismatic" here refers primarily to a style of worship characterized by lively singing and nonliturgical informality; many charismatics also emphasize speaking in tongues, healing, prophesy, and spiritual gifts. "Evangelical" describes Christians who emphasize biblical inerrancy, salvation through Christ alone, proselytizing, and the importance of personal conversion through being born again.[3] The religiosity of AAC shares a great deal with other evangelical groups at the U of I and on other campuses, particularly its multimedia experiences in an informal and celebratory atmosphere and a counterculture conservatism.[4] For the majority of Korean American Christians, AAC was familiar in every way, from its expressive, informal style of worship, to its songs and daily organization of religious life, to its theological tenets. Not surprisingly many Chicagoland youth ministers and Sunday school teachers have passed through AAC and the seminaries where many AAC ministers trained. Korean America is overwhelmingly Christian; although scholars report a variety of percentages, there is widespread agreement that Korean America is majority Protestant Christian and that the figure rises about 10 percent with the inclusion of Catholics.[5] Additionally, it is widely reported that in comparison with other ethnic and racial groups, Korean Americans attend church more regularly. In Chicago, for example, 78.3 percent of Korean American church affiliates attend services at least once a week.[6] Chicago's large evangelical youth-oriented churches and youth congregations of multigenerational churches are again not unique. Likewise, most campuses with sizable Korean American student bodies have wholly or largely Korean American churches, although in keeping with developments at the U of I, the increase in multicultural and pan-Asian churches is widespread. What appears to be somewhat unique about AAC is its independent, nondenominational status, as well as its size. Further, while certainly not the only university with a large Korean population (including South Korean and Korean American students), the U of I is distinctive. Indeed, in 2008 it was the top receiving university of South Korean international students. Interestingly, South Koreans constitute the only international population at the U of I with more undergraduate than graduate students, reflecting in large part South Korean nationals who studied abroad before entering college. Indeed, AAC is but one, although by far the largest, of many Korean churches; others cater more to specific Korean populations, such as South Korean international graduate students and their families, Korean American resident families in town, and South Korean undergraduates who also studied abroad in their pre-college lives.

A large body of literature documents the role of the ethnic church in immigrant life, and there is considerable agreement that in the Korean immigrant case the church is the primary social organization through which people find social networks and social support, as well as meaning.

It is hard to overestimate the intricate Korean American Christian network that AAC, a handful of seminaries both in and outside of Chicagoland, and a small cohort of northern suburban churches compose. As *the* U of I Korean American touchstone, everyone had something to say about AAC. Detractors expressed the feeling that their university coethnics "might as well have moved their mom and their suburban home [to college] with them, while they were at it." Indeed, many Christian Korean Americans had traveled to the U of I area a few to a dozen times over the course of high school for religious events. For these students, the U of I was quite literally the campus where AAC is located. In what many would consider extreme cases, students came to the U of I to attend AAC. Jane, the high school suburbanite, described her high school connections with AAC this way: "We've been kind of involved with it back in high school. 'Cause my Bible study went to AAC, so we would go back and forth for lock-ins and retreats even while we were in high school and even though it's a college group." Not surprisingly, Jane's high school Bible study leader was a U of I graduate who had been active in AAC. Jane described her high school group of seven Korean American girlfriends, all of them fairly devout Christians, who wanted to come to the U of I. Only Jane briefly considered applying elsewhere, to Northwestern: "They all wanted to come here. Yes, because of the academic factor, but largely because of the church factor. And actually I was the only person who wasn't so much like the church factor but like the home factor was more affecting me. But, yeah, the church was a huge incentive to come here." Jane recalled her arguments with these friends in high school: "I'm like, 'Why are you—it seems like church is your whole life. I don't think that's right—you should think about it. Why don't you get more involved in school or stop hanging around just church friends all the time?'" Jane was unwavering that when it comes to choosing college "studying . . . should be *one of* the factors." Those who wanted to stress the excesses of the U of I–AAC connection often talked about the growing number of Korean American students at the regional community college, Parkland, who moved to the area to be able to attend AAC and with the hopes of someday being able to transfer to the U of I.

Thus Christianity, and particularly AAC, was at the heart of the uncomfortably comfortable Korean American comfort zone, that zone that troubled ideal notions of a multicultural college experience and personal development. One student who decided to distance herself from AAC put it this way: "I felt like it [AAC] kept me from being who I originally was." She wanted to "break away from" the AAC "mold," "stereotype," and "restraints." She described how easy it was to get "trapped," to "fall into it without even noticing," to lose one's "originality," "creativity," and "sense of being individualistic."[7]

Although mired in the image of the Korean American mainstream, for some AAC nonetheless offered its adherents a challenge to that status quo, to the model minority images of striving, instrumental families.[8] As such it provided another way to enact certain liberal ideas of universal humanity. So, while it troubled outsider Korean Americans for its ethnic particularism (i.e., its largely Korean American participation at the time) and for the way it seemed synonymous with a particular lifestyle and trajectory (the comfort zone), many of those in its fold found there an identity beyond the contingencies of race, ethnicity, class, and the like.[9]

In this way, those Korean Americans who, from the perspective of AAC detractors, should have been most troubled by their own ethnic intimacy seemed quite unfazed by it, for the church in its own way offered a critique of these racialized images. It is worth pondering how a largely ethnic and religious space could afford this critique. Thus the "challenge to college" in this chapter's title refers to this religious version of intellectual and personal growth in lieu of that offered by the university. For many students, the secular university failed them in the liberal venture; it was instead the church that fulfilled this vision of human development. I realized early in my research that I needed to take religion seriously when a student told me she did not take notes in one of her general education courses. Her reason: "Unlike at church, [there is] nothing to take with me."[10]

Affiliation with AAC posed an equal challenge to family as students differentiated their own Christianity from that of their Christian parents; they described parents who at best were simply less observant, and at worst were entirely hypocritical or heretical. Their parents' ethnic Christianity typically stood precisely for that mainstream constellation of upwardly mobile, striving, status-oriented, and instrumental desires. Like the youth congregations nestled in many of the larger Korean American as well as nonethnic Chicagoland churches, AAC offered an evangelical Christianity different from the more formal liturgical variant of the parent churches. Youth Christian practice is typically more fervent, ecstatic, and musical; most observant students I spoke with were not strangers to speaking in tongues, personal testimony, or other forms of spiritual experience in their own lives.[11] It was in this context that some students proclaimed even their faithfully church-attending parents to be spiritually wanting or even religiously immature.

Perhaps it can be said that Christian and non-Christian Korean American students join all students in a critique of their middle-aged parents' values. However, as I argue throughout this book, what is distinctive here is that this rejection is racialized; it challenges not only particular parents but relentless stereotypes of Asian American immigrant parents and families. Perhaps it is ironic that with this challenge these Christian Korean American students echo the criticisms that some of their non-Christian Korean American student colleagues lodge against Korean American Christianity itself! Here we must take note: nearly all of the students in this book grappled with racist images of the upwardly striving immigrant, whether they claimed that their family (or even their family's Christianity) embodied that very stereotype or (at least intermittently) that their family was somehow distinctive. These images are present, and often disturb, as they navigate college and take stock of their own family.

THE CHRISTIAN CHALLENGE TO THE UNIVERSITY

At the first weekly meeting of the 1998–1999 school year, the head pastor of AAC, after singing out "We are filled with the Lord, not empty," offered, "This is why this [i.e., AAC] should be *the best party on campus*, right?!" In quick succession, the pastor hit all the recreational nodes of college social life: alcohol, sports, and parties. He told the congregation, "Fill yourself with the words of the Lord, not with wine." And he urged the students to rejoice in church "as loudly and enthusiastically" as fans do at sporting events, counseling that "the words 'Don't be emotional' are ridiculous." He added that "small groups" would serve as their new "families" and that they should pray that they grew "close."

"The best party on campus"

"The best party on campus" was much more than an occasional weekend gathering. The church offered a veritable shadow campus calendar, a roster of nearly daily activity. Small groups were the locus and organizer of much of that activity; that the pastor offered them as surrogate families is telling, for they were to be held responsible for their fold.

Taken together, the shadow campus calendar and surrogate family were designated to subvert the dangers of the secular college experience, both in and beyond the classroom. One former member said of the congregants, "They want to be safe. Especially in the college atmosphere. . . . There's this fear of, like, the sex thing and the overdrinking, and getting into drugs. So they [AAC] like to take care of their students."

One cannot but be impressed by the time demands AAC made of its students, with its nearly round-the-clock activity: weekly small group Bible study, Sunday services, meetings with prayer partners, weekend social activities such as mini-Olympics, large group Friday night worship, daily morning prayer, revivals, retreats, lock-ins, volunteer activities, not to mention daily quiet time for personal prayer and reflection on specific Bible passages. One small group leader, Cindy, admitted that the church demands a large commitment, but she insisted that college kids have "a lot of time" on their hands with "only two to three classes a day," and so it was "better the church" than "not so edifying activities" take their time. On the one hand, college was a precious time for critical growth; on the other hand, college kids had "a lot of time" during which to stray. One student ruminated on his own wasted time: "I remember my freshman year when I was taking art classes and stuff, I felt like it was really, it should have been more *time consuming* than it was for me. But at the same time, I look back at it like, even the *times* when I had to work on projects and stuff, even though I was swamped, I felt like there was *so much time* that, I mean, I did my fair share of goofing off and I did my fair share of playing basketball and hanging out with friends, but at the same time, I felt like, I think back and *there was still time* that I still had and it's just a matter of—I just kind of squandered and what not."

Beyond its full roster of activity, AAC also tutored students in a veritable philosophy of time. Small groups were designated to train students to account for their time, and their members were held responsible for each other's judicious time management. They were accountable in all senses of that word: students were to take stock of their time, to be held responsible for it, and to narrate their use of it. Sophie, one of the small group members, described small groups this way: "Basically, the purpose of small group is perseverance. . . . You cannot persevere without *accountability*; you cannot persevere without singing to one another. . . . [The pastor's] phrase is 'singing to each other every day and encouraging each other.' . . . Especially since they're area coordinated, you live with them: you're going to see them, pretty much, if not every day of the week, you're going to see them a lot. . . . It's sharing, sharing to encourage, to build each other up, to keep each other from falling, to persevere, to keep each other *accountable* until the very end, until Jesus comes and says, 'Well done, my good and faithful servant.' That's basically the idea of small group. Basically."

Taking Sophie's description to its logical extreme was the time chart that was distributed through small group meetings in February. Students were handed a 24/7 chart calibrated by half-hour units, making for 336 boxes. Prior to handing out the sheet, Cindy led a discussion on accountability and urged, "You know, we have . . . how much . . . three months left until the end of the semester. . . . If we hit mid-May, guys, and [you] have had no change of heart at all [in a heightened and pleading voice], then I'm going to be held *accountable* for it! I'm going to be judged before God! At the pearly gates." As she handed out the chart she instructed, "Keep yourself *accountable* for each half-hour block of your life. Do this chart for a week and it will reveal a lot about our lives." She went on to tell them to draw a contrast between time spent in "neutral" (i.e., of little positive value) activity and "time spent with the Word and with helping someone in need."

This discourse on time presented students with an interesting contradiction: on the one hand, a fear that with *so much time* they could easily fall prey to all sorts of secular temptation, but on the other hand, the sense that the time for serious personal religious development was in short supply. One student described the inevitable onslaught of adulthood and the work world: "Once you start your work, your work can become who you are. I think you should be shaped before you get out of here. Either that, or once you get out of here there's even more things that can take you away from *who you're supposed to be*, in a sense, just because you're too busy or too lazy." Becoming "who you're supposed to be" was designated a time-sensitive college project, and one that required faith.

"Intimacy, not intensity"

Time management and accountability aside, Cindy set "[religious] intimacy, *not* intensity" as the theme for her small group that year and called on the phrase repeatedly. Small group leaders tended to be seniors or recent graduates; Cindy was a recent U of I graduate who had stayed local with a teaching job. She was well-known for her dynamism and emotionally engaging leadership style, and we were advised that hers would be a good group to follow. It was as if Cindy knew that observers might look askance at the time demands, the intensity, of AAC and wonder whether constant activity masked some sort of lack. With AAC's intensity as a near given of the church's image and daily life, she sought to highlight the church's meaning, its intimacy. Interestingly, she spoke explicitly of intensity as a feature of Korean American immigrant life, and with intimacy she meant to intervene in pejorative images of Asian or Korean America. Here again is the thread that runs throughout this and subsequent chapters: the myriad ways that Korean American students and collectivities challenge prevailing racialized stereotypes. In the opening minutes of the first small group meeting Cindy introduced the theme this way: "We all know this: as Asian Americans, our parents are different from other parents, *they're intense*. They don't just go to work and come home. They work fifteen hours at the dry cleaners so that we can have a nice house. . . . Well, I'm reminded of a distinction I once heard from a preacher: there's a difference between intimacy and intensity, and sometimes we even confuse those in our personal relationships. *What I want for this small group this year is not necessarily an intense group but an intimate group.*" Cindy thus charted a distinct course for her small group, one that rejected, or at least distinguished itself from, Korean American parental intensity, such as that of the life of dry cleaners. Her statement also acknowledged, however, that it was in fact those fifteen-hour-a-day immigrant parent jobs that made for the students' leisure, the excess time, that needed to be organized by small groups and AAC (i.e., rather than through jobs to support college fees and living).

In early November Cindy explained intimacy to the small group this way: "We think that if we serve so much, running around, doing our prayer partners, doing praise night, et cetera, that if we serve so much, then this will bring the love of God. But the love of God comes first. This is my big thing and I'm going to keep saying it over and over again: *intimacy, not intensity*. That's my desire for my life." Nonetheless AAC was intense. This contradiction was not lost on students as they struggled to make sense of, to narrate their spiritual search and growth in relation to their busy secular *and* religious lives. When AAC detractors, and even internal critics, mentioned the well-known rumor that AAC had once been listed as one of the top-ten cults in America, they were grappling with both AAC's religious intensity and ethnic intimacy, arguably the church's two trouble spots. One student described the cult rumor this way: "You know, [AAC] people usually like to study together, eat together, so it really is your social group. That becomes who you are, AAC. I think that's why it can be considered a cult because it takes you away from other people, other social groups, and it gets kind of exclusive."

AAC's religious intensity was troubling for its Korean American members precisely for too nearly echoing just the sort of ethnic intensity Cindy highlighted, the intense small entrepreneurial variety. Ethnic intimacy, the plurality of Korean Americans in AAC, was troubling both for running against the grain of liberal human development and, in a different vein, because color should not matter in the eyes of God.

"Ask God to change you"

I began this book on the liberal promise of college, the promise foremost to help students develop over the course of college: the college graduate should be and feel different. The AAC church articulated a similar call for its members: to grow and transform over the college years. The church's call, however, was to allow the divine a hand in this change, a very different picture from the liberal individual guiding his or her own growth. To underscore this religious point, Cindy reminded the small group of Romans 12:2: "Do not be conformed to the pattern of this world but be transformed." She told the students that they must overcome worldly tendencies in order to be able to ask that "God change [them]."

The divine hand posed a challenge to the secular self as college agent. "We need to keep praying if we want to transform," one student offered a small group. A second student echoed, "God wants us to transform. It's not just our doing. *Even if we want to stagnate*, He's going to help us. *God will change you.*" To this the first student responded, "We also need to come down from the mountain. . . . We're so selfish. . . . We really need to listen to Christ."

Henry took the floor at one small group meeting to answer Cindy's question, "What are your greatest challenges or areas of growth?" "I have a big problem growing [pause], no pun intended." Because Henry is short the group members laughed. He continued seriously with a speech about growth, college as a vulnerable time, and the relationship between the church, his major, and the university: "I'm like, do I grow first and that makes me do [good] things? Or is it the other way around, where I do things first and that makes me grow? And then it turns out that I'm doing neither. . . . College is a vulnerable time for us. I feel like I haven't grown enough *to take anything with me* when I graduate. This semester is the first time I've started taking notes at Friday large group. . . . But now I feel like I have another chance—I'm starting a new minor right now, so I'll have another year here. I'm so grateful that God allowed me to stay another year. . . . I mean, the main motivation was the minor and stuff, but I see now that it gives me another year at AAC. . . . I have another chance." As Henry talked about a fifth year at the university, one "allowed [by] God" (and afforded perhaps by *intense* parental work), we heard him negotiating between secular and religious growth, musing about more time for his academic minor but also celebrating a fifth year at AAC and the chance to "take notes" at church.

Many students spoke, as Henry did, about church learning in relation to college learning. For some, it was church that was doing the better job, giving them more to "take with them." They also described how the university was falling short in its mission to educate, enlighten, and inspire. Julie, for example, suggested that while the church calls on students to be global citizens, jaded professors do little more than "teach to the grade." It was Julie who first told me that students typically take notes at AAC, and that while she always did so at church, she took notes only occasionally in her university classes. The college professor in me was taken aback, imagining the college classroom to be the major education venue. Julie explained that her class notes were different from her sermon notes (from my perspective, her approach to her sermon notes was exactly what I would like students to do in my courses): "When I'm listening to a sermon, it's more that I'm not writing down exactly what he [the pastor] says. I'll take what he says and I'll be able to think about it and then write myself notes." As for her college classes, she said, "It's just like rote memorization. . . . Whereas in church, the concepts are always linked with examples. When I'm in one of my classes, I don't feel like I'm learning about life. I'm *not* learning about *who I am* and *who I should be*." Julie described the AAC pastor who told her that her purpose in college, away from her family, was to "grow as a human being." Later in our conversation she elaborated, "[The pastor challenged me to] look at myself individually, locally, nationally, globally. . . . Our pastor tries to stress we're not just someone at the U of I, in Illinois, in this nation, we're someone *in the world*. As far as college students go, this may be a generalization—I think we're all just really selfish. It's us, *it's me*. The way that society makes you feel: look out for number one, number one is you." By "society" Julie referred broadly to American norms and more specifically to American youthways, reminding us that ethnic America does not have an exclusive hold on instrumentality, but that the charge ("It's me") takes on particular meaning in the lives of students of color. Although Julie admitted that there are some professors who challenge students to think about "who you are," the status quo pales: "They've taught at the university for *how long?* They just realize that all they [students] seem to care about is the grade. They cater to that. After a while, they [professors] seem to get burnt out."

Like Julie, Phil also looked favorably on his church learning in comparison to his general education courses, highlighting the relevance or "power of application" of church learning. But unlike Julie, Phil gave credit directly to the Bible, particularly the *Life Application Bible*. He placed blame for college weaknesses on the absence of "guidance" that would have directed him to more meaningful classes. As for the Bible in relation to secular texts, for which he relies exclusively on "Mr. Cliff" (i.e., CliffsNotes), he said, "It's more inspiring. It's more, you can relate to it more, not divinity-wise. . . . If there are problems you can look it up in the Bible." Indeed, Phil "looks things up" in his Bible almost daily (easy to do with the indexed *Life Application Bible*). When asked about university guidance he said, "If there was an advisor . . . I would have chosen a little bit more wisely." Didn't Phil have an advisor? How did he fall through the cracks? Phil imagined that there were many students who, like him, "probably regret" their choice of courses: "Like, I should have taken something that was more relevant."

Catherine was more generous than Phil or Julie on the university; for her, the strengths of AAC and of her liberal arts classes had equal weight: "I think liberal arts are key to understanding, like, everything, understanding a lot of why things are the way they are. . . . They're a much bigger part of, like, society, life, you know, and it's, I think it gave me a greater understanding, especially anthropology, about people, behavior, it makes you a lot more, I don't know, not compassionate, I guess, understanding, just see why things are the way they are." Catherine compared this learning to her experience at AAC: "[The head pastor]

54

encourages people to take notes. It's almost like going to class and, you know, they ask you to apply things to your life and try to see the connection between faith and things in your everyday life." Like other AAC students, Catherine spoke of "application," hoping that both church and college could make an immediate difference in her life.

Unlike Julie and Phil, Catherine figured that it was the university that set the tone and AAC that followed suit: "Because they know that people here are more academic." While each of these students had a different perspective on the relationship between AAC and the university, they shared a profound sense that the university's secular mission was not the most important path in their lives.

If Catherine and others facilely compared the benefits of AAC and the liberal arts, it was the matter of a "divine hand" that most emphatically distinguished students' Christian and secular college worlds. It was here that students struggled to accommodate both church and the university, to figure themselves and their own hand in the course of things. It was here that we find perhaps the greatest challenge to the secular university. At one extreme, students spoke summarily about the sin of hubris and the idea that they are going it alone. Most, however, wavered, wanting to allow for divine plans but struggling to make way for their own place in the world.

Telling was the 1998 AAC opening meeting, "How to Survive at U of I," that paralleled the university's own secular orientations. The pastor emcee told the newly arrived freshmen and returning upperclassmen, "[AAC taught me] about myself, about what my major was going to be . . . and about where I fit into God's plan," thereby establishing AAC's singular role in academic guidance. In the first Sunday sermon of that year the head minister described the "Christian life" as "walking in uncertainty": "We don't know where we're walking." He then spoke to the specificity of college: "Even in this intellectual setting, this university, we still walk in faith." With these comments, students' academic planning was relinquished to some combination of the church and divine inspiration.

When Cindy asked small group members to jot down their favorite Bible passage, three students selected the same favorite, Jeremiah 29:11, "For I know the plans I have for you." Indeed, the passage came up during a number of my interviews. Liz, another AAC small group co-leader who had been born again when she "responded to the altar call" in eighth grade, turned to this same Bible passage when she talked about her major and how she came to change her major. She described her impasse this way: "I think even while I was all confused, while I was wanting to switch out of business but then my parents were, sort of, not wanting me to, and still not being sure about even what I wanted to switch into, I was very, like, 'cause you know sort of like as a Christian, you sort of feel like *God has a plan for you*. So, like, 'God, What do you want me to do?' I don't know. So, I felt like I was really searching, like, trying to find out what God wanted me to do about it." Liz contrasted her parents' desire for upward class mobility, wanting her to stay in business, with God's plan. "Sort of an understood thing" for Liz was "not to just make a decision on [her] own but to prayerfully consider it." The term "prayerfully" was new to me, so I asked her what she meant. "It's in the scripture," she answered, and proceeded to quote from Jeremiah 29:11: " 'For I know the plans I have for you. Plans to prosper you, not to harm you,' things like that." Then, like so many other students I spoke with, she dug into her backpack for her Bible and cited the verse: "Oh, okay. It's Jeremiah 29:11. 'For I know the plans I have for you, declares the Lord. Plans to prosper you and not to harm you. Plans to give you hope in the future and then you will call upon me and pray to me and I will listen to you.' " She described becoming born again in similar terms: "It's basically just acknowledging that you need Jesus as your Savior . . . that you can't save yourself. . . . Basically, it's sort of like a turning point of, like, living on your own, like depending upon yourself, and changing and then accepting . . . and depending on Him . . . for everything." Despite having become born again in eighth grade, it was in college that Liz truly transformed, becoming able to depend on God. In her early college days she found it "really foreign" when people spoke about "what God was doing in their life." It made her feel "uncomfortable," she added. At that time, church was "just almost an automatic thing . . . something that [she] just did." It wasn't until her sophomore year that she became "more serious about Christian life." She spoke about wanting to be like the others, "wanting to have this same relationship with God that they had." She subsequently "worked hard" on her relationship with and became "more open" to God, even seeing the transition from high school to college as moving from "insecurity" to "just knowing that God is working through the struggles in [her] life."

Sophie too spoke of God as the prime mover of her college life. She described her painful religious struggles: "A lot of guilt and a lot of pride wrapped together and a lot of fear. Fear of what God wants me to do and I'm scared to let go of the things that He's asking me to let go of." It was a boyfriend that she was being asked to let go of because she realized, "I love somebody more than I love God." She described the struggle in religious terms: "But I just think, I really think God's using this time to make me know Him better." Later in the conversation she came to the matter of college itself. She spoke of her wish to set aside her boyfriend, school, and her reading and writing from her faith. But she claimed that they were in fact "church issues" and that there was no real way for her to somehow stand "in the middle." Appreciating that life and church necessarily meet, she continued, was "the only way to be truly happy and content."

For these students, AAC thus posed a considerable challenge to the university: it offered its own variant of human development; it asked students to manage college via the church; and, perhaps most profoundly, it called on them to question their own hand in this very management and development.

THE CHRISTIAN CHALLENGE TO FAMILY

Many Korean Americans questioned the authenticity of their parents' religious practice and went to some lengths to distinguish their own practice from this ethnic one, even as they were ensconced in a largely ethnic church. I do not mean to suggest a paradox, but instead to treat seriously students' struggle over how to carve out personal and religious identities against powerfully racialized images of the ethnic group. The distinction is challenging given the aforementioned remarkable figures of Korean American adult Christian church attendance. At the more generous end of the spectrum, the second generation merely echoed the sociological literature on immigrant-generation Christianity: that it offered new immigrants an important ethnic support network, one that can be both comforting and critical to immigrant survival because of networks that make a difference to livelihoods (e.g., securing clientele for small businesses).[12] At the other end of the spectrum, this sort of Christian practice was antithetical to real religiosity. As one student put it, "There's a difference between just going to church and doing all these things as opposed to changing your views and having it *really* affect you. . . . My parents are just primarily focused on doing things and going to church. I think that's mainly the difference." "My parents," another woman explained, "have a different viewpoint on religion, more as it's some kind of social control on people, a way that people explain the unexplained kind of thing, rather than *a way of life.*" Parents too were sometimes troubled by their children's Christian intensity. Some parents worried about their children's considerable time commitment to the church and feared that they were being led astray from school and other secular matters.

Robert, like many students I interviewed, posited Koreanness against Christianity. He considered his family as, for the most part, uniquely (really) Christian. Indeed, a considerable number of students did think of their families as "really" Christian, but they usually stressed their distinctiveness in the landscape of Korean America. With this we return to an overarching theme: in a racialized America it is distinctive Koreans who belie pejorative racialized images.

"I'm not trying to be Korean, I'm trying to be a Christian"

For Robert, it was having a ponytail that marked his Christian identity as being in opposition to his Korean identity. "Christian" and "Korean" stood for radically different ways of understanding college and life. Robert spoke of college as a crossroad where nominal Korean American Christians like himself (i.e., kids from church-attending families) faced a decision between being sincere, born again Christians or Korean. He described a contest between a lofty, spiritual journey and a Korean narrower or worldlier path. As to Korean (in that worldly version) Christianity, he had this to say: "I think Koreans have the idea in their head that Christianity is just the best religion in the country . . . so we're going to make it our religion now. So you gotta be, we just gotta look like a Christian family even if we're not. We have to be the best at everything. We have to make the best cars, we have to have the best jobs in industry, stuff like that. So, when it comes to Christianity and Koreanness, 'If two things are the best, well, they just have to go together.'" Then he regaled me with humorous stories of relatives who asked salesmen for "the best" of this or that, knowing or caring about little other than the status of the product. For Robert, going Korean meant that "the big part of your life is your job, is making money, is getting the mutual funds, is finding the best 401(k)." The "Korean route" meant backing away from the church, attending only sporadically: "If I had time, I'd go." It also meant living intensely, and secularly, in the way that small group leader Cindy had criticized. In contrast, going Christian, in his sense of an authentic religiosity, stood for an examined life, one not narrowly instrumental. As for college in the examined life, he said, "School's still a big part of your life, and you're required to do well in school to honor God."[13]

But Robert's main point was that in the case of his own family, the generational contrast didn't work because he thought of his parents as authentic Christians and as such atypical Korean immigrant parents. Over several years Robert never tired of telling me that his parents were "different," just as Jim described his parents' distinctiveness for wanting him to experience the world broadly. Robert described his parents as "weird . . . unlike any kind of Korean parents you'll meet." "In what sense?" I asked, and he offered the following story, laughing all the way. And with this he came to the matter of his ponytail.

> Well, okay, let me tell you one little story. I have this friend. One day we were going to come to my house with a bunch of our friends and watch a movie, so I had gone to pick him up at this place. And he was wearing these really short shorts, but he didn't realize it. And he had a really long shirt on so it didn't look like he was wearing any pants. It looked very strange. I didn't say anything about it and I took him to my house and my parents came home. And [my friend] gets up and says, "Hello Mr. and Mrs. Lee." . . . What's the first thing my father says? Not "Hello," not "How you doing?" but "You're not wearing any pants." This is like completely typical of what my parents will do. Uhm, *I think my parents really strive to be Christians more than they strive to be Korean.* I guess you can kind of see that in, like, just my hair. My hair is long, which is unacceptable in Korean culture, but my parents are not [preventing me from wearing it long]. . . . [When my parents asked me about it] I'm like, *"I'm not trying to be Korean, I'm trying to be a Christian."* I'm not saying I'm growing my hair long to be a Christian, but [Christianity] doesn't say it's wrong. It's an aesthetic twist for me, and my parents said, "Okay."

Robert then told me that his father and paternal grandparents never had a problem with his hair, but that his mother, aunts, and uncles had "taken longer to come around." Robert thus distinguished his parents by asserting that they were more authentically Christian than most of their generation, that they were not, as was often implied, faux Christians. For Robert, his ponytail was all about appearances; more specifically, it meant that he and his parents were *not* obsessed with appearances. He contrasted his parents with "typical" Korean parents who he suggested were quick to register measures of status rather than to make jokes about bare legs (i.e., a trivial aspect of appearance). This was clear in his descriptions of what it was like to visit Korean Americans friends' homes, where he encountered a steady stream of questions that he considered "a completely Korean thing."

Robert described the typical Korean parents' "third degree" when he went to pick up one of his friends: " 'What's your major? What kind of driving record do you have?' And then I got this great twenty-minute speech about life and not wasting time. I felt like I was taking him out on a date or something like that." He continued with more generic observations about Korean parents' questioning: "Like, 'How many languages can you speak? You only speak two? What's wrong with you?' I'm like, 'I speak one-point-five.' And they're like, 'What did you get on your last report card?' . . . And there'll be other things, like 'Why don't you talk Korean to me?' " In contrast were his parents' questions: "The first question is usually 'What's your name?' and the second question is, 'Do you want pizza?' " When Robert told me this, as when he described his father asking about his friend's bare legs, he laughed heartily because of how jarring, or rather how refreshingly lighthearted, these anecdotes struck him in the landscape of Korean American parents.

Robert's college impasse, whether to be Christian or Korean, nonetheless came down to appearances: his hair. He said that he had always known that college was the "breaking point" when "most people stop going to church." I interjected, "You heard that growing up?" and he answered, "Growing up, college, everywhere. College is the breaking point. And I really think it is." He elaborated, "You're away from that [Korean] culture. . . . It's kind of like, now you're here and you come to a leap of faith, so to speak. You either make your choice to be Korean or a Christian, and it really separates like that, honestly." In another conversation he described the fork in the road this way: "If you're, like, a Korean Christian person, you come to a point where you ask yourself, 'Is this all there is to it?' And you start to see contradictions and things like that in what your father is telling you is Korean and what your minister is telling you is Christian." It is interesting that Robert offered this generic generational tug-of-war even as he detailed precisely the way his own parents departed from the stereotype.

THE EVANGELICAL CHALLENGE

Robert went on to say that he was at the "leap" point, ready to leave the "culture" behind but still not sure about Christianity. When he told me that he felt "pressure" to decide, I asked, "By who?" He replied, "I honestly don't know. God, my peers, my parents . . . my grandparents." He admitted that not all Korean Americans come to this point: "A lot of people never come to this leap of faith, and they're just going along happily with this blind kind of 'duh' . . . Korean version of Christianity."

I do not want to leave you with a sense of Robert triumphantly exiting the ethnic fold. Once we had a long discussion about his "ending up in engineering," which turned into a lament on the fateful inevitability of ethnic tendencies in his life. "I've been fighting it for a long time. Like, I'm not going to be an engineer. Every Asian person becomes an engineer or a doctor. I'm not going to be an engineer." He summed up his situation with a similar lament about his parents' small entrepreneurship: "We eventually decided to do what other Korean people do, go into dry cleaning. It's kind of like my life: I try to avoid doing what other Korean people do, and it just kind of ends up like *I end up doing what they do*." It was hard work for him to carve out a religious or even a secular life against the ethnic grain, the shallow, unflattering portrait of Koreanness. The ponytail, a corporeal matter, a feature that speaks everywhere he goes, was meant to doubly distinguish him: for what it said about himself *and* his family.

"You can't bring your car to heaven"

The "real" Christian life was about something other than what Robert described as the Korean parent success-oriented third degree. Cindy, the small group leader, summarized: "[There is] even conflict in . . . the things they [parents] teach us to live for: you know, the American dream. Have your two-car garage and your picket fence and make a lot of money, and, you know, 'We're busting our butt at the cleaners twelve to sixteen hours a day so that you can have a better life.'" Liz, the student who was counseled by her pastor to "prayerfully" switch her major, transferred from a well-remunerated discipline to a low-paid service career track, a switch that both baffled and bothered her mother: "I was talking with my friend. . . . I always had this, for some reason whenever I imagine myself in the future, I imagine myself poor for some reason. And then my friend's like, 'Me too.' It's so weird." Liz described her family's material struggles as being "not necessarily poor, like living in a shack, but . . . ," and how it was thus easy for her to imagine a very different life from the one her parents had so carefully planned for her.

Another student spoke of his parents this way: "Instead of serving God, it's like 'Get good grades!' " This student was seriously considering becoming a missionary, renouncing the well-paid career track he was on. He described the decision in terms of his own previous material indulgence and his longing for the "simpler life" of Africa: "I feel like I've indulged myself into the world. . . . I feel like, even basketball and things of the world . . . and I'm a really big fan of cars. And then this summer I asked myself, I wonder what's going to be in heaven, and then I was like, basketball is a worldly thing, and then God all of a sudden [told] me, 'It's like, *you can't bring your car to heaven,* you know that right?' I said, 'Why?' 'It's a thing of the world.' I'm like, 'Man, are you sure?' and He's like, 'Yeah.' . . . So, I'm just thinking, man, I should give this all up, and I was thinking 'Africa' because it's so humble there. . . . I'm just so things-of-the-world, but I feel that when you have less material wealth, then you're actually a happier person." This remarkably intimate conversation with God (whom he called "Man") speaks to students' interest in imagining alternative career tracks, far from the well-worn mainstream trajectory.

An October small group meeting which discussed the preceding Sunday's sermon and Bible passage, "No Servant Is Greater than His Master," suggested a similar challenge to the mainstream. Cindy's group members had been stumbling over this Bible passage and broke into groups to discuss it. Sophie spoke up three times to say that she still didn't understand the passage. On her third attempt at an answer, Cindy asked, "Sophie, does this make sense?" Sophie didn't respond and Cindy asked again. Sophie finally muttered, "Huh? Sorry, I wasn't paying attention, I'm totally out of it. I just realized that I don't have my keys." "That's okay," Cindy said, and picking right up from this mundane and secular interlude, she launched into a mini speech meant to definitively explicate the passage. She began by reminding the group members that they are elite college students and ended with the story of one of the congregation members, a doctor they all knew, to teach that following his example they must be Christian servants first and doctors only second.

You know, only one percent of all the people in the world ever get the opportunity to have a college degree. This puts us in a really elite position in the

62

world. All of you will become doctors, engineers, writers, et cetera. . . . We're bound to be successful, but will that become your identity? . . . No matter what your position will be, you're not greater than Jesus—*you'll always be a server of Christ*. . . . As a Christian, this is who you are: a servant. . . . You know the doctor who came back here? . . . When he was here before *he was one of those people who really had a servant's heart*. I mean, like, if someone needed to get to Washington, D.C., he would jump in his car immediately and drive them without a second thought. Then when he became a doctor . . . someone asked him for a ride to Chicago and he was really calculating. He thought, "Okay, if I leave now, can I make it home by eleven o'clock? . . . Can I make it and still get enough sleep to get up in the morning for work?" Then the person was late and delayed the trip by a couple of hours. So he thought, "Well, okay, I'll get back by two a.m. and I think that's still okay. *After all, I'm a servant, right?*" Then the person delayed the trip a few more hours and he started to get ticked off. The person sensed this and said, "Never mind, I'll just get someone else to do it." Later on someone said to the doctor, "You know, you've changed so much, *you're more of a doctor than a servant.*" This hit him so hard, so deep because *he had always thought of himself as a servant.* Now you'll see him at every event tending to people's needs. . . . When I see him, I feel so challenged myself because *he's a servant, not a doctor*, at his core.

With this story Cindy brought her small group to the heart of the conflict between one's secular (and in this case highly remunerative and arguably service-oriented) career and religious practice. There are several points of note. First, the doctor was not called upon to forsake his career but simply to be an ardent church participant. Second, the service the doctor called himself to was not missionary or service work with the needy, but service to the (ethnic) church fold. Recall the pastor's exhortations about the church and the small group as family. We can perhaps appreciate this moral tale this way: unlike those students called to low-paying jobs who more clearly renounce mainstream or parental ethnic expectations, this is the story of a doctor, an adult who set an example of career-religious-ethnic balance.

KOREAN CHRISTIANITY: *"THE GIRLS WOULD BE IN THEIR CORNER"*

The challenge AAC posed to family and the university was perhaps most poignant for women because of its gender-specific ideas about career expectations and family obligations. For AAC detractors and even ambivalent insiders, the church's gender conservatism was a constant topic.[14] Complicating matters was the stigma of ethnic patriarchy: Christian and Korean vied for blame in many students' accounts. Sophie's slip of the tongue was telling: "I don't plan on *submitting to my husband* and I don't plan on *giving my career away for a family* and I don't have any of the same values as [my roommate] that she thinks *is the model of a Korean, not Korean, I'm sorry, a Christian woman,* you know." Interestingly, by the time the church had become significantly pan-Asian in the middle of the first decade of the twenty-first century, it was Koreans who single-handedly bore the charge of the excesses of patriarchy; by that point, although the congregation was 42 percent non–Korean American, it was widely accepted that the culture of the church was nonetheless decidedly Korean.[15]

Three issues came up regularly: that women in particular were encouraged by the church to veer away from the more intense and well-remunerated professions to choose service occupations; that the church hurt the reputation of nonattending Korean American women: and that the daily division of labor in the church was chauvinistic.

Many people, men and women, described, and on several occasions imitated, what Sophie called "the typical AAC girl." "[My roommate is] probably just, like, the typical of the typical," Sophie said. "She's, like, 'Miss Korean Christian woman wanna-be the mother of ten children and submit to my husband,' you know?" Despite these mocking comments, Sophie went on to describe her roommate as a faithful friend who had been very helpful as Sophie carefully crafted her own Christian college path. Sophie nonetheless accepted the AAC ministry's religious and gender conservatism.

Liz, whose "prayerful" change of major I discussed earlier, described the pastor's response to her original major: "Yeah, he was very like, 'I can't imagine you in business' . . . 'cause I think he was saying, like, 'Business, it seems like you have to be pretty cutthroat' and things like that. Well, just more assertive, like stronger, I guess, than how I was." This is exactly the sort of gentle gendered coercion that another female student objected to: "[AAC members] were basically all clones of one another. . . . I know people who would come in with majors. They would want to be pre-med or engineers. By the time they'd leave, they were more into education or pharmacy or nursing. There are so many people

64

in AAC, 'ladies,' who came in engineering or pre-med, but just decided to switch their majors all of a sudden into education. You know, how AAC has those so-called ladies' jobs." Another woman similarly objected to this sort of career choice, in which "the woman sacrifices herself for the guy while the guy kind of, you know, does whatever": "A lot of people disagree with it when they come in [to AAC] freshman year . . . but when I see some of those girls now, they've changed. It seems like they've come to accept, like, oh, you know, not that they don't want a job. . . . A lot of them go into education. But they go into things that are safe for women. . . . I have nothing against education, it's a wonderful field, but I don't think you should go into it just because [you're told] that's the only thing you can do or that's the thing that's expected [i.e., by AAC]." These remarks ask us to consider how the liberal college project is gendered in the church context. This woman also protested the gendered division of labor in the church itself: "I saw just a lot of differences, and the girls would all be in the kitchen cooking and then the guys would come in and, you know, goof off, and then they would feed the guys, and then the *girls would be in their corner.*"

Students described the consequences for women who left the church, a "reputation thing": "They would just put judgments on you." One woman reported having confronted these self-appointed judges, saying to them, "I don't understand where you came up with that conclusion because that's just not correct." The term "ladies" said it all for her: the church set out to fashion just that, and as for those who had strayed, well then, they weren't very ladylike.

Although often spoken of euphemistically, it was clear that the church's impression of nonpracticing Korean American women was that they were sexually liberal or "loose." If there was one thing well known about AAC it was its stance on dating. One of the members of Cindy's small group summarized, "AAC dating is not dating, it's praying. . . . You pray for him [someone you have strong feelings for] as a mate and you pray for him in general *as a person,* and then you can't help but start loving him as a *Christian brother,* you know what I'm saying, *as a person.*" Notably absent was sexuality. A woman prays for "him" not as a male, but "as a person," "a Christian brother." Later, this student continued, church leaders "will kind of like, not mediate exactly . . . but guide you through it [dating] . . . decide whether it's meant to be." This was what for some was the infamous "red light, green light" system in which ministers were said to grant permission to proceed with romantic relationships.

The church's detractors took stock of its illiberal practices, of the ways it infringed upon personal freedoms. They also balked at its illiberal demography, its Koreanness. Detractors argued that AACers had forsaken the liberal promise of college, instead hovering near the ethnic fold and the image and trajectory of the mainstream churched Korean American (girl) in Chicagoland's northern suburbs. Herein is the irony of AAC, for its adherents managed their own critique of that very mainstream with their own Christian challenge to college and family.

Race and gender were cornerstones of this critique. In an excursus on pride, Cindy made it clear that Christian humility was particularly important for people who were not "Americans," by which she seemed to mean Americans of color. Small group, she explained, was meant to help undergraduates overcome their pride, which isn't a problem "for Americans [i.e., whites]": "You know, to some degree America values that sense of self-confidence, self-importance . . . as long as you don't become totally self-absorbed." White Americans, she seemed to be suggesting, can be striving, instrumental, and even proud, but she called on the largely Korean American members of her small group to accept Jesus' value system, one "so radically different than the world's value system." She described helping students to transcend the prevailing (white) American idea "I'm number one." Cindy was fashioning a particular ethnic subjectivity, one decidedly not instrumental and striving (the "plan" was God's), and with particular gendered hues. The church then subverted liberal notions of secular growth at college while at the same time managing to challenge illiberal images of *the* Asian American.

In one AAC detractor, Mary, we will see that the liberal project is gendered far beyond religious circles and that the racialized critique of the university exists both inside and outside AAC.

It might seem impossible that AAC, the quintessential Korean American church, could be seen as "white," and yet that is just how Mary saw it. I introduce Mary to take up the Korean American margins that chapter 1 introduced. As a non-Christian, poor, second-generation city Korean American, Mary was off the map of the U of I Korean American mainstream. But she directed her most persistent charges of exclusion not at white Americans, but at that Korean American mainstream epitomized for her by AAC, from which she had felt so painfully excluded, foremost for being poor. I argue, however, that for Mary AAC stood metonymically for "white America." I think of Mary's criticism of the church as naming larger racist and classist exclusionary practices, including those of the university. That Mary focused many of her criticisms on Korean Americans spoke not to the absence of other exclusions; rather, it indicated that she took for granted that the university had excluded her, the daughter of poor immigrants. That fellow Korean Americans, and Christians at that ("And they call themselves Christians!" she once quipped), had excluded her made them an easy target.

Like so many of her cohort, Mary shared a well-elaborated liberal dream, at least in her early days at the U of I. She entertained both a universalistic vision of self for which class, gender, and race should not matter, as well as a keen interest in the liberal arts and her own personal intellectual development. She became increasingly aware, however, that her race, class, and gender had thwarted her college dreams. Between the lines, she made it clear that the university's multicultural embrace was tenuous at best. In this vein, AAC's exclusivity spoke to segregation at the U of I more broadly.

The students I feature in this and later chapters have not

been chosen for being representative of Korean American college students generally, U of I Korean American students, or even those students I interviewed. How did I decide to feature these particular students so prominently? The answer is twofold. First, it almost goes without saying that as ethnographers, portrayers of some element of the human experience, we introduce those people we have come to know well (Mary, for example, kept in touch and often wanted to touch base). Second, I have chosen particular students because of my conviction that their particularity can help to communicate what I have learned over the course of many more conversations with many more people and that I have enough of a sense of the larger lay of the land that I can effectively communicate their particularity, placing them on the map, as it were. Mary extends this book's discussion of U of I Korean American ideas of the normative life because it so elided her. While her college disappointments were greater than most, the fault lines, the logic of her struggles were nearly universal among the population I seek to introduce here.

Mary's was largely an account of college and the deferment of liberal dreams. But she was also of two very different minds. On the one hand, she echoed her father's deep-seated belief in the liberal American dream in which her family, poor immigrants, can succeed. On the other hand, her own college experience as well as her increasing awareness of her parents' bleak prospects in the United States challenged that America and the American college dream. By the time Mary left college during her senior year (she would eventually graduate), it was her father's unreality that had come to matter most. By then it was eminently clear to Mary that race, class, and gender had conspired to curb her college dreams. Her disappointments were many: her parents, her brother, her Korean American coethnics, American education, and immigration itself. With Mary I introduce this book's foray into the intergenerational coordinates of the liberal project in which immigrant and American college dreams meet or collide.[1]

COLLEGE DREAMS: "FORGET ABOUT SEX, FORGET ABOUT RACE . . ."

Like other spokespersons of universal humanity, Mary longed to make her way in the world on the basis of her own attributes, not the contingencies of birth, bearing, or even education: "*Forget about sex, forget about race*, it shouldn't even be there" was how she put it when talking about college admissions. Mary joined nearly all of her generational Korean American cohort in contrasting this universalistic sense of being with Korea and all that is Korean: "*In Korea*, they judge you on everything but yourself: who you are, what you did, and what family you come from, and how much do you make a year. Everything is 'So, where's your résumé? Let me see what kind of a person you are by your résumé.' " Recall Robert, who stressed his parents' singularity precisely by pointing to their very different litany of questions ("Where are your pants?" and "Do you want pizza?"). As her father repeated to Mary endlessly, Korea is a place where a poor man like him, who wasn't college educated, could garner no respect. As he pointed out to me in a conversation in which Mary was present, America wasn't that kind of "small, regional society" in which a man's "face" (or reputation, *ch'emyon*) could hold him back. He had longed to emigrate to America, where "children who live well can think about becoming firemen." In the era of his childhood in South Korea, such strivings for a less prestigious occupation had been unthinkable and spoke to the humanity of America, where it was the human being who mattered. Mary, who immigrated at about age four and was comfortable speaking Korean, once groped for the English words to describe why her father had balked when she mentioned the possibility of his retiring to South Korea: "And I'm like, 'Why?' and he's like, 'Korea is the kind of society where if you don't have a lot of money . . .' I can't, what's the word in English, *taejop* [treatment or reception], you know. And just, people treat you like you're nothing, like they don't give you any respect if you don't have that kind of money." Mary spoke at length about her father's ideas about South Korean "shallowness . . . materialism . . . [and] vicious atmosphere." Against these damning critiques, immigration and a college education were assigned a tall order: that Mary and her father alike could be judged on the basis of themselves alone.

Mary's early college dream to become a professor answered to these hankerings. When she first told me about wanting to become a professor, she described the lives of her "female professors" (I listened intently!) and the riches of a college town: "Just always being around learning. Being on top of what's going on in the world. . . . Being around students, young people all the time. There's this kind of energy when you come to campus that you don't get anywhere else. . . . I go home, I walk around, it's different. You get on the CTA [Chicago Transit Authority] bus in Chicago, it's different from getting on the MTDS [Metropolitan Transportation District buses] over here [in Urbana-Champaign]. It's just a completely different environment here—that energy." She went on to describe the college town through her parents' eyes: "They love coming down here. They're like, 'Can we come down here, and there's like this youthful energy here and this is the kind of place we want to live in retirement.'" An academic career, that "energy," was for Mary about being able to "do what [she likes] to do." In the fall of her sophomore year, she spoke about not caring about material things, houses and cars: "As long as I'm happy with what I'm doing [material things don't matter]."

The American university offered a present and future that was decidedly *not* Korean. Her discussion of her South *Korean* Korean-language teaching assistant spoke to the contrast she meant to make:[2] "The thing is that I think a lot of his philosophy on education was traditional Korean or, I guess I shouldn't say traditional, but what Korea is going through now. . . . So a lot of things he was doing were, like, more Korean than American, what we're used to here in American universities . . . the lack of structure. When you get here in a classroom, right at the beginning of the semester, you're given a syllabus: everything is laid out, this is what you're expected to do . . . and these are the grades you are going to get. Really, there was hardly any of that." The teaching assistant tried to defend himself, offering, "Well it has to do with Korean culture and because this is a Korean classroom, that's what you should expect." Mary prided herself on retorting, "That's ridiculous because this is an *American university*. I mean that might work in Korea, but this is a Korean-language classroom, not a Korean school." Structure, rationality, a contract—these were the touchstones of Mary's American university and her desire to join its professional ranks.

"I just wanted trees, maybe some hills, no corn, definitely no corn"
And yet not all American universities were the same in Mary's calculation. As for many in this book, the U of I was a default school for Mary. Yale had been her dream, William and Mary (a small East Coast liberal arts college) a close second. When I asked, she explained that there were real differences between the U of I and a place like Yale. She followed with examples from one of her friend's reports on college life at Cornell: things there were better organized and the curriculum was "more structured." She spoke of other differences, particularly of looking through

the bibliographies of her college texts to find that "everyone's from, like, Ivy League or some big school." (I chimed in, defensively, to say that most authors published by the Ivy League university presses do not teach at the Ivies.) But there was more: "If you look on television, I hardly ever see a U of I professor interviewed on PBS." Mary's images of college were spun in part from the media and the ad hoc experiences of friends. But perhaps her most vivid college images had to do with the look of the campus: she and her classmates imagined that college should have a particular look, that it should look the part of the American university. When she vividly described William and Mary's tree-filled campus, I asked if she had visited. She hadn't, but she had studied the catalogue. Item for item, Mary's ideal campus was all that the U of I was not: "*I don't know why* the trees were such a big thing to me. *I just wanted trees, maybe some hills, no corn, definitely no corn.* Nice buildings, like, old buildings. I like old buildings." With "I don't know why," Mary spoke to the robust college image that she had fashioned from friends, media, and college materials themselves. It is noteworthy that the U of I is in fact a tree-lined campus with many late nineteenth-century buildings. Indeed, not long after Mary and I spoke, a movie about Harvard was filmed on the U of I quad. These realities aside, clearly it was important for Mary to register her disappointments through the look of the place. Her liberal dream was spun of such faint traces, or perhaps poor indicators, of prestige: the look of the quad, TV shows, and the like. However, what really mattered was that Mary wasn't confident in her ability to access the best of *even* the U of I.

Smiling and striking a melodramatic pose, Mary spoke the mantra of so many U of I Korean American students: "I wanted to go *anywhere but the U of I.*" Even more dramatically, she flared her hands, flung back her head, laughed, and added, "I dreaded it like a nightmare, like, 'Oh no! Anywhere but this!'"

Corn and lack of hills aside (on these points no one can question her accuracy: corn as far as the eye can see and nary a hill), it was the university's perceived low standards, its mediocrity, that Mary definitively charged with having thwarted her liberal development. Her sense of mediocrity, though, much like her ideas of campus prestige, was based on indicators other than excellence, in this case on the campus's familiarity, its high school–like quality. When we spoke during the summer after her junior year, Mary was very critical of the university's general education requirements. She claimed that the classes were "high-schoolish" and a complete waste of time. Further, she could not make sense of which classes counted and which didn't. Offering anthropology as an example, she asked, "Why does it matter what type of anthro course we take? That's my point. Why limit us?" When she complained about the prerequisite system for courses, I interjected, "So the system seems kind of random to you?" "Yeah," she answered, "very random. Or maybe it's not random and I think that's even worse. That they would *actually* make a judgment on what is fit for gen ed and what's not!" With these thoughts, Mary challenged the university's authority to curtail her freedom, to determine what would make for her liberal (arts) education, for her development in college.

In one of our last on-campus meetings, I remember smiling when Mary said, "Did I ever tell you about how disappointed I am with college?" She had, again and again. "I'm so disappointed by college education in general. I mean, I don't know if all universities are like this, but I feel like, oh my God, *it's just like high school all over again.* I'm not finding the kind of life here, like, the education here, that I expected, that I thought I could get if I wanted." She pined for something "more in-depth, more involving . . . something more sophisticated than the watered down sort of stuff you have in high school." She harped again on the system of prerequisites: "[They send you] all the way back to number-one basics. . . . You start *all* the way back at the bottom again. . . . Like, how many times do I have to read *The Scarlet Letter*? . . . Repeat, repeat, repeat." When I asked whether the U of I was really so different from any other American university (I was on the defensive again), Mary broadened her charge: "That's how American education is—always thinking about the majority." From there she escalated to a biting finale: "Don't they call . . . college education 'higher learning'? What's the point of calling it 'higher learning' when it's not higher?"

Mary's critique of higher education generally and the U of I in particular did not stop her from blaming herself for "ending up" at the U of I or from fretting about her own ability to fit in academically (at least with students in the humanities). With one voice she shouldered the burden herself; with another she echoed Jim on the ways the university excluded *her* and questioned the truth of prevailing university images and ideals. I thus offer Mary's two minds, both already at quite a remove from her harsh criticisms.

Mind 1: *"I got what I deserved"*

When Mary blamed herself she adopted that American ideology which asserts that with only a little more work, if only you had tried harder, you could have had it all: Yale, William and Mary, the whole gamut. With this mind, she echoed her father's immigrant American dream.

When she hoisted the world on her own shoulders, Mary blamed herself for ending up at the U of I, for not having tried hard enough, and she described herself as "lazy." She preferred to believe that extreme effort alone can conquer all: "If there's a will, there's a way, that's what I believe. If you really, I mean, there's no school in this world, *or in the United States,* that's going to say 'No!' if you really, really want to get in. If you cared enough about your grades and your school record. . . . They're not going to reject you if you have straight a's—Do you know what I mean?" Of course, this bold assertion hardly holds for higher education in the United States, nor in most of the world; such assertions echo her father's immigrant dream, fictions and all. When I asked about her own dream school, Yale, and about her brother's dream school, Johns Hopkins (he had just then decided that he would be joining Mary at the U of I), Mary said, "I feel like I deserve, *I got what I deserved.* I think it's fair. Even though, I mean, sometimes I'll just sit there and feel sorry for myself. Well, this is what I used to think, like, God, you know, if it had been any other year I would have gotten in. . . . But no, you have to deal with what you have and what situation you're in. . . . I didn't work to my full capacity, so *I got what I deserved.*" She extended this logic to grades, even as her own were faltering. She argued that grades should not come as a surprise: "By now, if you don't know what kind of grade you expect [it's your problem], because we've been in school so we know how the system works." She elaborated that students learn over time how to "gauge themselves": "You know that if you put in *this* many hours into *this* type of paper and do *this* kind of research, you know what you're going to get." Taken together these statements paint a rational picture of effort rewarded and fairness (if only . . .).

Mary once admitted to me that she hated tests and did much better on papers. Nonetheless she defended tests as the most rational means of selection by college admission departments: "Test scores make everything so much more efficient. I totally agree that a lot of tests do not really test the skills that are necessary for whatever you are applying for."

I had made this point. "Yet, I look at it this way: if you want it bad enough and if *that's* what you really want to do and try hard. . . . Most of us are not stupid. . . . If *that's* what you want, if you want *that* job, if you want to get into *that* school, you will try to get *those* scores." Mary's "that" and "those" made a particular statement: in a rational system, there are rational standards and rational measures to match, and the rational system is the liberal system. That Mary didn't have the résumé, the family background or the cultural capital that some other college students had, shouldn't matter by these sorts of calculations. But such was the thinking of only one of Mary's minds.

Mind 2: *"What about my repertoire?"*
Over the course of our many conversations in Mary's sophomore year she spoke with great determination about her desire to become a humanities professor, her hard-hitting comments on "higher" learning aside. But by the summer after her sophomore year she had begun to give up and spoke about the possibility of law school instead. This change of heart spoke both to Mary's faltering confidence in her ability to really become a professor and to her escalating sense of economic necessity (i.e., a higher paying job) on account of her parents' financial troubles.

From her earliest days at the U of I, Mary struggled with measuring up, fitting in, and maintaining standards, particularly in her liberal arts department: "Is my intellectual level up to par with the rest of the upper percentage of this academic institution? . . . Do I read the *New York Times* enough? Am I up-to-date on current events? Do I know enough literature, quote classics or high-class literature? *What about my repertoire?*" She claimed that in addition to a "repertoire" "those that want to become intellectuals have personal standards" and a number of other dispositions: "You have a *certain* vocabulary. You talk a *certain* way. You take *certain* classes. You do *certain* things." In contrast to rational notions of achieving "that" or "those" goals she listed earlier, with these remarks she admitted to "certain" things one needs to have to be successful. At the end of her sophomore year Mary described an occasion on which a colleague at work looked at her, as she said, "like I was an idiot," when she admitted that she hadn't read Christina Rossetti until college and that she hadn't read Keats since junior high.

With these accounts, we find Mary struggling over whether Mary herself (i.e., as opposed to her background, "sex, race" and the like) can make the grade, *even* at the American university, *even* in the familiar Midwest, *even* at a public university, and *even* at a university whose faculty purportedly don't appear on PBS. *Even* in her sophomore year Mary once explicitly raised the possibility that she would not realize her dream of being a professor and described how she might end up reflecting on her past: "Like, what did I do with my life? . . . I don't want to look back and think, 'What did I do? I regret this so much.' I hate regret. That hopelessness, like, I can't go back into the past and change things because that's life." Mary was unable to envision herself on the path to a professorship, which in her estimation necessarily required time at an East Coast private school: "I'm just afraid of a kind of social environment. Remember I told you I always had my heart set on the East Coast? If I moved there, I'm afraid it's going to be a completely different place than the Midwest that I'm used to. Also it'll be a private institution where a lot of people will be from high-class families. I'll be, 'Oh no, what if I don't fit in?' I don't know." It was here that Mary most boldly referenced her class (as well as regional and implicitly racial) background, as she worried about fitting in, about being accepted by "high-class families" in a "completely different place."

LEFT BEHIND

Mary's college trajectory, from dreams of becoming a professor to practical plans, echoed her changing portrayal of her father. What began as a celebration of her father's enlightenment, optimism, and deep belief in America (distinguishing her parents from the Korean fold, as we have seen with Jim and others) ended as a relentless critique of his lack of reality, conservatism, and even delusions (and his Koreanness). Mary's senior year spiraled downward as her parents' financial situation plummeted: she dropped out both semesters, suffered a breakdown, and left for South Korea, where I met her during what would have been the summer after her graduation. That Mary could think about heading to South Korea spoke to her comfort in Korea, a grandmother she was still close to, and her social circle at the U of I that included many South Korean nationals, including Min, who had introduced me to Mary.

Mary's Father, Take 1: *"In America . . ."*

Early on in our meetings Mary talked a great deal about her father, most often in admiring terms. Most positively, it struck Mary that her father had managed to leave much of South Korea's "résumé" society behind (a nearly ubiquitous Korean American image of South Korea), that with the help of a maverick (i.e., not mainstream Protestant Christian) religious practice he had found peace with his station in life. Mary once put an age to this transition, proclaiming that at twenty-nine her father had gotten over not having been able to attend college. In our first meeting, she described his reconciliation this way: "My dad would say, 'Oh wow, some people might look at me and pity me or they might say, "Yeah, you just have such a hard life." ' But he's like, 'Right now, I'm the happiest person and I'm just totally satisfied with where my life is going. I couldn't ask for anything more. I'm completely content.' I'm like, 'Wow, Dad!' " She stressed that her father did not pressure her the way other Korean immigrant parents did, that instead he believed in her and in her future. Recall the accounts of Jim and Robert of their parents' liberal exceptionalism and note the *patterned* way in which some Korean American youth discern their parents' *singularity*.

Indeed, when I met Mary and her parents together (she could understand and participate in Korean-language conversation; this was often not the case with the other students I interviewed), her father offered this liberal view of her education: "We've watched what has happened to many children around us—it is torture to be forced to study something you don't want to, but enjoyable if it's something you want to study. If you can find something you like, you can live out your life more joyfully, less dully than others." At these words, Mary exclaimed in English, "My parents are so cool." Her father continued optimistically:

In America, even if you choose the most unpopular discipline, if you work hard you can get a job. So I don't have any twisted ambition [*yoksim*] for Mary. I'm not thinking about her becoming famous or earning a lot of money. As long as you don't get caught up in those sorts of useless thoughts [he had been talking about people's enormous ambitions in South Korea], and if you think only about living a healthy [*konjon han*] life, whatever you study, even if it is something unpopular, in the United States *you won't end up being left behind*—it isn't that sort of a society. As my wife says, when it comes to a "good life," how much does it really cost to make ends meet? Of course, if I had a bigger house or a bigger car I might think differently—it might be a different story—but if you intend to live with a minimal car and house, then *as long as you graduate* from college and make twenty or thirty thousand dollars *you can live well and save money.* So you have to ask yourself, "What is my perspective on life?" Is it a dreamy, ambitious [*hohwang*] life perspective or not? That's what makes the difference. And Mary doesn't need to worry: if she wants to become a professor and she tries hard and it doesn't work, then she can become a [high school] teacher.

These comments speak to the component parts of her father's American dream: that in America, barring "twisted ambition," it is easy to live a good life; that hard work promises a decent job; that the modest life is still a "good life"; and that even a modest salary is sufficient. Pretty quickly, though, these optimistic proclamations ring a bit hollow; for starters, even in the late 1990s a household income of twenty to thirty thousand dollars would have hardly made ends meet, let alone allow for the purchase of a house or car. Not to mention that Mary was not heading so easily toward graduation, one of her father's minimum requirements for even the modest or scaled-down plan.

Mary's Father, Take 2: *"Is anything worth it?"*

As the years of our conversations continued, Mary spoke less of her father's peace of mind and more of her frustration with his economic and business failures. There were so many failures over the course of her college years that I could hardly keep them straight. They were in a business affiliated with dry cleaning, a largely Korean American sector in Chicago and many other cities. I remember once trying to understand what it was that they couldn't sell—the machines, the business, or the space—but in any case the bottom line was that they had located the business in such a smelly place that they could not sell without huge losses. Once Mary summed it up: "I'm sure they're better off than when they first came here, but [they have] just been through so much work and toil and never having even a Sunday off. Seven days a week. Just working, working, never had a vacation. To this day, they've never had a vacation. Sometimes I wonder, is it worth it?" When I asked her "*What* wasn't worth it?" she answered, "Just everything. *Is anything worth it?*" Adding to these bleak calculations, she wondered if "God was punishing" her parents: "Do they really deserve this kind of a life?"

I have yet to mention Mary's mother, who spoke quietly at our meetings, often along different lines. Her mother's quiet pessimism was easily overshadowed by her husband's optimistic onslaught. While Mary's father was busily sketching a sky-is-the-limit future for Mary, her mother had no problem naming Mary's disadvantages. In Mary's presence she matter-of-factly explained that the "real reason" Mary didn't get into Yale was because they were poor, although she didn't elaborate on how this had worked. Over her college years it was clear that Mary had come to agree that personal circumstances did make a difference. Already in the summer after her sophomore year she described "getting sick of school." She began to wonder about her "endurance" to be a scholar and said that she now wanted "a secure life, a secure job." "Right now," she continued, "we [i.e., her family] have absolutely no monetary power to do anything. And I think, you know, all those little situations [with my family] just really encourage me to go out there and find a high-paying job." By her junior year law school was on the horizon. That year I asked about her earlier graduate school plan, and she answered, "I don't know, thinking about the future scares me; it depresses me." "Why?" I asked. "Because I'm never sure what's going to happen, what I'm going to do. There are so many things I want to do, scared to do, I don't know."

When I visited Mary in Seoul, she explained that she had suffered a "mental breakdown" and had grown "tired" of school: "Every element in my life was going down." "I just couldn't handle it any more" was how she summed it up. She told me that she had been "completely isolated" in her college apartment and that she "basically starved." Her weight had dropped to eighty-four pounds and she had recuperated a bit at her parents' apartment. She contemplated counseling, but knowing that it would "cost money," she ended up in Seoul.

In Seoul we spoke at a girlish café in a popular college student neighborhood where Mary seemed at home. There, amid frilly tablecloths and waitresses dressed like the girls on Swiss Miss canisters, Mary was more critical of her parents than I had ever heard her be: "It's just horrible—this whole situation [laughter]. I mean, I can laugh about it now, but it's not really laughing, laughing, it's just . . . I have this philosophy—I don't know if this is cruel to think this. If there is such a thing as fate, then this is their destiny and there is nothing I can do. There is no compromise in their lives, in terms of business, their marriage; they're just so stubborn and old-fashioned." I asked her to clarify. "There were plenty of opportunities to lead—at least for my mom—an easier life, just be a waitress. We wouldn't have been rich, but wouldn't have been in debt—all the emotional struggle!" Distant by then was Mary's praise of her easygoing, "cool" father, content with his world and cavalier about Mary's future.

When we met in Seoul I was horrified at the sad reality that Mary could have been starving in her room, so alone. It both explained why we had fallen out of touch that year and made me reflect on my own complicity as a university agent. I pressed her about meetings with advisors or other university personnel—hadn't anyone noticed this emaciated, distraught young woman? Where was campus counseling or psychological services in all of this? This was all Mary had to say: "I told the dean, 'I'm thinking of going to counseling,' and she said, 'Make sure you do that.' Well, you know how bureaucratic our school is." With this remark, albeit one that surfaced at my own nervous urging, and with her earlier comments, Mary named class and race, the ways people like Mary struggle in high school and college. We can hear the echo of Jim's portrait of the university bureaucracy: "Have a nice day! . . . Nice talking to you."

LEFT OUT

In my portrait of Mary thus far I have stressed her enormous efforts to take personal responsibility for her failings, particularly through her defense of the American meritocracy, her resignation to the rational system by which excellence is identified or rewarded. Gradually, however, she found again and again that the causes of her exclusion at school and eventually from school were well beyond her control.

In Seoul at issue was no longer simply her father's personality, or even his unreality, but her family's poverty: its effects on her, her schooling, and her life. Mary was naming, head on, the effects of economic instability on her ability to manage her own college trajectory and life course. In the meanwhile, there had been other developments: her mother had been diagnosed with cancer but couldn't stop working; her parents had been sued because of debt; and she, of course, had been unable to focus on her studies. She related to me her new perspective: "I mean, you know about our financial situation—just my uncertainty about the future. I always had that fear of failure—wearing me down."

On giving up the dream of graduate school she said, "I figured money is important after all. If it was just my life, I might have made a different choice, but always that, always the fact my parents were there, so . . . All of last year, just worrying about my parents kept me up—I don't think they know, I don't show it—try to be optimistic in front of them. . . . All our lives, basically since we got here, it has been like that. It used to keep me up just worrying about this. And now I am just, like, *numb*. My mom, getting sued, and the whole thing with school—now [I'm] just *desensitized*." Numbed, desensitized—Mary described her resolve at that point to hem in her world so that she could proceed with her own life: "Now instead of stressing out about the future and all these things that are going on in my life, I just set small goals for myself, and now what I'm really concerned with is graduating and getting into a good enough law school to get a decent job."

Not all of this awareness of the limitations of class mobility can be credited to her parents' worsening circumstances. When I looked back at the transcripts of earlier conversations with Mary, I found moments that presaged the bluntness she displayed in Seoul on the topics of class and college. One conversation on Korean American Christianity, a tireless topic for Mary, had taken a particularly gnarly course. Mary spoke about the money in the church: "Those ministers driving around their little Cadillacs, and, you know, their nice two- or three-story homes." In the spirit of adding insult to injury, Mary then mused angrily about "federal grants and scholarships" for "preachers' kids": "They actually call it that!" The conversation had turned whimsical, if cynical, and she proclaimed, "[Someday,] if I'm rich . . . I'll start a fellowship for 'cleaners' kids.' " Here Mary pointed out the middle-class contours of Korean American Christianity, or at least the image of the Korean American mainstream.

To Mary, the church was precisely the sort of place where stereotypes about the city, its poor schools and its bad neighborhoods, thrived. Churchgoers could never have believed, she protested, that her city schools and neighborhood were decent. She and her family attended a suburban church until she was in fifth grade, when they left, feeling humiliated. She remembered her father's description of the tithing system, and something about a man getting kicked out of the church because his name was at the bottom of the list of donors. "They had no problem just sitting there and putting other people down" was how Mary described the classism of Korean American suburban churchgoers. "They turn people against one another," she said, and concluded, "I find from my experience and other people's experience that church people are just the worst hypocrites. I can't believe that they could do that . . . and call themselves Christians!"

Mary was matter-of-fact, though, that religion was hardly the issue: "When I say AAC . . . *I'm not referring to religion at all.*" When she detailed what she was speaking about, however, instead of referring explicitly to class she spoke of "Americanized Koreans." "Americanized Koreans exclude" and make people—and here she meant poor people—"feel like they don't belong." "Despicable!" she exclaimed.

For Mary, AAC connoted a pejorative mainstream, statistically and otherwise: "Okay, this is going to sound really stereotypical and stuff, but if you want to belong to a group like that, you really have to be a conformist. And I don't, I don't conform. You act in a certain way, you dress a certain way, you go to the same church, you meet the same friends." She never tired of charting the troubling intimacies of Korean Americans: "Check out the web pages of Korean people on this campus. . . . Just look for the Korean last names. And you will notice something really funny. You know how they put links of other people's home pages? They're all the same. You see the same home pages. *The links are all the same. Links of links of links.*" The "links of links of links" are those that excluded Mary, those built on precisely the social or network capital (i.e., who you know) that she lacked. "Links of links of links" for Korean Americans and "repeat, repeat, repeat" for the U of I: such were Mary's idioms for the two troubling intimacies of the U of I as she tried to realize her college dreams.

"What does religion have to do with race?"
Throughout the years we spoke, it was as if Mary were conducting her own ethnography on the racial exclusivity of Korean Americans generally and AAC in particular. For Mary, that her own social circles were racially diverse was an important mark of her difference from other Korean Americans. It was also, however, a mark of her exclusion from mainstream Korean America. Mary described her surprise at segregation at the U of I generally: "I think the U of I is very diverse. I think it's very segregated and that's what I'm not used to because at [high school] . . . there is segregation wherever you go, but it was much less so than here, at least I think. I had a lot of African American friends [in

high school]. . . . Whereas here, it's kind of like the unspoken taboo. *Like, no, you're a nice Korean girl, you don't hang out with black friends.* I find that so disturbing." Mary joined other Korean Americans whose social groups were not exclusively Korean or Asian American in stressing her divergence from the Korean American mainstream. Noteworthy, however, was that while Mary pointed to Korean Americans who segregate, with these remarks she also held the university responsible for being more segregated than other places and for its "unspoken taboo" (i.e., against racial mixing).

Mary struggled to understand AAC: How was it that a "bunch of Korean Americans that can't speak Korean" congregate in exclusively ethnic circles? She called AAC "artificial," meaning that theirs was an artificial way to claim "Korean identity": "I mean, if you want to learn what it is to be Korean, how about trying to talk to your parents? Have a decent conversation with them!" "Despicable" for Mary was "the fact that they're using this artificial identity that they've made for themselves to exclude others." With this remark, Mary referred equally to the exclusion of urban non-Christian Korean Americans like herself and of non-white racial others. Wrestling with the hypocrisy of it all, she suddenly exclaimed, *"But what does religion have to do with race?"* It was a critical comment: religion should be universalistic (the liberal vision). How could it exclude (her and other non-middle-class suburbanites) this way? At another time, she put her critique this way: "If they weren't racist, why wouldn't they hang out with black people, white people, Hispanic people? They don't. Well, some of them do, but most of their friends are Asian, so I think that's a clear indication of, maybe not such blatant racism, but it's there."

But Mary wasn't unequivocal. She described her "strange theory" about the segregation of her Korean American classmates at the U of I. She described "freedom" and spoke of her classmates' "choice" but also registered the perils of "multiculturalism": "Okay, I have this really strange theory. . . . Why does [segregation] happen? And I was thinking maybe this is, like, one of those side effects, results of multiculturalism. Because the fact that in America there are so many different cultures and you're given the freedom to be whatever you want, right? . . . So I'm thinking maybe because they're given that kind of freedom, they choose to go more of the extreme rather than spread themselves out." Interestingly, she went on to point out the irony that it was in faraway South

Korea that Koreans were increasingly interested in learning about the rest of the world. Although she seemed to blame Korean Americans for segregating themselves, in contrast to their more cosmopolitan brethren in South Korea, it was revealing that she also registered segregation as, in its own right, a "side effect" of multiculturalism, even as it was touted as the pathway to the American dream that college was to nurture. With this, Mary rendered multiculturalism an ideology that also licensed racial exclusion, her own, and perhaps even that of her squarely middle-class suburban coethnics. I take these comments as a quiet concession to the fact that perhaps the university itself might have had something to do with the ethnic segregation she observed at AAC. On one occasion in her junior year, Mary was almost sympathetic to the Korean American mainstream scene: "Once you get into the whole Korean scene, it's hard to come out and to, like, sort of see other potentials around you. Like, yeah, there's a black person sitting in front of me. Yeah, I could be that person's friend. That never would enter their mind."

It was in 1999, arguably the pinnacle of multiculturalism, that Mary offered these comments on segregation and multiculturalism at the American university. Her charge—that in the name of multiculturalism, classism and racism are rampant—was devastating. She longed for a multiculturalism in which race, class, and gender wouldn't exclude her and was disappointed that they did. Interestingly, in her junior year (and during her troubled senior year as well) her social circles themselves became largely Korean and Asian American, focused particularly on 1.5-generation immigrants and Asian nationals studying abroad at the U of I, a group that she comfortably called FOBS. Perhaps Mary would have been comfortable pondering her own social circles as another of the "side effects" of multiculturalism.

"He's definitely more white than Korean"

Mary had a foil: the successes of her younger brother, Michael. Michael's path spoke to how gender and race worked together. Mary figured that it was his gender that had allowed him to be "more white" and endorse a host of American values.[3] But in some ways Michael was oddly both "more Korean" and "more white." Mary described Michael's patriarchy and pride as "old-fashioned" and his selfishness and other unflattering traits as "white" (and later "American"). "My parents are always saying that he takes after my grandfather, my dad's father. So I guess, in that sense, he's kind of *old-fashioned*. Like, I can't really put my finger on it, why he's that way or even what specifically makes him *old-fashioned*. Sometimes he expects a woman to be a certain way—in little ways: 'Please, the woman never pays,' or 'I hold open the door for women,' or, I don't know. There's just something about him. . . . He's definitely *more white than Korean*. . . . Seriously, I mean culturally and the way he thinks and the people that he hangs out with. *He's so white*." Through either lens, however, it mattered that Michael was a boy: Mary stressed that Michael was neither bothered nor burdened by the family situation in quite the same way she was. She described his relationship to their endearing youngest brother this way: "Michael's very, like, 'Here's me and here's you.' Don't invade my space sort of thing, you know . . . which I think is very *American*." She recalled how he treated a South Korean cousin who had been kind to Mary on one of her trips to South Korea: "He couldn't understand the fact that we had to be good to this person. She's a guest in our home, a relative. . . . It's like a cultural thing" (his old-fashionedness aside). Once she put it this way: "He doesn't have a large capacity to just sort of understand and forgive."

It was in Seoul, though, that Mary's critique of Michael was most pointed. It was then, as she reflected on the ways her own life had come to a standstill, that she took note of the gendered way he had managed to stay on course, seemingly unaffected by family crises: "It's hard to know what Michael is thinking. He is the type to just go after what he wants. . . . Honestly, we don't have a very good relationship. . . . We are very different in what we want in life. . . . *I don't think he would ever give up his dreams about his own future to help [our parents] out*." Mary thus registered Michael's resilience and selfishness in the face of family trouble as American or white.

Michael's optimism, both about his own future and about the value of a U of I education, was remarkable to Mary. He put it simply when I spoke to him (we met several times): "I figure, like, you're at a top, Big Ten school. You're gonna graduate with a bachelor's or a master's and it's gonna be internationally recognized—so why worry?" It is interesting to listen to almost parallel remarks from Mary in her most optimistic sophomore year: "I don't want to be poor, that's for sure, but I always have this certainty, like, oh, come on, I'm going to at least graduate from college, which means I'm going to have a bachelor's degree at least in two fields. . . . I don't think I'm going to be poor, dirt poor, at least not like my parents. . . . I'm not going to be unemployed." Here she paused for a long time. "At least I hope not." But Mary's initially optimistic comments ended on a worrisome note, confident of little other than that she wouldn't be "dirt poor," a far cry from her brother's bravado, "Why worry?" In Michael's comments we can recall their father's unmitigated immigrant optimism. Not surprisingly, it was hard for Michael to understand the profound way in which Mary's college career had faltered. He simply said that he "couldn't understand": "I came to the conclusion that she's twenty-one, twenty-two now, and she just needs to tough it out on her own." His claims were harsh: circumstance shouldn't matter.

For Mary, Michael and AAC were somehow white, standing for those aspects of normative middle-classness that elided her. And they were white in their exclusivity, their disregard for race and class Others, such as working-class Korean Americans like Mary and other students of color. It was thus Mary's perceptions of AAC's racial exclusions that spoke to exclusion itself and hence, if ironically, to whiteness. Most important, the AAC churchgoers were white for being like the university and its white student majority. From these Mary felt left behind, left out. In her more sympathetic moments, she wondered how white (in this metaphorical sense) AAC really was after all and whether its ethnic segregation could be so easily understood as a matter of its own making. Of course by then Mary's own social circle had narrowed to the sort of Korean Americans who she figured wouldn't have fit in at AAC. If Mary began her college account with liberal ideals, by the time she dropped out hers was a litany of exclusions. That she most often named other Korean Americans (e.g., AAC members) or her own brother spoke not to her naïveté about the workings of the university or the behaviors of its white majority, but to the pain of these most intimate (ethnic) exclusions.

When students go to college they bring their families with them; family hopes, conflicts, economic fortunes or misfortunes, all make the journey to this supposedly independent college life. To delve further into the impact of the family presence in college trajectories, in part II I focus on one family, the Hans. The reader will meet five of the Han second-generation cousins and three of the Han siblings from the immigrant generation. Through this single Korean American family I continue to examine the intersection of liberal college ideals, race, class, and gender.

CHAPTER THREE

PART II: A FAMILY

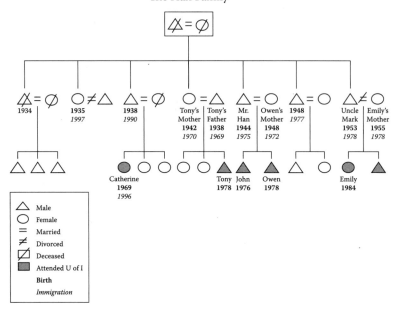

Figure 1. The Han Family

4 AN (ANTI–)ASIAN AMERICAN PRE-MED

Owen's college story is quite different from Mary's. He was a successful pre-med student from a squarely middle-class suburban family who found his way to a top-tier medical school. These differences aside, Mary, at least in her early years, and Owen shared a similar university project: to grow and develop as universal human beings. As it had for Mary, the university also disappointed Owen in this vein.

Mary made it clear that she had not felt welcomed at the U of I and had been disappointed by her college experience and by her parents' desperate circumstances. Owen's struggles were different: it was precisely *as a successful Asian American pre-med male* that he struggled with his liberal project. His was a struggle against the powerfully racialized images of the instrumental striving immigrant family with its son, the doctor. The conundrum was this: how to conform to obvious contours of a racialized stereotype while retaining one's singularity and the liberal project of the American university ideal. Owen's case is distinct from Mary's in another important way: in contrast to defiantly secular Mary, religion was at the heart of Owen's college struggles. In his liberal quest, Owen wrestled over how to make sense of the contingencies of his birth: his family's Catholicism and his Korean ethnicity. The secular university that met Owen disappointed him *not* for being secular—he reconciled with that—but because it refused to engage him in his own spiritual and intellectual struggles. Those spiritual and intellectual struggles were inextricable from his struggle as a Korean American on campus. This chapter features Owen not because the university forsook him miserably—it didn't—but because it disappointed by failing its mission to provide a reason for students to reach across racial and other boundaries or to exit the ethnic fold.

88

A LIBERAL EDUCATION

Owen asked a great deal of college. By the time I met him when he was a sophomore, he stressed that he "only had three years left," recalling the "preciousness" of college that many Christian students described in chapter 2. Most of those three years would be whittled away by his science requirements. Clearly, in Owen's reckoning life ended after college. In my early forties when I talked to Owen and his college cohort, I was sometimes made to feel as if I should now be comfortably ensconced in that part of life in which no further personal development could possibly happen! The problem with postcollege life (that is, if there was one) was this: career and family would likely leave little room for loftier matters, not to mention that for Owen the whole point was to figure out *now* precisely how to proceed with life, including career and family. Owen emulated a senior he once heard give a leadership seminar. The senior represented for Owen "[people] who know themselves because they know what they want out of life and where they are going and they are always trying to *understand themselves* . . . people that are *open-minded* and people that think about things, *different aspects*." So Owen's electives bore a weighty responsibility.

Three years later Owen was still talking about the philosophy professor he mentioned to me during our second meeting early in his sophomore year: "Whenever I make an appointment with professors, I think back to that philosophy professor I told you about a long time ago." The professor made a big impression on Owen, but not a good one; for starters, he had told the students in his small seminar class reserved for freshmen that they should not become philosophers: "It isn't a good field to go into." His apparent lack of interest in and even degradation of his own field had bothered Owen, but an early visit to the philosopher's office proved much more troubling: "The whole time he didn't even look at me, he was, like, staring off somewhere. He put his feet on the table—so I left." The professor had also seemed unengaged about the course material, "really indifferent about everything": "Like, he wouldn't get personal with his students much. It'd be, like, *he's the professor* and he, like, lectures, and *he asks the questions*." Owen had hoped that a small freshman seminar would offer a chance to "get to know the professor." But there was even more: the professor's angry retort to a question that Owen had posed. Owen admitted that under the

CHAPTER FOUR

pretense of asking about an upcoming paper he had in fact gone to the professor's office "to talk to him about theology." The question that provoked was this: "I should have asked him if he minded if I talked to him about it, but it just came out that I asked him if he believed in God, and he said 'It's none of your business.'" Needless to say, the course didn't proceed in the way Owen hoped it would.

All college graduates can recall a bad professor, an indifferent one, and even one who blew them off during office hours. I begin with this story because it speaks to resounding themes in Owen's narration of his college career. He had high hopes for that part of his education that was to be most liberal, his nonscience education, those classes beyond his major and premedical preparation. Of a liberal education Owen expected the chance to broaden his mind and to develop as a person. His call was grand: this liberal education would answer abiding personal questions about how best to live. For Owen, the humanities, more specifically his electives, were to answer this lofty call. The humanities were to be "about life," unlike his required science classes: "[In] biology, you learn facts. I'll *take that with me* but it won't be as meaningful. *It's not about life*, it's about science or something. [It's not about] life in general —how to live life." Here we can recall the many students in chapter 2 who worried about having something to take with them over the course of their college years. Owen began a notebook in his freshman year for just this purpose, for jottings meant to live on beyond college, but unlike his AAC classmates he expected to fill the notebook with inspiration from his classes.

As the grand opening to Owen's liberal university, the freshman seminar was weighty; after all, it was designed to be intimate, it was for freshmen only, and it wasn't science. It was not asking too much to expect a passionate professor, one deeply committed to his subject, and an intimate environment in which Owen would meet the minds and passions of his professor and classmates as he addressed personal questions about life generally, and his own in particular. The professor had disappointed: his offhand remark to students about philosophy, his cavalier attitude (i.e., his legs on the table and averted gaze during office hours) and authoritarian mode (i.e., *he* asked the questions) all showcased his lack of interest in students' personal and ethical development.

Let me, though, turn the table for a window on the humanities professor in the context of the late twentieth-century university. I do not mean to hold court or to revisit the scene of the crime. In contrast to the large lecture, the format of many of the offerings that satisfy students' general education requirements, the freshman seminar is designed to offer a personal touch to the freshman experience at a large and imposing campus. Although for quite some time hiring and promotion have paid lip service to the importance of teaching, one would be hard-pressed at the research university, the sacred mantle of the U of I, to say that professors are really rewarded for excellence in teaching. One would also be hard-pressed to say that professors at this sort of university have received real training in how best to conduct an intimate freshman seminar. The professor in question might well have been out of familiar water. Perhaps that is why he ran the seminar as though it were a large lecture. That the professor took the time to steer students away from careers in philosophy perhaps speaks to his sense of the value accorded what he does, both in and beyond the academy. At a large research university with a distinguished College of Engineering and many highly ranked science departments in the College of Liberal Arts and Sciences, humanities professors realize that their game is hardly the most important one on campus; they are assigned shabbier offices in older buildings and often are remunerated with considerably lower salaries. Their liberal dreams too have perhaps been dashed. The professor's suggestion that the students not pursue a career in philosophy might have been better kept to himself (or to the company of sympathetic humanities colleagues), but it is perhaps not the best yardstick for measuring either the professor's interest in the students or his love of philosophy.

But I have yet to examine Owen's query to the professor about his own belief in God and the professor's curt reply. Some readers might insist that the rest of Owen's story hangs on this one-liner, that the professor acted the way he did because of boundaries that Owen transgressed, and furthermore that Owen's entire experience of the course was tied up in his hopes for a personal engagement about faith. Owen wanted the professor to unveil his faith, and perhaps to engage him on the matter as well. With this we come to the contours of the secular university: Owen's question—he admitted that he should have warned the professor— crossed a line, a line that prompted the professor's curt response, "It's none of your business."

Over the years of my conversations with Owen there were other courses and other professors that he singled out. There was the chemistry professor ("He did not really care about us") who told the students that what they were learning would never really matter: "[But] at least you're disciplined in waking up at seven-thirty. That's the thing you could take from his class." Owen wanted to take more than that from college. Later he tried again with the faith question, with a grader for his class on archaeology and the Bible. When Owen mentioned "inconsistencies in the Bible," the grader told him that another student had the same concerns, "but that's as far as the conversation went." Owen was frustrated that there were no discussions in the class: "See, the thing is, he [the professor] said we're not supposed to reach a conclusion through this class, so I guess [discussion is] not really that important for him."

One of Owen's medical school interviews during his senior year recalled the philosophy professor and this litany of other professorial mishaps: "I'll probably remember it for the rest of my life—it was *that bad*." As for the interviewer, "he wasn't *even* a doctor. . . . He was, what was he?" He had been "totally disinterested" in Owen, as had the "indifferent" philosopher. Owen was outraged. Fifteen minutes into the interview the interviewer announced that he had no more questions: "For him to be out of questions, for him to be disinterested, like, right when I walked in, he looked, you know he was rubbing his eyes . . . he started talking about going home and stuff like that . . . like 'I'm going home to have a beer.'" Owen was aghast. After all, the medical school's website had promised a panel interview, something "very informal, very conversational." Instead the interview was "superficial, unprofessional." "*All that work*" coming down to little more than "whether or not you kiss their butt."

While Owen waited for his own disastrous medical school interview, he chatted with an Indian American applicant about her earlier interview: "[She] said that, well, she was Indian and the interviewer was Indian and her question was like, 'What kind of Indian desserts do you make?' and those kinds of questions. They have nothing to do with medical school, so I was like, 'What's the deal here?'" This was Owen's prelude to his own story. In Owen's there was no conversation, not even of the hackneyed ethnic variety, let alone one that had recognized his humanity.

The interview that went best was the one at the medical school that became Owen's first choice (and which he attended). In that interview, he said, "[I could] talk about myself and my philosophy of things." Predictably, he yearned for an interviewer who wanted to get to know him personally. Convinced that the more caring interview reflected the school better suited to him, Owen outlined for me the many services this school offered its students and added, "That makes me feel special, I guess, and makes me feel like they care about me." One can see what appealed: Owen's full humanity had been registered.

PREMEDITATED PRE-MED

Despite Owen's carefully sculpted electives, beginning with that freshman seminar on ethics, he was nonetheless a pre-med. Not lost on Owen was that the Asian American pre-med conjures its own image or stereotype. While certainly the pre-med can easily pose as an instance of the so-called model minority (i.e., excellent students who do it all on their own and who make it hard for the rest of America to compete, an image that has deservedly been debunked as a myth by many people), I suggest that for Owen the idea of the Asian American pre-med spoke foremost of the image of the pushy Asian American family, interested only in status and material success. Owen went to enormous effort to let me know that this was true neither of his family nor of his own constitution, that his parents were not pushy and that he was not personally interested in wealth. He thus needed to establish himself as an Asian American would-be doctor with a difference.

Owen once argued that the best way to distinguish among college students was according to "*what* types of careers they wanted and *why* it was important to them." It was with this classification in mind that he figured he was different from most Asian Americans: "I actually think that the majority [of Asian Americans] would be either, well, probably doctors or something 'cause that's what maybe the parents wanted or seemed to [them], like, maybe an honorable goal for them to attain." His own experience, he stressed, was not like that of a high school Korean American friend whose parents "really pressured her" to go to Yale: "I don't think my parents pressured me at all to do anything. 'Just be whatever you want to be and that's fine with us. Just as long as you can make a living out of it, that's fine.'" (Recall Mary's early accounts of her optimistic father.)

Owen often spoke implicitly about white students, their career choices, their rationales. He was intrigued by those he observed in his elective courses, wanting to know how they thought about their careers. He imagined students who hadn't been pushed by their parents, students with "their own" reasons, students for whom a career was less important. For these non–Asian American students, "religious reasons," for example, might be a key factor: "They think that the career should revolve around religion or that the career shouldn't be the only thing that you should devote your life to. . . . So maybe that's their reasoning—why they're doing other things." Although the image of the non–Asian American student motivated by religion more than career might seem odd, and particularly odd in relation to Korean American religious fervency at the U of I and in general, Owen's interest was in self-directed lives, driven neither by material rewards nor conventional prestige. For him, these students stood at the other end of the spectrum, far removed from the "typical" Asian American college student. As for the place of material rewards in his own life, he put it this way: "I just want to, let's see, as Seinfeld put it—I was watching him on *Larry King Live*—he said, 'It's not so much that you have money, just so that you don't have to worry about it.' " Perhaps it was the laid-back pose itself that appealed.

Over his college years Owen entertained another career: research science. This option found its way into our conversations in two ways: as Plan B in case he didn't get accepted to medical school, and as an alternative lifestyle in which a career would figure less centrally. (I stopped myself from mentioning that research science was hardly an easy fall back plan.) Owen imagined that the research track would leave room for "the family part and the quality of life that [he] would be living." Without skipping a beat, this is what he said to me next: "This was a thought that just came up: . . . In high school, like on the ACTs [an aptitude survey administered with the exam], they always ask you if you like to do stuff with your hands. And I'm someone who always took things apart, and even when they're broken I'd save them and take them apart. Whenever they came up on exams [i.e., questions about mechanical aptitude], I'd put 'No' because I wasn't gonna add to that sort of thing, because when I get results back it would say you'd be a good carpenter." A few minutes later he added, "So I'd say 'No, I don't like working with gadgets or stuff like that.' That's not me, that's not what I want to be." On the one hand, he raised the possibility of a less career-focused life like the one he imagined non–Asian American religious students might choose, one that would allow him to focus on family and quality of life. On the other hand, he was wary of anything but a highly professional life and thus rigged his answers to the career survey for a desirable outcome: a medical field rather than a mechanical one. He reassured himself, though, that the answers he plotted for the "right" outcome were genuine: "Yeah and all that [also] was true."

If being a doctor was about something other than prestige or money, and if it meant sacrificing personal pleasure and family life, what it offered Owen was "meaning," the sort of meaning he was pursuing through his imagined liberal university: "I've always wanted to be a doctor and it kind of gives meaning to myself, like helping other . . . I think [the point of life] is helping people and finding out what you're supposed to be doing." In a lighter vein, he once contemplated what he might otherwise do if he didn't go to medical school: "If I wasn't going to med school I'd be a writer or a cook or something along those lines. Or a poet. . . . *Deep and to the point*, that's my style. That's, like, I like to write poetry. Or if I didn't have to do anything, I'd play tennis." "Deep and to the point" strikes me as an apt phrase for thinking about Owen's expectations of the liberal university. As for tennis, he once sketched the political economy of Chicago's northern suburbs in terms of high school tennis teams: the whiter the team, the better in tennis. It is not too great an interpretive stretch to suggest that the life of the poet or tennis player was colored white for Owen.

RELIGIOUS TRUTH AT COLLEGE: *"YOU KNOW, THE UNIVERSITY"*

Owen brought a religious quest to college, one that sometimes bristled, as it had with the freshman philosophy professor. If asked to summarize his college religious project, this is what I would say: quite firm in his belief in God and his own ability to realize an ethical life, what concerned Owen was why he should adhere to any particular faith over any other particular faith—why, in short, he should be Catholic. Owen put it this way: "I mean, if it was Islam . . . then meeting at sunrise, at lunchtime and something in the mosque and the prayer thing and stuff like that; if it was Jehovah's Witness go door to door knocking; and

Catholic? Then I guess I'd have to be going to [the Sacrament of] Reconciliation which I haven't gone to for a long time."[1] For Owen, the truth or status of the Bible as God's word was part and parcel of this debate. It often seemed to me that he yearned for a pure faith, unmediated by the human hand that sculpted religious practice in this or that religion. Further, understanding that religious doctrine is prescriptive such that Catholics pattern their days and religious practice one way and Muslims another, Owen simply wanted to know *how he should live*. And he wanted to figure this out sooner rather than later, for college was short, and for that matter "so was life," as he once told me: "I think I've put off this thing too long, and to be true to myself and true to God, I have to find out what the *truth* is and if there's *something I should be doing. . . .* If I'm supposed to be doing it, then I figured, it depends on what denomination I'm in so that's important to me: *to find out my purpose, if I do have a purpose.*"

As Owen selected his college electives, he again and again sought Truth, even as he realized that his courses made no promise of it. In his biblical archaeology class he struggled over the relationship between mythology and religion, which challenged his very understanding of the Bible. The professor, he admitted, had given fair warning: "You can't have it come to a conclusion whether or not religion is true or not."

Certainly no one could have solved Owen's doctrinal quandary. As to the professor who warned that the course would offer no conclusions, Owen mused, "Well—he's not supposed to come to a conclusion, I guess. *You know, the university* . . . I don't know. I should go talk to him. I haven't spoken to him yet." Owen desperately wanted to ask him if he was religious, but he wavered: "I don't want to ask him, you know, 'What's your religion?' He'll probably say that I'm not supposed to come to a conclusion and, but I would have asked him if he minded if I asked him, 'Through your research and everything, have you come to a conclusion about the existence of God?' But I don't know. I'll ask him, like, in a couple of weeks."

"You know, the university" was Owen's succinct comment on the tension between some of his desires and his coursework. But over the years, despite the urgency of his doctrinal quandary, I think that the struggle, the very lack of a conclusion, had in fact won his affections. With this reimagined liberal project the university fared better in Owen's eyes. By the spring of his senior year his tune had changed a bit. He reflected on the biblical archaeology course from a year earlier and on subsequent philosophy electives, concluding that the eternal search is the very stuff of humanity: "Not so much truth as learning how to find truth." About the question of evidence for the biblical flood, he said, "What does this mean to the Bible story? . . . For the pursuit of truth, you have to understand why we think the things we do today and a lot of the philosophers are actually trying to answer the questions of our existence, and of course they didn't come to any conclusions. . . . Why do we ignore certain things that our emotions tell us, [such as] that we have a belief in the spiritual? Why don't we use that as evidence? Because that is part of our inherent understanding of things."

Just as Owen was coming to these sorts of ideas, he was also doing something that he had been "about to do" all through the years we spoke: taking a university credit course with a campus-affiliated Catholic priest. Owen said that all the other kids in that class knew one another and chatted about this or that event or religious retreat. "So, I'm the only one who's sitting in the corner." But he had plenty to say about the course and its place in a university curriculum (it did, after all, "count"): "[The priest is] very presumptuous that *there is truth*. . . . He criticized Western philosophy, the Enlightenment, what were their names?—like Marx and all those people. He said, you know, that they're all wrong . . . you know, the humanism, domination of man over religions. . . . But it didn't seem to me, like, you know, that was their intent to just . . . He seemed to me that he was very presumptuous about things, like *there is a truth*. . . . Of course, he was teaching a Catholic religion class so I guess he had to take that position, but it was different for me because it wasn't, like, a secular class." Perhaps Owen's search for truth was all along nothing other than the search for good company with which to struggle, to grow, as one should in a university. Or perhaps Owen had changed.

If we think of the philosopher that so often figured in Owen's talk as a sort of narrative device or reprieve, a prop for telling a good story, we can similarly think about the priest being unwilling to engage the key questions (or at least, so it seemed to Owen). Owen looked to that part of college, the electives beyond his required pre-med courses, to provide meaning, to satisfy his liberal hankerings. And while those hankerings perhaps transformed over the course of college (with a good debate prevailing over the answer), both the philosophy professor and the priest had denied Owen his university due.

WHY KOREAN? RACE AND RELIGION

For Owen, Catholicism may not have solved the Truth question, but it posed an important ethnic question: "Would I be Catholic if my parents weren't Catholic?" Although his parents had long since stopped going to church regularly and did not even care whether Owen and his brother attended, they still insisted on prayers at mealtime: "They ask either my brother or I to pray, and I have a real problem with that. . . . It just seemed meaningless to repeat all that. . . . I'd say, 'Do I have to?' And then I'd rush through it real quick and that would be it. I guess it's because I hate hypocrisy." In much the same way that he questioned the practice of Catholicism ("Why this way and not some other way?") he also wondered "Why Korean?" "Really, the only Koreans I associated with were people who were Catholics, who were born in the United States and could speak fluent English and things like that." He asked why he should be or live one way or another in the name of being Korean: "I think there's a lot of tension in race. . . . My opinion about my, how comfortable I feel being a Korean, I mean, I've been thinking about that for a couple of days. [About] the reason that I don't fit into the Korean American society. . . . As I see it, it's because I don't feel comfortable being in that position. You know, having *the assumption that, the assumption is put on me that I speak Korean, that I do Korean things and things like that.*" He then described the "awkward feelings that came with" answering in English when he had been addressed in Korean by adult Korean immigrants: "I think it's really expected of Korean Americans [that they speak Korean]."

When Owen described for me the narrow spectrum of Korean Americans with whom he felt comfortable (i.e., English-speaking, American-born Korean American Catholics), he set out to distance himself from a range of Korean Americans: recent immigrants, Korean-speaking, city-dwelling, Protestant, evangelical, Korean-centered, ·and so forth. He was, I suggest, struggling with affiliation, race, and genealogy, and with how he, an Asian American or Korean American pre-med at a large research university (and one that draws heavily from Chicagoland's

Korean America), was likely perceived. Owen cared about images and expectations that were foisted upon him.

Perhaps if I had been younger, male, and Korean American or had asked more directly (these are always rather difficult thought experiments), the matter I take up now would have come up earlier, but my hunch is that it didn't because it was intensely personal for Owen and went to the painful center of some hard things. Two years into our talks, shortly after we discussed the mandatory prayers at mealtime, the conversation went this way:

Owen: Well, I don't know if I should talk about this. I never talked about my girlfriend in high school. She wasn't Catholic and she wasn't Korean. . . .

Nancy: And that pissed your parents off?

Owen: Yeah, big time.

Nancy: Was it that Jehovah's Witness girl?

Owen: Did you come to that conclusion?

Nancy: Yeah. . . .

Owen: Okay, I didn't want to talk about it, but it was her. . . .

Nancy: So that was very threatening to your parents?

Owen: Yeah. They grounded me, but they couldn't ground me because they didn't have time to drive me to school and stuff, so they didn't take that away from me. . . . *But they were really upset and that bothered me a lot.* . . . If Catholicism was the right religion, they shouldn't have problems with me questioning it 'cause I should come to that conclusion. . . .

Nancy: You guys broke up?

Owen: Yeah, over religious things. . . . And it wasn't working out anyway. Maybe we were together so long out of rebellion. I don't know.

Nancy: So that started the course of your parents worrying about you religiously? [I knew that Owen's parents did not like the extent of his religious interest and that they worried about his getting involved in a cult.]

Owen: Yeah.

Nancy: Do they know that you're going to Circle [the Korean American Catholic student group]?

Owen: Yeah, I told them I go to church. Actually, they don't want me to go to any religious group, study thing or whatever. . . .

Nancy: Why?

Owen: They think I should be concerned with medical school and studies and stuff, and I probably should be at this point [i.e., junior year]. . . . But this is *the only* time I actually have to pursue the other things anyway. I mean, when am I going to?

Nancy: Right, that's a good point. When are you going to do it later?

Owen: I mean, I can't keep putting it off, I've put it off long enough. . . . How did you come to the conclusion that I dated her?

Nancy: I just figured it out.

Owen: Women's intuition or something?

Nancy: Right!

In case the reader wonders: I figured out who Owen's girlfriend was because over the years of talking to him about religion, a number of times he had referred to a Jehovah's Witness friend from high school who was always there to offer *the* answers to his religious questions and to suggest a religious blueprint for living. He once told me that at one point in college she said to him, "Okay, just write down your questions and send them to me." I think that the matter of this non–Korean American Jehovah's Witness high school girlfriend was intensely private in large part because of the negative light it cast on Owen's family.

Perhaps what bothered Owen most of all was his parents', foremost his father's, unexamined relationship to Catholicism and Koreanness. With this account we can explore the complicated way Catholicism and Koreanness were intertwined for Owen. (Once he made this slip of the tongue: "That friend of mine isn't Catholic, I mean isn't Korean.") At issue was not merely the matter of his parents' narrow-mindedness, but the heavy hand with which they administered the family. In the discussion about pushy parents I described Owen's investment in a view of his parents as untraditional, not pushy, and most important not typically Asian American. But here was evidence to the contrary, evidence of parents wanting their son to keep to the ethnic and religious fold, evidence of his parents wanting him to be a conscientious pre-med student rather than a spiritual seeker. Over three years of conversation there was only one thing that Owen told me off the record, and I will not, of course, quote it here. But I will share that it too revealed details of his father's conservativeness. (During the weeks that I waited to hear from Owen about this chapter—I wanted his approval—I worried most about this sentence; when he didn't bring it up, I even flagged it!) These were sensitive matters because they made his family vulnerable to the very ethnic stereotypes that Owen was so invested in defying, both in his own life and in his account of his family.

BEYOND THE FOLD

Owen was the first to admit that he could have been more "social." "I can be social, I just, it hasn't interested me until, like, recently," was how he put it the spring of his senior year. He also described not having felt the need to make friends, what with "friends from high school, friends from home, family friends," and he had never lived in the dorms, instead sharing an apartment with his older brother, John, for the first two years and with his paternal first cousin Tony for the last two. But I submit that Owen had in fact been interested in diversity. No doubt, for Owen, religious diversity was the subject he talked about most, but as I have suggested, his doctrinal struggles, like his ethnic struggles as a Korean American, were really about encountering diversity, different ways of patterning one's days. In his sophomore year he was explicit about his desire to meet new sorts of people: "Well, the people I've met so far haven't, have been, like, the same kinds of people I met in high school. . . . It doesn't open my *perspective* about people and ideas and things like that." He continued, though, "This is what you get with a state school," and he mentioned the college life of one of his cousins at the University of Chicago: "People on her floor came from all parts of the world and had different ideas, and that's the kind of thing that I wanted to experience at college. And after that [i.e., college], you don't really have time to develop your thoughts about the world and things like that. This is the time to do it."

These misgivings aside, Owen was nonetheless consistent in his confidence that the university was a "good deal" for the money, although once in his sophomore year he was blunt about the finances that had drawn him to the university: "My opinion about the school—*If I had a choice, I wouldn't go to this school.*" By his senior year these were his reflections:

> I'm satisfied with my education but not so much with the *entire experience.* I mean, I think I have always expressed that opinion since I've been here . . . but I think I've become more satisfied with the education here over time. But, I mean, out of college *I still expected more.* But, I don't know, just kind of knowing, like, myself, I probably would say that about anything anyway 'cause *I'm always expecting more,* but in this case, I think it's, *I mean I have the right to expect more. . . .*
>
> I mean, I'm not entirely disappointed. . . . I mean, I'm proud and happy to be graduating with my degree. . . . In that sort of sense, I am satisfied. . . . I think I got my money's worth, and otherwise, well, again, like I said before, it's—the education you get—is *definitely dependent on you.* Of course professors and teachers have a good deal to do with it, but ultimately it's up to you. . . . If I had been more social I think I would have been happier.

Owen's evaluations were conflicted: he had gotten his "money's worth" but he felt that he had the "right to expect more," especially when it came to the "entire experience"; he couldn't really complain because a person's education is "definitely dependent on" the person; and finally, had he been more social he would likely have been "happier." By this time Owen had been accepted into a reputable medical school, and as such the university had been "worth it." "The right to expect more" harkened to Owen's great expectations, his liberal dream. As for what he should have made of his own education, we meet the American individualism and optimism that we found in one of Mary's voices as well; with this voice, Owen himself was responsible for the unremarkable passage of his four college years. His regret that he might have been more "social" spoke to his having missed out on more fun and on more diverse and interesting company.

We began with Owen's great expectations breached in the college classroom and with his struggles to wrest himself from the stereotype of the Asian American pre-med student. He began college with a quest for religious Truth and ended convinced more of the truth of the quest itself. Throughout, he wrestled with liberal disappointments in his family and the university. He had longed for inclusion in the white university against images of "pushy" Asian parents who directed their children into high-paying professional jobs. His liberal project was fundamentally and thoroughly anti–Asian American.

To understand something of why the university could not fulfill Owen's liberal yearnings it helps to roll the camera back and include in the picture Owen's extended family and the university in the landscape of family desires. In this vein I briefly introduce the family farm and Owen's brother and paternal cousin.

THE FARM VERSUS THE UNIVERSITY

To date, all of the second-generation members of the Han family residing in the United States have gone to college; moreover, so far, all of them have graduated in a timely fashion. At one level, then, it makes little sense to pose the farm against the university. I do so, however, to call attention to ways in which for some Korean Americans, family can, at some moments, serve as a refuge from America, even as Korean American families most often deeply embrace the American dream. This familial or ethnic challenge to the university was most clear in the lives of two members of the Han family second generation, first cousins John (Owen's brother) and Tony, who are the subject of the next chapter.

For the Hans, the farm was a veritable symbol of family, and by extension of ethnic networks and even segregation. The farm was the project of Uncle Mark, one of Owen's paternal uncles, and together with him represented a street-smart entrepreneurialism that was at odds with certain liberal university ideals. For the second-generation Hans, the farm and Uncle Mark together conjured an image of familism (or family-centeredness), ethnic segregation, Korean patriarchy, and a way of being in the world in which education didn't figure so centrally.

On 20 December 2003 I joined the Han family Saturday Christmas gathering; also present were three of the immigrant parent siblings, members of the second generation from five of the families, and various friends. For an anthropologist the party was a dream come true: five of the second-generation children whom I had been meeting for years alone or in pairs and a few of the parent generation all in one milieu, a ranch home with a sprawling addition in the back (perfect for a large Christmas party) in a squarely middle-class Chicago suburban neighborhood. The party was held several days before Christmas because six members of the second generation were off the next morning for a long-planned trip to Hawai'i.

I was most excited to finally meet Uncle Mark, the tailor, the youngest of the Han parent-generation immigrants and the father of Emily, one of the second-generation cousins I had been meeting. I had heard so much about Mark, his largesse to the extended family, his rough-and-tumble spirit, his sailor language, his huge reputation as a skilled tailor, but most of all his farm. The farm (which no one really farmed) was Uncle Mark's baby, nearly one hundred acres two hours southwest of Chicago, a place where the extended Han family had been retreating for weekends and holidays for over a decade. The farm stands out: it isn't very often that first-generation Korean immigrants purchase tracts of land in farm country. By that Christmas the only structure to be found on the farm was a large lean-to; I was told it was the kind one finds in the sort of rural Korean village where Uncle Mark and his siblings spent their early youth. That evening, though, Mark ceremoniously unfurled blueprints for a distinctive house that he planned to build there, nearly 80 percent of it a single room to preserve open space for Han kin into the future, a room designated for nothing other than the gathering, in private, of this large extended family, with occasional visits from family friends.

It was not until that Christmas party evening that I learned something about the origin of the farm. Mark explained that in 1992 the entire family traveled to a rural state park for a family barbecue. Korean countryside barbecues are hardly light fare; neither are they quiet or short-lived. As they unpacked the grills and various paraphernalia, Mark said, "People looked at us as if we were monkeys." "Like monkeys," he repeated again and again. Then and there he resolved to buy a place where they could all go comfortably. The farm, the symbol of Han family solidarity, was in one sense a refuge from the racialized gaze at a large ethnic family performing kin ties in the American landscape. But the story is more complicated. Several minutes later in our conversation, Mark told me another reason the Hans stood out that day: "We arrived in cars that were nicer than any that had *ever* been there!" Mark was describing an ethnic performance that was also classed, perhaps in ways that for the onlookers competed against prevailing images of immigrant families.

AN (ANTI−)ASIAN AMERICAN PRE-MED

Owen's paternal cousin Tony described the extended Han family this way: "I think of us as a big network. . . . John [Owen's brother and the oldest male cousin in the United States] is probably going to be the head of the family once all the members pass away . . . like in [the] next century." A conversation about the possibility of two of the other cousins becoming doctors gave meaning to Tony's sense of a network: "But if both of them go into medicine, we have too many doctors. . . . We need someone in accounting, we need someone in business, and you know we need someone who's a lawyer. I just think as a family, we have to just, you know, just kind of build resources as a big family . . . like *a huge network of people referring someone else to someone else*." The family was to offer resources, and hence it needed to cover several career fields.

Tony was matter-of-fact that he and his two male cousins, who were then at the U of I with him, "don't really care to integrate with the entire university": "We're pretty content with what we have, I guess." He lived with Owen, who also described a family-based social life for some of his years at college. For Tony, the comfort zone was narrower than the ethnic circles we met in part I of this book; it hovered around family itself. And family mattered most in his thinking about the future, in part because it was family, not necessarily his individual university degree, that he calculated might secure that future. It is in this sense that we can think of family as being in competition with the university, as well as thwarting the university's diversity initiatives.

Tony had dreamed of auto racing since he was a boy, majored in engineering, and early on hoped to work for one of the big American auto companies. With middling grades in his junior year, though, he began to fret over what an engineering degree would *really* promise. He spoke skeptically about "hard work that *supposedly* pays off in the end." When he told me that he was thinking about transferring to the College of Business, he brought up Uncle Mark, whom he described as "mentality-wise pretty young" and who was encouraging him to go into business: " 'Cause, like, if I were to graduate with a business degree I'm sure *through family connections* I could probably get a job with some investment firm because Mark has a lot of friends who are pretty high up there." Tony once described Mark as the "anchor of the family," adding that he thought of himself as "family-oriented in the same way as Mark." That by his junior year Tony described himself as not really caring to "integrate with the entire university" was in large measure a sign of his very resignation to the limits of what college offered *him* (he did, though, graduate in engineering).

Like the contemporary American university imaginary itself, Tony's university imaginaries were conflicted: on the one hand, a university that rationally conferred opportunity commensurate with achievement and fostered personal development, and on the other hand, one that didn't really offer much after all, managing only to move people through in segregated cohorts. The retreat to family, a network of resources epitomized by the farm, was thus posed against the university.

5 FAMILY VERSUS ALMA MATER

Although Owen was intermittently critical of the U of I for the ways it thwarted his liberal education, he ultimately embraced the university, its project and promises. I argued that Owen worked hard at his liberal education against the grain of racialized images of an Asian American pre-med student. Although he didn't speak specifically about race, I asserted that race was implicated in his careful crafting of his education and in the personal religious (liberal) struggles that figured at the core of his college education.

In this chapter I focus on Owen's older brother, John, who Tony predicted was "probably going to be the head of the family" in the future, and his paternal cousin Tony. John's and Tony's travels through the U of I were quite different from Owen's, both on the matter of race and ethnicity and on the question of a liberal education and the very purpose of college. John named race, was outspoken about racism, rejected the liberal premise of college, dismissed diversity, and made light of the importance of college altogether. In so doing he was brazen in his celebration of ethnic, familial, and even patrilineal segregation. He emulated Uncle Mark, his family focus, his rough-and-ready qualities, and his having made his way without college. In that vein, Tony too rejected aspects of the university and described being quite happy with his largely kin and ethnic network. Tony also admired Uncle Mark and had much to say about the importance of family, ethnic networks, and the practical world. But Tony had another side, one that understood his cousin Owen's (and Owen's dad's, his maternal uncle's) liberal hankerings for education for the universal human and the experience of diversity. Like Mary, Tony was of two minds. With John and Tony we continue this book's focus on race and college.

Like those of so many families that came of age in the tumult of the immediate post-Liberation (1945–) and Korean War era (1950–1953), the life courses of the Han siblings diverged enormously: while the two oldest Han brothers secured four-year college degrees, Owen's and John's father managed to get a night school degree while working, and the youngest brothers (Mark among them) did not head for any higher education at all.[1] In this single immigrant family there are radically distinct ways of being adult men that reflect differences of education, employment, and lifestyle. These men figured largely in the second generation's ideal selves and futures. Owen and John's father was educated, was a skilled nine-to-five worker in an American company, and championed the fine arts; Uncle Mark was a less educated, self-employed, workaholic entrepreneur tailor who lived for recreation at the farm. Where Owen's inclinations echoed his father's, John emulated his uncle, who was doing just fine without a college degree. So too did Tony in part emulate Uncle Mark against the grain of his own highly educated father (not a member of the Han patrilineage).

Students bring their families with them to college, but families do not bear on each and every member in the same way.[2] Although the vision of higher education, and certainly the aim of every alumni organization, is that each family seamlessly incorporate the university into its family structure—wearing the same sweatshirt, attending the same athletic events, and holding the Alma Mater equally dear—the college experience is in fact variously refracted through the prism of family, leaving brothers, cousins, mothers, and daughters with their different takes and trajectories.

JOHN: "COLLEGE . . . IS A WASTE"

John had no liberal romance with the "racist" American university. He pitted family capital, namely, his own ability to secure connections and work though the family, against the university. John was not the only college critic I met over the course of my research, but he was an extreme and interesting one, in part for being Owen's brother. Of course, in parsing differences between siblings, one could look at a range of psychodynamic or even genetic causes, but the factor I focus on here is family, particularly John's unique position at the helm of the paternal cousins.[3] Although he did not speak about his father to me at length, he did talk a great deal about his uncle Mark, with whom he clearly identified.

Although second generation, John was very matter-of-fact about his position (in a Korean cultural sense) in the extended Han family as the eldest male of the cousins in the United States. "I was brought up for that role from the beginning 'cause everybody saw me as that and so I'm just grown into that." John told me something I had already heard from three of his cousins: that he spent a great deal of time helping them and the family generally. "I was the oldest one and I had to do a lot of work for, not just my family, but everybody else as well." What sort of work? "Loose ends, like setting up the phone company, taking care of this, taking care of—just a lot of loose ends that would require English . . . stuff they would have no knowledge about." In immigrant families with limited English, the case of the majority of Korean immigrants of the era of his family's immigration and even of many today, it was often children who took on this family labor.[4] As for why it was John and not the eldest cousin, who is a girl, John said, "*It's a boy thing. . . .* I was always [interested in] the family kind of thing and it wasn't like that with her." As to his younger brother, Owen, John was again perfunctory: "From what I know of Owen, I don't think he sees the family situation as I do." He said that when he headed out to visit the cousins, Owen's take was "Why bother? Unless there's something I have to do." If John was resigned about his kinship niche, it was clear that the role and its duties were at the heart of his sense of self: "It makes all my relatives happy. . . . They call me, ask me to do this, this, this, fine. Often I pick them up from school or drop them off. I do a lot of that kind of work."

John did think that this "boy thing" mattered when it came to his education: "I have more pressure, like, I'm the first one out of here, out of high school, into college, out of college, into a job and all that stuff . . . 'cause I have my brother, my cousin, and then below, down there, there's like six others, I think." And John had been honing a skill set to match; in high school, for example, he began tending to the family's financial paperwork: "I pretty much put everything into organization and enter it into Quicken . . . so I pretty much take care of all that." Owen, on the other hand, seemed to have little understanding of family finances. As for ending up at the U of I, John minced no words: "The U of I was a financial given." Knowing firsthand about the family coffers, he didn't apply elsewhere. This said, John and Owen's family appeared to be solidly middle class, but as we know private higher education is becoming increasingly unattainable, even for the middle class.[5] Given his role, John described the commensurately "bigger impact" that money has had on his life in contrast to Owen's, making him more motivated by it than his brother, who stressed that it was not his primary focus.

An Ex–Pre-med

Through his junior year John, like his brother, was a pre-med student, majoring in a science. Uncle Mark, with whom John described having "a lot in common," found him a job that summer at an investment bank. John was a quick convert: "I saw the life there. . . . It would be so much easier as opposed to going to med school and residency and all that junk. . . . So, after I came back I dumped my [department] degree, my additional [department] double major idea, and I dumped all those classes I didn't need and I took a lot of easy classes." When I asked whether he had any worries he responded, "I'm told that everything's okay, just graduate and get out of here." As to whether the summer job and the future it promised could have been secured without his uncle, John was unequivocal: "No way!" Uncle Mark's friend, an Irish American client, had found John a job working for a Korean émigré. The story went that the young man had been deeply impressed by John's wholesomeness and family orientation; "[Making the Korean émigré] feel corrupt and dirty" was how Mr. Han described it to me. Uncle Mark's client convinced John that business was a better route than staying with pre-med: "[He told me that this is] a once-in-a-lifetime opportunity that you should not bypass." The client had gone further, advising him to drop out, but his parents prevailed: "[The client] was like, 'Forget college 'cause you don't really need it. . . . Anyway, [your major] doesn't really help you.'" Over time John embraced the client's perspective wholeheartedly: "I think you can survive in the world without a college degree and do really successfully. Only reason that many people go to college is because [of] that idea that a college degree will help and all this stuff like that, but I mean, academically at least, I think it's not so much. I mean it's, like, up to a point, it's, like, how much you do and then after that it's how much you don't do, how much you know, and who do you know." John questioned the import and meaning of a college education and suggested that what you do and who you know matter more. His critique of college, however, was about much more than its future utility.

John juggled several ideas about the U of I, some of them odd bed-fellows. He criticized the quality of students, the quality of the education itself, and intermittently his own attitude. He described the lack of ambi-tion and drive that characterized U of I students generally: "A waste of time . . . waste of time would be too harsh, but there's, like, so much more that we could be putting in, and getting out of it and, like, people here are not driven and ambitious." He spoke of the U of I as easy to enter: "It's easy to fall into that category [i.e., of people who are not driven and ambitious], to just waltz through." Getting more personal, he admitted that he and a friend had discussed their university experience: "[We] were talking about this and felt that there was so much more we could do but we don't." He had disparaging things to say about "aca-demic dishonesty and dis-integrity" at the U of I: "You have no idea how much I know, that's why I think that college . . . I think that a lot of the classes aren't really classes. They're just for people to enroll in and get an A and get nothing out of and they're, like, really pointless classes. *And so that's why I think college is a joke.*" Most people just "waltz through taking those easy classes." He counted himself among those who "actually do the work and deserve the grade," but he described the many who "get the same grade and do no work." "I don't think it's very fair," he added. He told me that in his senior year he took the time to write all of this down on the senior survey, which he dubbed his "anonymous grading of the university." He conceded that one does "mature through college," but that "after that it's just a party—kind of free time."

John and most of his Korean American generation agreed on the matter of growth at college. He too had bargained for much more: "I fig-ured I'd probably, I was going to get some big, I don't know, understand-ing about life or some revelation or something out of going through college and maybe learning something that I wouldn't have learned, or, I don't know, just something big or whatever. . . . But after going through it, I mean, I enjoyed my time here . . . it was a nice period, and what I really gained out of it other than a [science] degree, I don't really know." Like Owen, John also imagined that things might have been different at a more elite school. Although his maternal cousin at the University of Chicago complained about this and that, not lost on John was her more cosmopolitan "social life": "Like friends and all this stuff, she keeps, she keeps visiting Texas and stuff 'cause her friend is there and something like that. She's going back and forth. I mean it's an interesting life 'cause you meet people from all over the place, as opposed to here, where everybody's from Illinois." I have discussed the U of I's troubling ethnic intimacy at length, but here John referred more broadly to the over-whelmingly in-state character of the undergraduate population, another intimacy. He imagined that the people at the University of Chicago would be more interesting not only for being out-of-staters but also "because they had to work to get into there": "It's not, like, an open-door policy like it is here." I corrected John that the U of I hardly has an open-door policy, and the University of Chicago is hardly immune to legacy admissions.

John wavered slightly, offering broad dismissals of the value of college on the one hand, specific criticisms of the U of I on the other, and on occasion admission of his own complicity as well.

"I wouldn't have minded an all–Asian American freshman class"

Wistfulness about out-of-staters at more elite colleges aside, John had little positive to say about even those outside of his immediate Korean American circles at the U of I. In contrast to Mary, who channeled her critiques of white racism through a critique of the Korean American mainstream, John explicitly described anti–Asian American racism at the U of I. He reserved his most critical comments for the ubiquitous "frat-sorority type of person" at the university. "They drive me nuts and so I just, like, avoid them." He described their stupidity, their "party this, party that," their "lower standards," and "that stuff, the symbols and stuff." He described pickup basketball games with them and "*their* cockiness, *their* attitude, *their* arrogance and stuff I just really don't like." It became clear that "frat people" was meant to refer to whites when he continued, "I tend to avoid playing with black people *too* for that matter."

In our last conversation together he described a racist incident at his cousin Tony's apartment. He was surprised that I hadn't heard about it yet from Tony. "One night we were dropping [Tony] off and on the third floor there was a group of, there's white people who live up there, and that night they threw an egg down into our car and it, like, they whipped it really hard so that it shattered the paint on our car." They reported it to the police, and although they didn't call it a hate crime it was clear that from John's perspective it had been. (On reading this chapter Tony had only one substantive comment: that from his perspective the egg throwing had *not* been racially motivated.) As for the guys in question, John said, "They're always throwing stuff. . . . It's not just them. . . . So that's why I suppose I get my opinions about them. I mean, like, it's general, it's generalizing the rest of everybody else based on a few people, but, you know." This racial caution aside, he continued, "Probably they think, 'Oh, this is college, I'll do whatever I want' kind of thing." He described what could make for poetic justice in the future: "After college I would like to say to them, 'Hey I'm in *this* position and you're in *that* position and ha ha' kind of thing. I'd like to laugh in their face. . . . 'Go haul my garbage' or whatever."

Although in passing John worried a bit about "generalizing," he was pretty certain of his ground when it came to white America at the U of I. As for his exclusively Asian American and largely Korean American social circles, he said this: "I suppose . . . because the impression I get for the non-Asian people I know or meet or run into and stuff and the more things that I get a negative view about, the more I shy away from them." It was also clear that he wasn't so happy about non-Asian students of color at the U of I. And he was staunchly opposed to affirmative action. He imagined that without it there would be more Asian Americans: *"I wouldn't have minded an all–Asian American freshman class."* John was certainly at odds with his brother Owen's interest in diversity and a liberal arts education.

John's racial map becomes a bit more complicated when we listen to him talk about the "frat kind of culture" of recently immigrated Koreans, FOBS, and South Koreans. Despite his interest in an exclusively Asian American freshman class, what bothered him about Koreatown, the dwindling concentration of Koreans in the Lawrence Street area of downtown Chicago, was its "being all 'Korean,'" that is, recent immigrants from South Korea. For John, young Koreans are "wasteful," "just not practical." Nor did he have any patience for AACers: "I'd probably be laughing the whole time." For his own part he was "conservative," not at all interested in the liberal dream of growth that Owen and his father shared. "All that impressionistic stuff, and that deep art stuff, I could care less." There would likely be caveats to John's all-Asian freshman class: that for starters they be conservative (i.e., family-minded) as he was, that they be practical (work-oriented, street-smart) as he was, and that they be non-white-identified as he was.

Despite differences between John and Owen, they shared an active imaginary of what college could ideally be like, although their imagined universities were enormously different, Owen's a liberal project, John's nakedly instrumental. Both of them were enormously critical education consumers interested in their due. While Owen finally reached some peace about his liberal education, John walked away disgruntled. This divergence perhaps reflects their postgraduation paths: where Owen built on his undergraduate career, getting into medical school, John forsook his college capital and ties by finding a job through family contacts.

TONY: "I'M KIND OF LACKING. I DON'T KNOW IF IT'S ME OR THE SCHOOL, OR THE MATCH"

Tony was explicit about the family as "a big network." He claimed that he, Owen, and John were "pretty content" and thus did not "integrate with the entire university." In the previous chapter we briefly met Tony at a moment of crisis and falling grades in his sophomore year, when he had begun to contemplate a move from engineering to business and the prospect of finding a job through Uncle Mark, as his cousin John had. Tony too sported particular college ideals and worried that the U of I had forsaken him, preparing him for a bygone America. His critique of college paled next to John's, but over the seven years of our conversations (the most extensive of my conversations with any student; he made great efforts to keep in touch) Tony expressed a number of negative thoughts about the U of I and college more generally. In much the same way that John quietly contrasted his wage-earning father with his much more ambitious, hard-working, and less educated uncle Mark, so too did Tony contrast Uncle Mark with his own, highly educated father. Tony's father looked down on his wife's siblings, thinking of the Hans as "lower level" and uneducated. While the Hans were merely "immigrants," his father described his own family as "coming here at their own free will, . . . seeking a better life," and having been "sent here as a student [*yuhak saeng*], a governmental thing." Tony reproached his father's pride: "You'll find this pretty funny, Nancy, but he thinks because he's educated, he's somewhat superior." (Although I didn't find it funny —that a Korean man would prize his educational attainment was commonsensical—I was completely charmed by Tony, who seemed to idealistically hold out for a United States in which credentials didn't matter.) Where Tony's father stood for elite education and an individually focused life trajectory, Uncle Mark was for Tony a paragon of extended-family virtue and entrepreneurial energy that Tony found neither in college nor in his nuclear or paternal family. About Uncle Mark he said, "He's the doer in the family. He's the *one with the land*. . . . Basically *he does everything*, well, not really everything, *himself*. . . . *He takes care of everyone else*. . . . *He's kind of a dreamer too*, to me. He always has ideas. I kind of like, I hope to be like him because *he's always thinking ahead*. Even though he doesn't have a college education, *he has really good business smarts*." For Tony and John, Uncle Mark and the farm stood for an approach to college, family, ethnicity, and the future that was distinct from the liberal ideals we met through Owen and that we will reencounter, albeit in a different idiom, in Mr. Han. Uncle Mark embodied the version of the immigrant dream that was self-made, optimistic, entrepreneurial, and street-smart—and he was the one with the land!

Tony had always loved race cars. His parents "were not pleased" that he had spent high school summers working as an auto mechanic. About his high school auto mechanics teacher he said that he was "very well-rounded, his brain [was] always picking up things, learning." That teacher had often told the students, "College isn't for everyone." Tony came to the U of I in engineering with concrete plans to work at "one of the Big Three, GM, Chrysler, Ford . . . as a designer." In the fall of his sophomore year he mused that by the time he knew whether he was Big Three material, it would be too late to change direction. His thoughts were indeed prescient, not because he ended up not being Big Three material, but because by the time the Big Three were ready for him, he no longer wanted them (and by then the Big Three were cutting more and more jobs). At that point changing course was no small feat.

By the end of his sophomore year Tony described himself as being "in that red zone . . . digging a hole for [himself]." He did not appreciate his father's explicit comments about what he already knew: "If you keep those [i.e., low] grades up, you're not really going anywhere." Later that spring he secured a summer internship. Over spring break he went to check it out with his parents; the plant looked old and his parents worried that he "would be doing some type of physical labor." The fact that he would be wearing "a uniform, steel-tipped boots, and a hard hat" probably contributed to their impression. By that late spring meeting, Tony's parents had capitulated to years of pressure and given him a car. He dreamed about racing it, though it wasn't a race car. "I wouldn't mind putting something like that on my résumé," he said, figuring that this might make him stand out. This was exactly when Tony began to question "hard work . . . that *supposedly* pays off in the end" and whether he would, indeed, stand out!

As for the internship, his parents' fears had been well founded. He had hoped to "be left independent to actually think instead of just being a robot." It was in the spring of his junior year that he began to think instead about the prospect of business and about asking Uncle Mark to find him a job. This was also the point at which he began to question engineering more generally; it was 1999, the market was still high, start-ups were booming, and he thought about transferring to business, maybe even starting something with a friend. "Maybe there's an easier way to get there—not that I want to be like the next Bill Gates, but . . ." As for where his uncle might come in: "I guess he has lots of friends who are pretty high up there." His departmental advisor was not opposed to the transfer, but the dean was, and Tony knew his parents would be as well. Someday the market would go down, the dean figured, and then the engineering skills would come in handy. But this didn't stop Tony from worrying even a year later that he would end up "doing the dirty work so that business majors can make money off of me." Tony was juggling the competing strategies of his uncle, his advisor, and the dean. In the midst of it all he was worried that he had veered off course, that he would end up "doing the dirty work." "Business" for Tony spoke to entrepreneurship, to the mantras of the new economies in which we are to be entrepreneurs of the self; engineering, on the other hand, stood for old skills, old economies. It was at this juncture that Uncle Mark could serve as a role model for Tony.

A part of Tony simply wanted a "fresh start"; the year had been hard at home as well, and more than making it big, he was worried about "being happy." His perspective on starting his career at one of the Big Three auto companies had also changed. Reluctantly he figured, "I suppose I would sacrifice and do that." A year later, at the end of his senior year, he was even more set against the Big Three: "I wouldn't buy any of their products. . . . I don't feel they're worth my money or my parents' money. . . . In my mind they come out with poor products." This was a sea change from his freshman year. He was thinking about staying for a fifth-year semester, a not uncommon practice, and perhaps related to his inability to find a job. He began thinking about the aerospace industry and was disappointed when he gave one of the companies his résumé: "They were like, 'Shouldn't you be working for Ford?' " By then Tony had begun to reflect on the limits of his training at the U of I. An interview with Microsoft had been particularly telling: "[The interviewer] basically gave me a blank sheet of paper and told me to design the interface of a toaster." He hadn't fared very well at the assignment. "When I think about it, what they'd probably be looking for, yeah like, not that I'm not capable of doing that, but it was just . . . *I guess they want people whose thought process is, like, with no bounds,* and mine's kind of the opposite because over here [i.e., in engineering at the U of I] we're kind of trying to train to keep costs in mind, keep manufacturing really in mind. . . . It definitely seems like the U of I tried to keep everything very practical." Tony thus began to register that his own undergraduate training in engineering and at the U of I didn't make for the likes of Microsoft with their "abstract thinking." Owen reported to Tony that on the television program *20/20* Microsoft was described as a "yard where people can just walk and think." Tony wanted to broaden his training by staying on for an extra semester, but his advisor disagreed: "Basically [he] forced me out even though I had the right to stay." He was told that he would be taking a spot, wasting his parents' money, and forfeiting his own income; the advisor called an extra semester "absurd." With these experiences and calculations, we listen in on a college senior worrying about whether he had been trained for a waning era, for a yesteryear cutting edge. Tony feared that he could end up doing grunt work for other people who would know what to do with blank pages and in empty yards. As for the U of I, it "kept everything practical" and closed the door when Tony groped for new ways to grow.

"A monkey could have done my job"
When we met in late July that summer after his graduation Tony had a retail job but was seldom given any hours and was pounding the pavement in search of a "real" job. Over lunch, he described a disastrous interview in a sordid neighborhood with a motley crew of interviewers who Tony figured gave him a hard time because they graduated from lesser schools than the U of I. He had begun to realize that his training in mechanical engineering was qualifying him for "old-style industry" like that one, but that even there the fit wasn't perfect precisely because he went to the U of I. And he had begun to think that he might have to

"pay his time" in Detroit, although by then he had hankerings to head for sunny southern California. It was a sort of destiny: engineering at the U of I, at least of the variety he had selected, had him heading for Detroit.

Tony did end up in Detroit. That he was underemployed there (he was, in fact, doing grunt work) didn't stop him from losing three jobs in less than two years. By that time it was 2002, and downsizing remained a generalized and palpable trend. It was all disconcerting. Design, the career Tony had cared about forever, didn't matter—only the "bottom line" did. He explained that on the job he was no more than a "babysitter" in a "very little box": *"A monkey could have done my job."* The economy was "tanking," he had "zero social life," he had started going to church, and he even took an extra job in retail to meet people but found it "like being in high school." He packed up, broke his lease, and headed home to Chicago. When we met, Tony was working for a legal firm dealing with the auto industry and was thinking about law school. He described how helpful a visit to the farm with Uncle Mark had been and how he hoped to stay local: "He's the anchor of the family. It's not that I owe it to him to always be around, but I want to. He's not gonna say 'Do this [i.e., move home]!' But he knows that I'm family-oriented." Here again, despite his own lack of education, it was Uncle Mark who was the beacon as Tony planned for law school and the flexible opportunities it would give him for staying in Chicago. (Tony is a lawyer today and has remained in Chicagoland.)

It was at this meeting that Tony told me sadly that his father saw no need for the whole family "to live in Chicago or any central location." He said that he did not understand his dad and that while "it would be nice to have those [his father's] qualities as well," such as the ability to stand alone in the world, for his part he would much prefer to have family around. Tony digressed and asked me if I had seen *My Big Fat Greek Wedding* (2002), a movie he had loved about a close-knit ethnic American family: "[It] definitely reminded me of Koreans." In e-mail correspondence after his graduation, I asked him if he wanted to choose his own pseudonym for this book; he wrote back, "As for the pseudonym, I haven't seen *The Godfather* in years but perhaps a famous Italian name." "Tony" stands for close-knit kin, ethnic family, and (staying in) Chicago.

Recall that in *The Godfather*, Michael's position as a "college boy" is interpreted as making him too sensitive for the family business. Initially

Michael sees college as a desirable way out of the narrow and backward family traditions, but, as we know, eventually he reconciles himself to the path of his father when family need arises and he comes to see the mainstream world as hypocritical and corrupt.

In his reflections on his college education, Tony regretted his lack of breadth, both in his college courses and his social circles. These were thoughts he had entertained during his college years as well; that the straight and narrow path hadn't been so effective perhaps only underscored what he worried he had been lacking all along. He also echoed some of Owen's more liberal ideals and with both Owen and John offered a concerted critique of the U of I.

"Well if they really wanted a well-rounded education . . ."
"College is supposed to be the best time of your life. You're supposed to make lasting friendships. Yeah, you're supposed to get an education, but along with the education is supposed to be basically experiencing things that you're not supposed to afterwards. In that kind of sense, I guess *I'm kind of lacking. I don't know if it's me or the school, or the match."* These were Tony's thoughts in his sophomore year. By our meeting two years after graduation he was certain that it hadn't happened, that he wasn't "well rounded." His engineering training had "shoved so much down [his] throat" and he wondered, "If I had gone some place else, could it have been different?" Recall that it was on the basis of his sisters' private college experience that both Owen and John had wondered about the limits of U of I, with its reputed "open-door policy" and its largely in-state population.

In his freshman year Tony told me that his sisters had wanted him to go to college out of state to get "exposure to students around the world." By his sophomore year he had begun to agree with his sisters: "[At U of I you're] never really hearing anything that's totally different from anything you've experienced. . . . It's almost like, like if I look at my life, I'm just moving along with the same people, like, continually." Here we must remember Tony's self-described social circles of cousins and a few Korean American high school chums. He had begun to think that perhaps a private, smaller school would have been different. We spoke a bit about the high ranking of mechanical engineering at U of I, but he said, "I don't know . . . I don't think it is such a big deal to be here. Personally I would trade, I mean, let's say some private school in, say, New York or something." As it had for Owen and for John, it was money that made Tony's decision; his sisters, on the other hand, had done well enough to win scholarships to private schools. And he told me again about his sisters' advice to leave the state: " 'You have to meet different people.' Just hearing that over and over again, I was kind of maybe hoping, but . . . I guess, in the back of my mind, I knew it probably wasn't going to happen." He wondered too whether he might have been more motivated at a better school with more people with "natural talent." "Whereas here a lot of people are like me. . . . I don't know, maybe I'll just be content with mediocrity."

Like so many of the students I spoke with, Tony was disappointed by his general education courses. For starters, he hadn't chosen them himself: "Pretty much my advisor told me which choice of classes I should take." He longed for "other views," but his classes were not offering that. By the spring of junior year he reflected, "Throughout my entire college career, I can't say that I've had much choice in what I wanted to take. . . . *If they really wanted a well-rounded education*, which they claim that they want to give us, they'd let us or they'd allot us to take some classes that we're really interested in. And if you do that, you won't get out on time." Again and again he spoke of being "disappointed." Recall his description of his forced departure from college (after four years), his "rights" aside. I asked Tony about his dream curriculum: "I'd probably take some type of courses, just to keep me interested, in the technical field, but definitely religion. I'd still like to take up Korean, some philosophy class too. Just something to broaden my mind. I don't want to be so one-track-minded and not know anything else except for calculus or heat transfers. 'Cause even that, like, to a layman, that doesn't mean anything anyway. . . . So I just want to be well-rounded, that's basically what it is, *and that's what the university claims that they want to produce*." Tony had a clear sense of the gap between the university's claims and its reality. He charged that whereas the university claimed it was committed to fostering well-rounded students, in fact it made it hard for students to branch out, even in the general curriculum. He had managed to take Korean but hadn't found time for religion or philosophy. He contrasted his college experience with what he gleaned from dinner-time conversations with his sisters, their interesting courses and the things they seemed to be learning. Classics, his general education course at the time of one of our meetings, was "not doing it" for him, even though, he admitted,

"It's about as fun as a lecture can get." Tony's charge of university hypocrisy was bold: that the curriculum, the advising system, and even the courses themselves were not adding up to the university's claims, their promise to him to become well-rounded. Never, though, did he blame the university outright.

One piece of the promise of well-roundedness was diversity. In Tony's case his circles became increasingly Asian American and even Korean American over the course of college. But he never mentioned the racist incident that John described or any persistent pattern of racism at the apartment building. By his sophomore year, when Tony spoke of his future he described at least partially segregated social circles: "In my whole plan, when I'm grown up, I want to be in a city where there's a *good Asian population* too. I'm going to have to find a wife and raise my children. I think I would want to stay relatively close to an Asian community. That would have to probably be, first of all, in a big city." In his freshman year he described his social circle as "pretty non-Korean" and himself as "pretty far" from a Korean American center where the "ultimate closest" would be AAC, "where everybody around you is Korean." By the spring of his senior year, however, he spoke of his isolation: his social circle was no larger than his cousins and a handful of Korean American friends from high school. Like many of the Korean Americans I spoke with, he reviewed the almost natural way his social circle had narrowed. In late spring of that sophomore year, Tony described "wanting to get back towards the Korean community": "I think I have more and more friends that are Korean now. . . . I might go to Asian or Korean type of functions. I guess that's where I see myself moving, closer to the Asian community." Here again we meet the racial narrowing of social circles at college and the matter of agency or causality: Who or what is at work? One plausible reading of Tony's case is that his circle indeed did narrow as he forsook his earlier college ideals that envisioned both particular academic and social lives and trajectories. Paralleling these college developments were his perceptions of Korean masculinity and ways of being in the world.

Two years after graduation in 2002, Tony reached the conclusion that the university had cared only about training him to get a job. Interestingly, at that meeting Tony's conversation touched on his father, Uncle Mark, and Owen and John's father, each one standing for different ways of being an adult man. Although his father had been the international student in the humanities who prided himself on being superior to the men in his wife's family, in his sophomore year Tony told me that his father had in fact never supported their training in the fine arts and that he was "conservative" above all, wanting "nothing too crazy . . . nothing to break the mold." In that 2002 meeting Tony described his father's perfunctory trip to Europe and how his father had merely been "glad to see it rather than enjoying it." Tony yearned for a trip that might have made a real difference, an impact. Owen and John's father, he surmised, would have deeply enjoyed it, and would have "dwelled on it": "It would have had an influence." Tony admitted that he was a bit more like his own father, and Owen a bit more like his own father. With his hankering to be well-rounded, it was clear that he too wanted to "enjoy" Europe in the way that Owen and John's father would have. What Tony had come to deeply question was his own college education that had been so much about "shoving information down your throat." But for what? He had by then learned how little of it he used on the job—"Less than 10 percent," he once told me—let alone the fragility of the job market itself.

For Tony, family and the farm were comfort zones, happy ones, if somewhat at odds with his original university ideals. It is important to recall, though, the history of the farm as a refuge from racism. Tony's college circles narrowed, as did his training, and although he spoke at much greater length about feeling hemmed in professionally, I am inclined to think of the social and the professional running in parallel. Where John wholeheartedly rejected the liberal project of diversity, well-roundedness, and education credentials in favor of the particular and the practical, Tony still longed for these ideals. Where John was perhaps more like Michael in *The Godfather*, ready to forget college entirely, Tony embodied Michael's inner conflict and was torn between family and a yearning to get away.

I close this chapter with an exchange between same-age cousins and roommates Owen and Tony. I bought them pizza on the eve of their graduation, and Tony spoke, as he had before, of some day moving to California: "I'll probably be labeled as, you know, I mean, I'm sure 'selfish' will come up because I'll be pursuing my personal, you know, personal interests over the family." He needed to "do certain things on [his] own," though, to prove himself after having had "all this help of the family." Although there had been differences of opinion earlier in the conversation, for the first time that evening Owen spoke plainly about their differences: "I don't know, we have different points of view. . . . I mean, my family definitely gave me *a good family background* and everything, but I don't think they gave me everything. . . . I don't feel any need to prove myself or anything." Owen's comments had been consistent: for him, family, and for that matter extended family solidarity, was about "good family background," a point of family distinction, against Tony's sense of "all this help of the family" (i.e., family and ethnic ties and solidarity).

Although a spokesman for the close-knit Han family, Tony nonetheless struggled over his future relationship to his family, a struggle epitomized in his wavering for several years after college over whether or not to relocate to California, a veritable Asian American or Korean American Mecca in its own right. His considering such a move recalls his father's wanting the children to strike out on their own, against his uncle's "family legacy." Tony's California hankerings do complicate any facile distinction between these two cousins: despite all of Tony's conviction about and commitment to the close-knit family, there was a part of him that yearned to walk away for a while.

Owen too deserves to be considered in all his complexity. Three years after their graduation I took the cousins out to dinner in Chicago. Owen was talking about the medical specialties that he was considering and he described being completely bewildered that *anyone* would go into dermatology or ophthalmology: "What use would that be to the family!" The remark recalls the economic logic of family that Tony spoke of when he considered changing his major to business and finding a job through Uncle Mark. This rhetoric of utility, let alone family solidarity, ran against the grain of Owen's liberal college imaginary.

We have listened to brothers Owen and John and cousin Tony reflect on the promise and disappointments of college. We have seen that family and fathers are inextricable features of the landscape from which these young men attended and in turn made sense of college. These chapters have revealed considerable heterogeneity of even brothers and cousins. What they share, however, with all of the students in this book are the same concerns: family, segregation, and race—ways to be educated, ethnic, and familial in a transforming America.

We have seen that Uncle Mark loomed large in the consciousness of many of the younger members of the Han extended family. Equally vital to the college trajectories of John and Owen was the figure of their father, Mr. Han, who himself entertained a powerful image of the American university. Mr. Han's education, employment, and immigration histories go far to explain what he asked of American life and institutions, and therein of the American university. Further, they explain how he set out to raise and educate his children. Mr. Han distinguished himself within the extended family by his artistic leanings, fine taste, higher learning, and line of work, particularly in relation to his two youngest brothers, Uncle Mark being one of them. Unlike his immigrant small entrepreneur brothers, he was a skilled worker in a small company. Mr. Han called himself "Mr. Culture" and prided himself on the tour he could give visiting relatives of the Chicago Art Institute. At the Christmas party that I described in chapter 4, he showed no interest as Uncle Mark pulled out the blueprints of the sprawling home he planned to build at the farm someday. Instead he appealed to me to join him in a discussion about the then controversial conductor of the Chicago Symphony Orchestra. I remember being torn, equally interested in both symbols of immigrant manhood, the farm and the symphony. In all of our conversations there were asides about high culture, such as the figure in the French film *A Man and a Woman (Un homme et Une Femme)* that resembled a Giacometti sculpture and the aesthetics of war as portrayed in the American film *Empire of the Sun*.

My being pulled between Uncle Mark's grand unveiling and Mr. Han's cultural tour was emblematic of the diverse influences in the lives of Owen and John. Among the Han siblings, Mr. Han stood for a particular immigrant male adulthood, one very different from that of Uncle Mark. This difference takes life in the college paths of the second generation. Picking up from the intergenerational equation of Mary's life, albeit one with significantly different gender and class contours, "intimate traces" refers to those aspects of family and immigration history that inform the present. The intimate traces of the students in this book are patterned by the particularity of the post-1965 immigration from South Korea. With these traces, I like to think of students like Owen and John in dialogue with their parents. I am as interested in real dialogue, those instances in which parents literally evoke their education and immigration history, as in communication that is not spoken outright. Most enlivened in the immigrant equation were palpable ideas of a democratic modern, powerful notions about a just society and about the full integrity and global membership of a country that had been deeply compromised by a colonial regime that affronted Koreans' dignity and humanity.[1]

AMBIVALENT CALCULATIONS: THE U OF I

Over the course of our conversations, Mr. Han's estimations of the U of I varied enormously. The university was intermittently low-quality and entirely unbefitting his children and an exemplar of the best of American public institutions. Not surprisingly, Mr. Han's evaluations sweetened over time as his boys' successful futures seemed increasingly secured. But I argue that these estimations echo South Korean modern history, in which both society at large and individuals in their own particular ways exercised their own development, both in the capital-D sense of economic growth and in the small-d sense of personal fulfillment. In the capital-D sense, it was global (Western) membership and emulation that was at stake. In the small-d sense it was about a personal modernity project, one almost always implicated in immigration. Varying estimations aside, Mr. Han sustained a quite singular ideal for the American university as an accessible, public institution that was good enough to nurture capable and motivated students to make something of themselves. His version of the American university would develop boys from a middle-income family like his who were serious and upstanding students and whose parents would continue to take an active hand in their education, as he and his wife would. As Mr. Han's personal history shows, the promise of being both good enough and democratic enough to welcome *his* boys was the very promise that postcolonial South Korean life had so mercilessly forsaken against the great promise of Liberation from the Japanese in 1945. Of course, good enough boys and good enough universities are hard to measure and describe, and in those gray zones Mr. Han wavered on the U of I and on his sons' preparation and potential.

With the salary of a skilled wage worker turned manager in a small corporation and his wife's salary as a nurse, Mr. Han told me matter-of-factly, he had not been able to save large sums, and so he had simply explained to his boys that two college educations at Northwestern were out of the question. He told me that the boys had complained once, "If you didn't want to send us to Northwestern, why did you send us to summer school there?" What precluded private college education, he explained, was his "simple" wage-earning life, which he differentiated from that of the striving small entrepreneur so prevalent among Korean Americans (with the highest rate of any ethnic group in the United States), and among his siblings as well. In the landscape of Chicagoland Korean America, Mr. Han was self-conscious that he had chosen not to become a small entrepreneur: "Of course, if I had needed to I could have gone in debt and started a company." The U of I was to answer the promise of a democratic society in which a man can make an honest wage in an honest job and still aspire to educate his sons for some measure of greatness.

Mr. Han thus asked a great deal of the U of I as the flagship public institution of the state, and not surprisingly the university did not always measure up. His first impressions of the U of I were terrible. For starters, the campus looked all wrong, not sufficiently centered or organized: "When you think about a university there needs to be a 'main complex' [in English] building and then the campus fanning out from it, but [the U of I] didn't have that—you couldn't tell one building from the next, or the school from the surroundings. . . . It wasn't like Northwestern or the University of Chicago, with their 'main building' [in English]."[2] On the defensive (again), I spoke of the U of I's quite traditional and clearly demarcated quadrangle, to which he answered, "No, it is too spread out. . . . You can't tell what is what . . . it is all mixed up." Nor did the dorms fit the bill. At one point he declared to his wife, "There is no way I can leave my children here." The concern, though, as to whether public institutions are good enough for Mr. Han and his family is an old story, with deep roots in the tumult of his family's history in war-torn post-colonial South Korea.

In another conversation Mr. Han worried about the feel or atmosphere (*hwankyong*) of the campus, concerned that it wasn't conducive to serious study, and even regretting that he hadn't sent the boys to Northwestern. *Hwankyong* has larger resonance than its most obvious English equivalents; it begins at home with households that are or are not conducive to studying and academic achievement, but with this single word one can easily refer to the class standing of a family and home life, and in this case the quality of a place and its people. Indeed, with this word Mr. Han was questioning the level and excellence of the U of I. He wondered what he "could expect" of a campus and student residences that looked "like that." He had things to say about the classroom atmosphere as well, complaining that the university was too big, as were the general education classes, and that lectures pitched at hundreds of students were downright "irresponsible." Further, the university disappointed him because it did not distinguish among its constituents. Specifically he called for honors classes for the more capable of the student body, as had been the case with the boys' high school (the U of I does in fact have a Campus Honors Program). That "outstanding students are given no special guidance" was, he charged, an "irrational" aspect of the university.

And yet in some ways the U of I did fit the bill for Mr. Han, as it allowed him (somewhat ironically) to distinguish himself and his family from the Chicagoland Korean American mainstream, which he described as generally holding nothing but disdain (yes, he did hold some) for the university. He described the way "snobbish" Korean Americans found the good enough university somehow wanting. In this vein he asserted that it was the continued support of families that made for a quality higher education, and he charged that many Korean American families were not sufficiently involved in their children's college education and personal lives. He outlined a university that should rely on the input and continued management of families, a university that blurred the distinctions between campus and home, an intimate university. With this voice, Mr. Han took the development project of his boys into his own hands, and the university was rendered a landscape that could allow for his sculpting.

Mr. Han told the following story about Chicagoland's Korean American or mainstream view of the U of I. He described a conversation at the farm with a Korean American friend. She was bragging about her son, who had been high school class president and had gone on to Duke University. The friend asked Mark's wife about her college plans for her daughter, Emily. When Mark's wife answered, "I'm going to send her to the U of I, where all her cousins go," the woman chided, "Don't send her there—that won't do." Emily's mother asked why and the woman replied, "If she graduates from there she won't be able to get married." At this point Mr. Han chuckled and said casually, "You have been to South Korea, Nancy, you know Koreans. . . . Korean snobbism is strong. What is it that I live for? I live diligently for myself and my family, but others live only to show off to other people." He spoke of this as but one "episode" (in English) to show Korean Americans' "perception" (in English) of the university. He elaborated that some Korean Americans evaluated the university this way precisely because of the large numbers of Korean Americans who attended, thus lowering its value. In a somewhat contradictory vein, however, he suggested that some of the disdain was instead about the large numbers of students who were unable to graduate from the university. When I suggested that a record of dropouts should instead encourage respect for the demands of the university, he replied, "It gives them bad feelings for the university . . . and then those parents speak ill of the place."

Mr. Han described several instances of Korean Americans flunking out of the U of I, including a distant relative. He outlined the typical path of Korean American high school academic stars who proceed to college only to fail: "In college, they become regular students and they no longer win prizes the way they did when they were star students. This happens because their parents have no access to the basic structure of their college lives, it's out of reach. In high school the parents managed everything—the special classes in school and the supplementary education after school—and their children succeed without ever having to really do anything. . . . But in college the kids have freedom and their parents can no longer manage things, so the kids let loose." He contrasted his own careful management, how he made sure that his sons' college education didn't become "out of reach." He and his wife attended all orientations and visited frequently, as often as every other weekend. He thought of their visits as "a source of endless energy for [his] kids." More literally, he always made sure to feed them steak dinners. As for the distant relative who dropped out (and more remarkable still was that the parents did not even know), Mr. Han reported, "I heard that the father had never even visited the U of I, so it makes total sense that he would end up dropping out."

Mr. Han offered these stories to charge Korean Americans of his generation with being snobs, as in the case of the family friend who worried about Emily's marriageability, and worse still with the cheap resentment of sour grapes. Further, he accused them of having neglected their parental responsibilities in guiding their children's education at college. He walked a fine line: on the one hand he championed families with enough cultural capital, namely, education and refinement, to both prepare their children for college and help them to succeed there, but on the other hand, he dismissed families who were interested in nothing other than the naked prestige of institutions, such as the mother of the student who went to Duke.

While the U of I did not initially measure up to Mr. Han's imagined university, against the landscape of snobbish Korean America it was nonetheless a fine public democratic institution that had served his children well, especially with the hindsight of their secure futures. Mr. Han's university was in part to be fashioned with the know-how and care of parents, a sentiment echoed in Owen's conviction that one's college education is the product of one's own making. Mr. Han's education, employment, and immigration histories offer a story of dramatic social flux that sheds light on these sometimes ambivalent calculations and on those of his sons as well. I take the time for this brief personal history to demonstrate that the college dreams and ideals of immigrant and second-generation children are necessarily tied to ideas that took on life in another world altogether. In the previous two chapters I attempted to make sense of the university lives of the Han second generation, with a particular focus on race and family. Mr. Han's history reminds us that ideas about race, family, and liberalism have transnational lives that begin in the home country. By relating Mr. Han's immigration story, I mean to consider his university imaginary in relation to its roots in South Korea's own gendered postcolonial modernity story. What follows is a *man's* history, a profoundly gendered one. The next chapter turns to women's stories, including those of Mr. Han's wife and sister, to underscore that these histories are powerfully gendered.

CHAPTER SIX

THE THREE CHANCES A KOREAN MAN HAS TO ROT

Mr. Han reflected on the ways South Korean society had thwarted the personal development of men like him. He once claimed that what he hated most about South Korea was that a man had three chances to rot: in cram school (for entering college), on the job, and in the military. I take up the first two chances here. Indeed, the imagined university we have just met emerged as the perfect answer to his childhood and early manhood in South Korea. He asked of this university nothing short of what he asked of America with his decision to immigrate.

Mr. Han recalled a South Korea that disappointed: where he asked for rational, well-organized, fair, and democratic institutions, he found instead militaristic, authoritarian, and irrational ones. He also called for institutions, schools among them, that would respect his personal talents and family background. He described a rational, democratic system that would preserve the integrity of elite human capital.[3]

Some information on Mr. Han's family background goes far to explain his sense of personal and familial entitlement. In the first moments of our first meeting, he communicated that his family had been prosperous (at least at one point), upstanding, and modern. He made sure to tell me that his father had received a modern education, meaning an education in a public school rather than a Confucian academy. He was also quick to establish that his father had been prosperous during the Japanese colonial period (1910–1945) as a rice collector and that he had been "qualified" (in English) for such a position because of his proper upbringing and upstanding manner.

Ideologically tainted for having been collaborators (rice collectors worked for the Japanese), Mr. Han and his family suffered at the hands of local "reds" in the aftermath of the 1945 Liberation and during the 1950–1953 Korean War. He described a wartime childhood in which the bomb-lit sky was strangely beautiful, and like so many of his generation he detailed childhood in the topsy-turvy world of ideological strife in which the South Korean forces ruled by day and the communists by night. In the immediate post-Liberation period Mr. Han's father was imprisoned, and during the Korean War he was always "about to be tried by the people's court" for his sins as a rich man and collaborator. His father's trial never came on account of the bribes that his family offered the communists. Mr. Han spoke of the fear of his classmates, the children of communists, when the South Korean regime prevailed. Such are the stories of every South Korean village and of every South Korean old enough to "know the war." It has already been many years since South Koreans began to note that those who do not know the war are members of an entirely new generation, a generation largely ignorant of ideological strife and abject poverty.

In this way Mr. Han recalled an illustrious family background, including prosperity and modern learning, that was marred by the ravages of war and postwar poverty. For South Koreans it is commonsensical that family standing either during the war or in its immediate aftermath was often out of synch with family history or upbringing. For many, Mr. Han among them, the indignities of poverty were particularly hard to bear. It was at a normal high school (i.e., that prepared primary school teachers) that Mr. Han's twin senses of rationality and entitlement were first and deeply insulted. With these details, Mr. Han began his narration of his inevitable emigration. (Hindsight is the brilliant author of the inevitable.)

A Normal School and the Military Revolution

When Mr. Han was in sixth grade his family divested of the only thing they had left, land, and moved to a nearby small city. Mr. Han took pride in telling me that he returned to the village only once, to participate in the elementary school graduation ceremony so as to accept the prize awarded the school's top student. He said that he continued to excel in the city's best middle school: "I was the law." His reputation and standing were formidable: he was a strong student and an award-winning artist and his was a family of repute and modern learning. His word was respected and his opinions held sway. All this to distinguish himself, his very modernity. But his father's attempt at a small business failed, and by the time he was ready to proceed to high school, the family coffers were empty. At that time entrance to high school was by examination and many of the most outstanding students, and "yes, of course, the ones with money," had left for Seoul. For his part he did well enough on the exam that he could have proceeded to the high school attached to his middle school as a scholarship student. But Mr. Han opted instead for a normal school and thus turned the hands of fate, or so he seemed to think. The logic of his decision was fourfold: his family did not have the finances to send him to college, a job upon graduation was assured, the school's being coeducational spoke to its liberal character, and one of the school's teachers who had judged his artwork in a contest had taken a liking to him.

Mr. Han joked about "struggling for Liberation" as a young man born on the eve of the end of the colonial era. He noted that he entered high school with the birth of the military authoritarian state, Park Chung Hee's 1961 coup, the first gasp of nearly thirty years of a heavy-handed military state. The coup followed the 19 April 1960 Student Revolution in which high school and college students took to the streets to protest the regime. Although Mr. Han never mentioned this brief exciting chapter preceding the military takeover, we can feel its eclipse in his encounter with the rule of law. Not far into high school, he fought with the principal, and a series of events led to the principal's beating him up. The story went this way. With the takeover, teachers who had not completed their military tour of duty were fired. Mr. Han was outraged. Three months had gone by and the teachers had not been replaced; he dripped sweat every day to walk there, for what? And where was the plan to replace the teachers? This is exactly what he said to the principal, who then charged, "You, you . . . who the hell do you think you are? How is it that you are so full of yourself?"

Mr. Han's brazen confidence, as he reported it, was about more, though, than his keen sense of rational action. And it was about more than fired teachers being replaced in a timely fashion. At stake was that he had "chosen" to attend the normal school in spite of the option to remain as a scholarship student at the college-track high school. "All of the other kids at the normal school were country bumpkins from poor families who had *no choice* but to come; I was the only one able to *choose* between the two." With this detail Mr. Han distinguished himself from his cohort, asserting his enlightenment and modernity, something he did repeatedly over the course of our conversations. Recall that his son Owen asserted his difference in another landscape a generation later. Mr. Han's classmates were bumpkins with none of his upbringing and modern garnishes (his own poverty aside), and the principal was a thug, a *kkangp'ae*, a petty agent of the military state. Thugs are the antithesis of Mr. Han's sense of self: they know nothing of law, civility, or reason, the cornerstones of the modern, liberal project. Although Mr. Han was distinctive for the extent to which he narrated his singularity, the touchstones of his stories are in fact familiar grist in the South Korean immigration narrative.

The ruffian principal was incited to violence on a different occasion. When the stereo system disappeared from the broadcasting club room, the principal accused Mr. Han. Although not a member of the club himself (he was in the art club), Mr. Han spent much of his free time listening to (*Western*) classical music in that room. He boasted that he had been remarkable as a freshman for taking first place in both the art and music composition contests. He reeled off the names of composers and offered an aside, one I heard several times, about how beautifully Owen had played Rachmaninov in high school. The broadcasting equipment was the good fortune of the normal school as the affiliate of the U.S. Peabody School. *Western* classical music and *American* equipment were among the many emigration-bound signs of Mr. Han's narration. What prompted the principal to hit him was the rational and entitled manner in which Mr. Han had defended himself against both the charge that the robbery might have been his and that in the first place he had no right to be hanging out in a club room other than his own. To the latter charge he purportedly responded, "Is there some rule that bars me from going there?" at which point the principal hit him, thug-fashion. "He didn't just hit me once or twice—he became totally irrational—and then he came after me with a broom." Mr. Han called him a "thug-principal" to his face and then bolted. Mr. Han's older brother, whom he described as a paragon of "logic and intelligence," visited the principal and even called the event to the attention of the local newspaper, but things settled down and Mr. Han returned to school. A lasting effect was that the principal marred Mr. Han's school record with a low grade for behavior, which barred him from becoming class president, as was his due. Upon graduation Mr. Han followed his siblings, who had meanwhile been making their way to Seoul, where he got a job as an elementary school art teacher.

I think of Mr. Han's story about his transition to high school this way: from "I was the law" to the arbitrary law of a military state. It was the law of the state that undermined his birthright, for his social standing no longer held sway. A normal high school had been foremost an economic imperative; the college-bound track had seemed a riskier option. Indeed, although one of Mr. Han's older brothers made it through college (as did he eventually, a matter I turn to below), neither of his younger brothers made it past high school. Mr. Han entered high school on the heels of a military coup. His own law faltered, as did rationality, good breeding, and democracy. His family capital and personal achievements, his modernity, was lost in translation. The normal school, its thug-principal and its country bumpkin students, were affronts to his very person.

A Civil Servant in Seoul

Given the structure of South Korean education and employment, it is no surprise that once in Seoul Mr. Han quickly decided to somehow make it to college. Then and today, consumer demand for higher education drove the exponential expansion of that market, a demand fueled both by the prestige accorded education achievement and by the escalating wage discrepancies between high school graduates and college graduates.[4] Years ago I told Mr. Han's immigrant story (and that of a half-dozen other fathers I interviewed) in detailed relation to data on the education and employment prospects of various South Korean age cohorts; the correspondences were quite neat. Further, I learned that the kin of Mr. Han and others who had not emigrated understood emigration in just these terms: as contingencies of age, timing, education, and character. Mr. Han contemplated continuing with the arts, but the "flow of the times" was such that to "justify" a college degree there needed to be the possibility of a "decent living," and so he first settled on interior design. But the call of family, the many younger siblings who needed financial support, precluded daytime college. Instead, he studied public administration at a night college because the family decided that a lawyer was well suited to the times.

The reward structure aside, it was Mr. Han's work experience that most forcefully pushed him to higher learning, and ultimately to emigration. His work as a civil servant teacher during the military regime again brought daily affronts to his sense of justice, rationality, and modern education. That an elementary school teacher was a civil servant was the whole problem. "Why?" I asked. "Why? I'll tell you why, and what I am about to tell you is really important," he said emphatically. And then he seemed to digress. (Digressions are, I have long been convinced, the gold mine of ethnography.) "After I came to the United States I wrote this in a letter to a friend in South Korea: 'I think of my life in the United States as the exercise of a *particular choice*: in the United States [a man] is less often tempted by injustice (or shady dealings).' " "Shady dealings" (*pujong pup'ae*) ran the gamut, from the likes of the high school thug-principal, to bribery and flattery, that other side of the rational, modern, and democratic. The temptations in the United States were fewer than those in South Korea, he told me; moreover temptation here was a matter of choice, whereas in South Korea "the matter [i.e., committing injustices] was forced." What Mr. Han meant by "a particular choice" became clear as he continued: "[In the United States] one can choose to live differently." The choice, then, was the very possibility of a clean life, in contrast to his sense of the ruin of men as they come of age in South Korea. "That is what I wrote in that letter and I still think so today. . . . It isn't that the United States is such a clean country either, but it is cleaner than South Korea—a point that I have stressed to my children. . . . In the face of shady dealings there, this is a 'utopia' [in English]." The digression came full circle (not all do): "I hated the life of a civil servant because of all of *that*—it had *nothing* to do with teaching." Furthermore, "The system hated *people like me.*"

It was against this human and historical background that this "episode" (in English) followed. In brief, his school's administrators had been cooking the books, and Mr. Han blew the whistle on them. The principal would later admit to him—they subsequently became friends—"That [i.e., being exposed] was the most painful moment of my life." Mr. Han spoke of blowing the whistle in the name of "the advancement of education . . . and new [i.e., modern] education": "When I put my finger on something, there is no escaping. I am a well-read man and I don't make my charges lightly. I prepare and I only speak when I'm certain. Owen is intrigued by this feature of mine."

It was thus again the injustices of the system, in this case, civil service employment, that left a man no ability to choose to rise above the fray. Emigration and a clean life were choices that a man could make. It was his own clean and modest life that would send his sons to public school, and that clean life that should promise democratic, public institutions that reward personal and familial virtue—exactly what Mr. Han demanded of the U of I.

South Korea thwarted both the realization of his attributes and bearing and a larger human membership. The United States, of course, is a very particular immigration destination, one that promised cosmopolitan belonging, or being at home in the world.[5] Like his son Owen, Mr. Han was interested in the liberal project of universal humanity, but with

Western culture as the acme of human achievement. For Mr. Han it was as if U.S.-educated adulthood (the one he would give his children) promised, in and of itself, that larger global citizenship. This said, he was not so quick to entirely forsake his Korean identity. He described a Korean potential, the Korea and Koreans that might have been if history had played its hand differently. The immigration project for Mr. Han, and for most of his generation in South Korea, is fraught, for it seeks to realize a project that both exceeds Korea, the project of a cosmopolitan self "at home in the world," and one that is decidedly local, the realization of a Korean self unaffected by the whims of history.

Mr. Han described his family's education and his early schooling successes: "All my siblings read lots of books and I was a good student when I was little, and since my education foundation was strong I could do whatever I wanted." Recall his having been "the law" in middle school. From there he spoke about the historical tragedy of Korea: "The war, revolution, military regimes . . . if only there had been none of that we could have become a really great state, but this is how it has turned out [i.e., all this injustice]." While on the one hand he underscored his own exceptionality for being able to transcend his times, he also sketched a collective portrait of the personal virtues and potential of *all* Koreans, a potential curbed by the contingencies or circumstances of history. For Mr. Han it was an easy jump from the people and country that could not realize their potential to his family's emigration.

> And it's the same thing [as the country] when it comes to me and my brothers and sisters. If you take our talents one by one, each of us had so much potential. If you really think about how we have all ended up, our talent has been so wasted. Things could have turned out better: we could have all ended up in more active positions, leading more productive lives. Of course, all of this does have something to do with our having been lazy and not continuing our studies. There is the fact that our perseverance wasn't strong enough, but there is also the fact of the destruction of our household after the war—that none of us were blessed with the continuous support of our parents. This is the story of how we all didn't end up going any further than this.

Mr. Han's humble thoughts on personal limits aside, featured here were siblings whose family background and national characteristics should have promised greatness. Certainly in his description of his early schooling we saw the bravado of greatness, a figure destined to cut a large human presence. We can, however, also recall Mr. Han's sense of his own modest immigrant life, the "simple" life of a wage earner, a choice that he described as having destined his boys for the U of I.

RAISING RESPECTABLE AND PRODUCTIVE
CITIZENS—OR DOCTORS, IF IT TURNS OUT THAT WAY

Recall Mr. Han's initial disappointment at the look and feel of the U of I; his was, after all, the artist's eye. It was an ambience out of keeping with the one he and his wife had sculpted at home. I turn here to that home environment and to the ways Mr. Han and his wife managed their children's education.

In one of our conversations Mr. Han described a household or family as a "cultural zone." He and his wife went to enormous efforts to limit their young children to that cultural arena. I learned about these sorts of efforts from many of the parents of Mr. Han's generation. He told me that people were impressed by his clear philosophy and his efforts to make good at it. He summarized with a Korean cliché: "You know about bean sprouts—in water they grow, but without water . . ." "Water" here represents the cultural zone and love. Like love, water is eventually absorbed, but the investment is the product: the bean sprouts or children. He worked days and his wife worked nights as a nurse so that one of them, or at least a relative, was always with the children: "We were dead set against babysitters because we didn't want the children to enter another cultural zone."

Tellingly, the names Owen and John, or the real names they stand in for, were chosen for meaning "well-born." When the boys came of school age they were sent to Catholic schools because John had been utterly silent in public preschool, perhaps, Mr. Han mused, for having been so indulged at home. Mr. Han took responsibility for sending the boys to what turned out to be weak Catholic schools with inferior facilities: "Had they been better trained early on, they could have become better students later."

Mr. Han claimed that his move to the suburbs was typical, precisely the mainstream ideal I have described in this book: "After some years you buy a car, and then if you are going to buy a house to get out of congested Chicago, you head for Skokie or the north suburbs, the suburbs where originally the Jews had lived." He continued, "Any chance I get to, I tell Koreans, 'We need to learn from the Jews—their wisdom about life, and their persistence in history,' I tell them that." (There is widespread South Korean and Korean American interest in Jews.) With this he returned to ambience or environment, to the "residential environment" that Jews had been able to fashion in the towns they settled in, ones with "strong service and social welfare facilities, most of all libraries and hospitals." It was this infrastructure that first attracted him to Skokie, their first suburban move.

As the boys approached the age at which they would transfer to public schools, Mr. Han moved from one suburb to another, from Skokie to Morton Grove, also a suburb with many Jews. Not lost on Mr. Han and many of his immigrant generation was that the Jews had been moving north with the arrival of so many new immigrants like Mr. Han himself. In addition to the presence of Jews, he followed the high school rates of national merit scholarships. While the rates at Maine East, which the boys attended while living in Morton Grove, were respectable, Mr. Han knew that the rates were higher farther north. There was a moment in which the family contemplated moving farther north, perhaps to Deerfield, and with it to Glenbrook North. They even put the house on the market, but it didn't sell and they stayed put. While Mr. Han thought that the boys might have studied better farther north, he also reflected that his children might have struggled there for being less academically prepared. Owen once told me that his father calculated that things would have been difficult for him and his brother farther north because their family would have been, relatively speaking, less economically prosperous than most, which might have affected the boys' confidence and personal development.

Mr. Han detailed the gentle ways he tried to assess his children's talents and guide them in the right direction. This said, it was clear that he had long nurtured the dream of the boys becoming doctors. "We didn't push them to become doctors, but we thought they might go that direction, so we created the proper atmosphere and opened up that path." In another conversation he put it this way: "We opened the gate but didn't push them." On several occasions he described what makes the medical profession so special, and each time he recalled the film *Dr. Zhivago*: "No matter what happens, you always need a doctor—like in *Dr. Zhivago*, where both sides of the 1917 Revolution, Bolsheviks and tsarists, need a doctor. Even if American society is destroyed and becomes a really poor country, people would still need doctors. . . . Doctors enjoy special social status, security, and compensation." Doctors, he said on another occasion, "can make a living anywhere, anytime." The medical profession was unaffected by circumstance; it would not, for example, be vulnerable to the circumstances that had precluded the full development of him and his siblings. However, when it became clear to Mr. Han that John was not well suited for a medical career, he struggled with how to help him veer away from that dream. Indeed, he described his own deep-seated frustration that John didn't yet "know himself" well enough to change course.

When the boys were still underclassmen, Mr. Han continued to think of his sons as capable students, but he had given up hope that they might become the large figures he had dreamed of: "My children are not exceptional students, which does make me sad. I once had such high expectations for them, but that part, the studying part, hasn't really happened." But he went on to describe his enormous pride in his sons' personalities, emotional health, and ethical character: "They are really good, and I'm not just saying that because they're my kids. . . . These days when I write letters, I always put it this way: 'My greatest joy is to witness a well-raised child.' " He was candid about forsaking ambition for them given their capacities and proclivities: "I used to want them to become big men, but that doesn't seem to be happening—their abilities are limited and I want them to become upstanding people.[6] So far, so good, they are really nice, really kind—if anything I wish they could be a bit more manly [sanae]. I have some regrets there, but you won't find two boys as nice anywhere." Here again we are reminded that Mr. Han's is a story about boys and liberal dreams with masculine hues. In his own case, the resolve and promise of a modern man had figured so prominently.

THE UNIVERSITY REVISITED

By the time Owen was squarely en route to becoming a doctor, and later when he was already accepted into medical school and John had secured a high-paying job in the financial world, Mr. Han's tune naturally changed a bit. Although I do not think that he would have ever echoed his son John that a college education doesn't matter, he did reflect on the United States as an "ability society," rewarding skills irrespective of education. He reflected that Owen had managed to find a community at the U of I with an atmosphere conducive to his development, the very atmosphere he had once feared might not exist at the U of I. Specifically it was the scientific lab and Owen's friendships with graduate students that he thought made a difference: "These days I really enjoy talking with Owen. There is so much latitude [yŏyu] to his talk, so much variety to his references. . . . I think it is because of that environment [i.e., the lab], don't you think so?" He claimed that Owen's personal and emotional development had reached a "high level." For Mr. Han, Owen had become a cultured citizen of the world, in keeping with his own immigrant project. He added that the graduate students in the lab often praised Owen's clothes. Mr. Han, who was always impeccably dressed when we met, made sure that Owen looked mature and well-kempt. He was, not surprisingly, delighted that the members of this "high-level" cultural zone approved, and had even praised Owen's clothes: "They said, 'Wow, how nice,' whenever Owen had on something new. . . . These days we have bought him lots of clothes, and my wife and I smile thinking about his friends there [i.e., who will appreciate these purchases]."

Mr. Han worked hard to assure Owen's and John's successes, nurturing the right ambience and opening doors without pushing. That the U of I looked better to him toward the end of their college careers makes perfect sense. The university had, in a sense, become a place that could answer to his boys' potential, a democratic institution that made good on their bearing and rearing. But Mr. Han never surrendered the idea that family plays a critical role in crafting a successful college education. At his most idealistic, he imagined democratic institutions such as the U of I that would let his sons flourish to the best of their abilities and allow them to actualize those achievements in the work world, the rational society that was so lacking in the South Korea he left behind. In his less optimistic moments, he worried about the quality of democratic institutions like the U of I, and about the vitality and even the quality of his own children. When he wavered in these estimations, he assured himself that he was raising good citizens, although less clear were the productive lives that would be granted such citizens. When everything seemed to have worked out well, the boys' good breeding, the careful childhoods and cultural zone he and his wife had afforded them as well as their continued investments and care, had allowed them to become capable *men* who could hold their own in American society. On the eve of Owen's graduation, and in a reflective moment, Mr. Han summarized his boys, the U of I, their child rearing (and more) this way:

> Over time I have come to see that this school isn't what I thought it was when I first left John off here. . . . It isn't as if most students could even take advantage of what a first-rate school [i.e., one more selective than the U of I] has to offer. What parents need to have given their children by the end of high school is the ability to digest whatever they find in any college situation. If that has not happened the child will not be "set up" [in English] for college, regardless of the college. If it is a good kid it doesn't matter where they go, they don't need to go to a Duke to survive in college. And if parents are not able to do that much, their children won't be able to manage even at a community college. In the final analysis, where they go isn't the important thing at all.
>
> Well, we've been talking about this for a while now, let me just tell you what it is that Owen said to my wife—not to me, he tends to share more intimate thoughts with his mother—when he received his acceptance to medical school. He said, "So, here I am going to medical school, and that means I'll be a doctor, and that means that you guys raised me well, thank you very much." . . . How gratifying that Owen expressed himself that way. . . . I can't tell you how adorable he is in my eyes. Well, there are many Korean parents who have raised their kids successfully in their own way, but it has really been rewarding for us. . . . And John too, his situation is good, and he is developing nicely.

Many streams of Mr. Han's narratives meet here, among them the sense that college is fashioned by the family, the confidence that he successfully raised his children (and the evidence of their appreciation), and the idea that the likes of the U of I are good enough.

But Owen once spoke to me about his shock and disappointment at his parents' euphoria over his medical school admittance. For Owen, who had invested so much in the idea of his development as an educated person, a project he understood was supported by his parents (and hence marked their distinctiveness among Koreans), his parents' glee troubled him for being so very typical, the modal response of Korean émigré parents. I consider this exchange between Owen and his parents, albeit one not necessarily explicitly spoken, in the context of the larger intergenerational project of education. We have seen that for Mr. Han, a doctor was many things at once: a measure of security, the realization of the "cultural zone" they had so carefully created at home, a profession that was impervious to the whims of history, and more. It would be wrong to reduce the profession to the machinations of immigrant striving, although this is precisely what Owen feared with his response to the euphoria. But it would also be wrong to ignore the ways in which Owen's liberal project was also intimately tied to his father's history and immigration.

John's successes also took on family meaning, although somewhat differently. In Mr. Han's account of John's employment in the Chicago financial world he exercised a particular gendered and classed immigrant family imaginary in which Korean family ties produce value in the heart of American late capitalism. To recall the story went like this. John was hired by the Korean émigré friend of an Irish American client of Uncle Mark. Mr. Han was stunned to discover that these financial circles were not all about education credentials, as the South Korean imagination would have it; all the more shocking was that John's 1.5-generation Korean American boss, purportedly the son of a professor in South Korea, was not even a college graduate. With hearsay from Mark, Mr. Han reported on John's initial meeting with the Irish American intermediary and the prospective Korean American boss. Speaking as if he had been there himself, Mr. Han described how the South Korean émigré boss had been very impressed by his wholesome and family-oriented eldest son. For Mr. Han, chief among John's masculine virtues was his familial allegiance at the helm of the many second-generation cousins. Mr. Han's third-hand observations on that dinner turned to kin ties and family culture to explain John's employment success.

I began this chapter with Mr. Han's ambivalent university estimations or imaginaries. From there I looked to personal and collective histories that have authored the cornerstones of these imaginaries, most particularly to Mr. Han's ideas about good enough public institutions for people of good breeding that promise in turn good enough lives. Neither Owen nor John, nor any Korean American of their generation, is merely living out his or her parents' histories or ambivalences. But I suggest that there are intimate traces of these histories in the second generation's own university lives and imaginaries. For the Hans, these traces took material shape, for example, at the moment Owen's path to becoming a doctor was secured and in the way Mr. Han accounted for John's successes.

Earlier I argued that it was the crucible of American racism (i.e., the figure of the instrumentally striving Asian American specifically) that could in part explain Owen's efforts to be a pre-med with a difference: an anti–Asian American pre-med. It was in that context that I perceived Owen's liberal vision of development in college as racialized. I examined the divergent workings of race and gender in the lives of Tony and John, for whom another Han adult male immigrant, Uncle Mark, had loomed large. With this chapter I hope that these contexts have met: race in America and immigrant ideals (which are at once South Korean modernity stories). Any attempt to neatly parse these contexts, to suggest where one lets up and the other takes over, would be foolhardy; life doesn't work that way. Furthermore, the contexts themselves are connected, for the modernity project at home is tied to the more than five decades of U.S. imperial presence in South Korea and broadly with the hegemony of the West as the locus of modernity.

CHAPTER SIX

7 IT'S A GIRL THING

The reader would think from my conversations with Owen's father, replete as they were with extended narratives of his history and aspirations, that Owen's mother, who didn't figure in these narratives, had never been present. In fact, she was present on two occasions but for the most part had deferred to her husband. This chapter looks at the intimate and often silenced traces left by the women of both generations in the Han family.

This chapter, I warn, sits a bit oddly at the near end of this book because it is almost exclusively focused on immigrant women. Their lives are necessarily different from the women I introduced in the first half of the book: Lisa and Jane in chapter 1, a host of college Christians in chapter 2, and Mary in chapter 3. In those chapters gender mattered, and mediated, being Korean in the Chicagoland suburbs and in the ethnic comfort zone at the U of I, being Korean American Christians in a largely ethnic church, and in Mary's case being a woman at college decidedly outside the Korean American mainstream. It was important to me that the chapters on Mary and Owen be arranged contiguously to bring their gendered contours to full light, while still appreciating the work of class and individual style and proclivity. Analysis is hard because life isn't parsed into simple discrete components (e.g., race, class, gender), though recall that Mary argued that her brother acted "white" and had the luxury of taking on college in that "skin," unhampered by family, not wracked by falling confidence. In this chapter, however, it is not segregation at college or even a mother's hand in the liberal promise of college that is at issue. Although one of the younger women's stories is explicitly about her education, the others are not. So what is my justification for this chapter? I have argued throughout about the importance of family, both as the site from which college dreams spring and as the hearth of ethnicity for immigrant and second-generation Korean Americans. If I end with Mr. Han, and earlier the resonant voice of Mary's father, I will have done an injustice. These families have mothers who spoke in a different voice and need to be listened to differently. The Hans, like all families, are a particular family, as are the Han women. Taken together, these women are eloquent on how family, education, and ethnicity can be quite different for women. By including their stories I do not mean to suggest that all Korean American women tell a radically different family, immigrant, or education story from that of their male counterparts, although in this particular case they do. But I do mean to suggest that gender very often does matter.

In the preceding chapters this book took a decidedly male turn, zooming in on men in the Han family: second-generation brothers and cousins and an immigrant father. Taken together, those chapters, those men, tell a story about race, liberalism, and college. I have argued that both the most deep-seated embrace and virulent rejection of liberal aspirations to universal humanity are profoundly racialized. I introduced Mr. Han's immigration strivings as the attempts of a postcolonial modern *man* to achieve full humanity beyond the contingencies of race and nationality. Similarly, in my discussion of Owen as an anti–Asian American pre-med student and of Tony and John as college critics, I considered the ways race and racism informed these young *men*'s relationship to the liberal college project, to develop young people beyond the affinities of race or religion, but certainly not beyond the affinities of manhood. In fact, in Mr. Han's reckoning, the university was to make "men" of his boys (although recall his comments that they were not quite manly enough). The college imaginaries we have encountered thus far must be understood in their gendered specificity, for they are not about immigrants and college students generally but about college boys and immigrant men. I have called this chapter "It's a Girl Thing" after John's explanation of how he had come to play the role of second-generation senior cousin, even though there was an older girl cousin—namely, "It's a boy thing."

Immigrant women have their own cosmopolitan strivings, and college women too both embrace and reject the liberal project (like Owen, John, and Tony, among others). With this chapter I assert that they do so with greater difficulty. The liberal project, like any other human endeavor, is gendered: women and men take it on in different ways. A caution is in order, however. Neither the preceding chapters nor this one is meant to be predictive, claiming that all men or all women will do this or that. Nonetheless I argue that liberalism, as we have seen it in this book in its postcolonial cosmopolitan and American university forms, has particular hues for immigrant women and college women, respectively. This global imaginary, its international and comprehensive reach, often comes harder to women.

CATHERINE: "HERE IN AMERICA . . ."

Catherine is one of the Han family's 1.5-generation FOB cousins from the only late-immigrating family (in 1990), that of the second eldest Han brother and now the eldest living son. Her story is one of remarkable efforts against considerable familial odds to pursue continued education in the United States in music (which she is now doing very successfully).

In South Korea as early as in college Catherine longed not necessarily to emigrate but to study abroad. She described being recruited by a visiting scholar at her college and going so far as to write the check. Study abroad for Catherine was more than a musical pursuit; as it is for so many people, study abroad promised an escape from local circumstances. Catherine described her objections to hierarchy, social prestige, and shallow measures of worth in South Korea (recalling Mary's father in chapter 3); specifically, she bristled at the senior-junior system (*sŏnbae hubae*) in which relations are governed by age hierarchy; at the way family background ("Who are your parents?") mattered; and at the obsessive attention to external appearances. She said that her father had always "liked America" and that she had grown up hearing about the workings of regional prejudice in South Korea that branded those hailing from the southwestern Cholla provinces (her own family's background) as inferior.

For nearly a decade after her college years, Catherine had not given up on her own "American dream." What was shocking to her, however, was that her extended immigrant family would not hear of it. The long and the short of it: continued study was not appropriate for a *daughter* in her thirties with family responsibilities for an ailing mother, a sickly father, and a mentally compromised sister. One of her aunts put it this way: "I've been observing you and I can tell you that you are not the studying type." The aunt didn't leave it at that, adding that study would be nothing more than an attempt on Catherine's part to escape familial responsibility.

Catherine found herself in a generational no-woman's land. Against the endless celebration of the immigrant cousins' educational achievements, no one could imagine anything for Catherine but a small business, the vocation of the immigrant brothers (with the exception of Owen's father). Catherine described the eldest sister in the Han family lavishing attention on all the cousins but particularly on the "boy cousins." She laughed describing study-abroad female friends at a Chicagoland urban university who would imitate the tone in which parents and other kin flippantly dismissed them: "*You're* gonna study? What for?" Catherine's musical ear aided her uncanny and often hilarious ability to imitate people. She didn't *tell* me what people said, she *acted* their remarks. She knew she was funny, that she could bring an entire cast of characters and caricatures to life. She cracked me up.

Catherine described the family parties in her early immigrant years, in which the immigrant generation sat upstairs, the second-generation cousins stayed downstairs, and there was no real place for her. Downstairs she could follow neither the English nor the humor; upstairs was everything she had hoped to leave behind in South Korea, including the unsparing voice of disapproval. Upstairs was a broken record, the all-knowing voice of early immigrant authority: "*Here* [in America] *this* won't do, *that* won't do, *those* clothes won't do, *those* manners won't do." Catherine's original sin was that she had come too late: "They treated me like a Korean, not like the rest of the cousins." "Hurry up and find your business, open a cleaner," was the reprieve.

Not lost on Catherine was that second-generation John had secured the role of senior cousin (for being the eldest *son* of the eldest *brother*), even though she was older and her father was older than John's. John had been matter-of-fact about Catherine's and her sisters' place in the family, describing all the cousins as "like brothers and sisters . . . except for [Catherine's father's] kids."

Catherine did manage to return to school, however, and thus resumed the trajectory of her much earlier dream to study abroad. More remarkably, after her mother's death her father and homebound sister first followed her younger sister to one midwestern town and shortly after joined Catherine in another midwestern town. All of these moves—her sister's first ("Why not go to the U of I with all of the other cousins?"), hers ("How can she leave her sister and father?"), and finally her family's ("How can they leave us? How can those girls possibly care for them?")—sent shock waves across the extended Han family. Catherine acted out the whole scene, including the hysterical visits of the aunt to the scene of the crime as her father and sister prepared to move. The charge was that her late-immigrated family had been ungrateful, that they had overstepped their latecomer status in this large immigrant family and eschewed their largesse and support (i.e., for leaving Chicago). By taking a second-generation-like (perhaps male) trajectory, Catherine had refused to stay in her proper place. She left a great deal behind, including the months in which she stood in for her ill father in one of her uncle's tailor shops; because she was unskilled, they had entrusted her to do nothing but take out stitches.

Catherine put her musical ear to good use, becoming fluent in English and equally facile at imitating a host of English-speaking characters, Korean Americans and non–Korean Americans both. She described having self-consciously "changed [her] personality" in order to set herself on the path she had dreamed of. Among her close friends were mostly non–Korean Americans who she said adored her and showered her with praise and attention.

Music for Catherine, like the liberal arts for her cousin Owen, was her way in the world, her humanity. "Music is my life," she proclaimed. She described what it was like to excel in music in South Korea, her criticisms of South Korean hierarchies aside: "When I played people looked at me different and said, 'I didn't know you were so good.'" In the immigrant crucible, however, at a distant remove from the promise of study abroad, her uncles had chided, "Having done well in South Korea means nothing here. There are so many good people [here]. Unless you're at the top of the top—even people with doctorates play the piano at a bar." In the basement of one of those uncle's shops, removing stitch after stitch against the painful refrain of her aunt's incessant criticisms of her mother and maternal line, Catherine had been far from music: "It was driving me crazy that there was no one around me making music, no one to talk to."

The uncles never tired of telling Catherine that "even the likes of them" (far superior to Catherine was the implication) hadn't been able to become more than small entrepreneurs in the United States, leav-

148

ing no room for "the likes of Catherine," for a woman, to become anything more. Catherine named it in English: their "damned pride," their "chauvinism."

ALL (ALONE) IN THE FAMILY: TWO HAN MOTHERS

I turn now to two women in Catherine's mother's generation to consider the gendered contours of their education and lives. These two women occupied distinct kinship positions: Owen's mother married into the Han family, and Tony's mother is a sister in the family who married out (Korean women retain their natal surname). For Tony, then, the Hans are matrilateral kin; as he himself once mused, "I mean, technically, I'm not even supposed to be on that side of the family [i.e., in relation to Korean patrilineal kinship reckoning]." Both women were nurses. Although they took stock of their lives in rather different terms, what they shared was their loneliness, their sense that they were alone in the world, in the family. Both of them spoke of being suspended, neither here nor there. Although to some extent this is the predicament of the immigrant more generally, I argue that theirs was a particularly gendered experience, one not articulated by men in quite the same way.[1]

Owen's Mother: *"My life here is suspended in air"*

In one of the conversations at which Owen's mother and father were both present, Mr. Han said that for his two sons "the cousins are like their real brothers. . . . They have their own world." Owen's mother agreed, but extended that world to the "children of *the three brothers*," taking time to note, however, that there was a difference when it came to the sisters' children (Tony and his sisters). She echoed what I had heard from all Han kin: that her eldest son, John, held a special position in the family, the very position that for cousin Catherine spoke to the family's sexism.

Owen's mother described her immigrant life as hard, much harder than the lives of her sons: "They speak English, so their lives should be better than ours." But she complained that they never had to take "serious stock of their lives" in the way that people of her generation did growing up in the Korea. Although she had taken pains to tell her boys that as minorities they would have to do better than whites and that as immigrants there was "something lacking in our parental support," she described sons who did not push themselves in the way that she had needed to push herself. They were, she said, "easygoing" boys, echoing her husband's description of his "nice" and "kind" sons. The reader might beg to differ on the accuracy of this description as it applies to Owen and his brother John. For her own part, when she thought about her successful nursing career in spite of a language handicap, she was not demure: "[I have] more ability than Americans. I am experienced and my skills are superior."

Owen's mother described her isolation as different from the other women in the Han family, distanced from other South Korean immigrants generally, and estranged even from her own siblings and parents. As for the sisters-in-law, three (and later four) of them in the United States, she thought of their "character" as different from hers. Two of them were small businesswomen, a point of distinction dear to her husband. She did not, however, mention Tony's mother, which is not surprising in the light of her patrilineal understanding of the cousins who "count." As for the larger Korean community, recall Mr. Han's discourse on their differences of bearing, style, and refinement; indeed Mr. Han told me that he and his wife once spent an entire road trip to Champaign-Urbana talking about nothing but those differences. She portrayed the Koreans this way: "They make no distinction between public and private space. For instance, at indoor golf facilities, every family member, children on up, make noise; and there are the grannies dressed inappropriately. They have no courtesy for people who want to practice." A moment later, however, she turned the focus inward: "There's an edge to our character—we aren't the sort of Koreans who easily become friends with Americans." On the Korean American front neither of them have had many Korean colleagues at work, although there are hospitals in Chicagoland with literally hundreds of Korean nurses. Several times she noted, "I am not that sort of open-minded person who accepts others easily." It is that "character" as well, she claimed, that explained how she "lived without being close to [her] parents and siblings."

It was clear, though, that such was a character in part fashioned by the circumstances of immigration. In the course of one of our conversations she did briefly blame her husband for never sending her back to visit South Korea. She returned only once, after twenty years in the United States. She chided him, "Even if I had no interest in going, you should have sent me." When he protested that he had told her to go, she re-treated: "The real reason was that I had no interest in going, concentrating all my efforts one-sidedly on my husband and children, at the expense of the other side [i.e., her birth family]." If a verbal retreat, we can still note her emphasis on caring for her husband and sons as what kept her away. In the conversation on their shared differences from other Koreans, Owen's mother echoed her husband's lead, but when he headed down memory lane with details from his past she again staked her distance: where Mr. Han detailed the many ways he had resisted authority, Owen's mother protested that the wrongdoings had been his for not following rules, for "bearing a grudge." Mr. Han weighed in, suggesting that she had misunderstood: "These were the struggles of an idealist." However, moments later Owen's mother wrapped up the conversation on very different grounds: "You were always thinking, 'I want to be special. I am a special person.'" It was clear that for Owen's mother, part of her husband's being "special" was his male privilege. The pretenses to modernity didn't ring so impressively for her.

Earlier in the conversation Owen's mother complained that they had not been saving money for retirement because of her husband's spending pattern; "easygoing" (as she had described her sons) and loath to work long hours ("like the uncles did"), her husband nonetheless wanted a "high standard of living when it came to clothes and food," so they had been unable to save. With these comments Owen's mother named her husband's pretensions and the costs they had imposed on her. In these conversational instances, she hinted that her husband (and his family) had contributed to her isolation among these "easygoing" men. For her part, though, she wondered aloud why she had spent her career "always dealing with sick people." "Sometimes," she said, "I wish I had a more comfortable job."

It was nearly ten years after her only trip back to South Korea that Owen's mother mused, "I feel lonely these days. I long for a friend to talk to. But I can't find anyone." As to the possibility of someday returning to South Korea, she said this: "*Returning? Where to? My life here is suspended in air.* This is neither a hometown, nor a new home either. . . . If my sons marry maybe it will be different. . . . When I went back to South Korea, everything seemed new, unfamiliar. . . . It didn't feel like home either. Same here. I am in between South Korea and America. Nonetheless, when the season turns, when the leaves fall, I cry longing for South Korea." On hearing this, allegations and all, Owen's father offered, "I do *not* feel lonely. *Even if I was here without my brothers and sisters* I would find other interests, like drawing." He did, though, agree with his wife's point about friends: "I do regret that I do not have a friend here. Of course, I never really tried either. Making friends is like an investment. I did not have room for that extra investment. . . . And if I were to have looked for a friend, he would have had to have some special talent, a talent that could capture my interest. Also, there are my brothers—we have been close to one another, and so friends were unnecessary." (Recall Tony's words on how familial ties had narrowed the cousins' social circles.) "Mr. Culture," then, having always thought of himself as "special," as his wife reminded him, could somehow go it alone. Clearly his brothers compensated for the lack of friends, that "extra investment" that he couldn't afford. But for Owen's mother the course had been a lonely one.

Braced by patrilineage, an "easygoing manner," and the arts, Owen's father brought the conversational stream to its logical conclusion: where his wife was lonely, he was not. Even as Owen's mother began on her sons' strong kin bonds, with John at the helm, *she* was lonely, suspended. She mused about *her* career, worried about *her* future, and regretted *her* distance from her natal family. Immigrant life had left her little space to "open her heart" to her own next of kin.

Tony's Mother: *"I want to study creative writing and reflect on my life"*

One of the first talks I gave on the basis of the research for this book was about how Korean American young men, women, and their parents talked about family or kin, and more specifically about how the idea of close-knit extended family works as an ethnic symbol.[2] In that talk, written not long after a meeting in 2000 with Tony's mother, I focused on the Han family and wrestled with a long story that she had told me. In part, I struggled over the story because it had baffled me. Why had Tony's mother taken so much time at our first meeting to tell me this particular story, and why had she begun our meeting with the story? It struck me at the time as being almost planned. In the talk I did venture an interpretation of why she had told *that* story on *that* day; that interpretation, as interpretations are wont to do, settled in my own mind as the truth. As I set out to write this chapter, however, in which I had long imagined featuring Tony's mother, I reread the transcript of the interview. I was humbled, if not a bit horrified. I had missed what I now think of as the most important reason that Tony's mother shared the story. Let me tell you the story, my first interpretation that I came to take for truth, and my understanding of it today.

The Story of a Friend: *"What sort of a girl?!"* The story was about an old friend. It began when Tony's mother was working as a nurse in an operating room at a hospital in Seoul. Her father had refused to support her schooling, and so she took this subsidized education path for women, although she never enjoyed the career. She befriended a woman who was at the hospital to visit a student she was tutoring, who had been admitted after a suicide attempt. The woman, a college student, began visiting Tony's mother at the hospital. "When she came, we would talk. . . . Even though I was stinking from the operating room, she would just chatter on endlessly. And I wondered, 'Why does she keep seeking me out and talking?' " The woman was a couple of years older and from the same region as Tony's mother. It was shortly thereafter that Tony's mother influenced her new friend's training in Germany.

> I don't know where that friend got her motivation, but because I was going to Germany [as a nurse, a very common migration pattern in those years], she decided to go to Germany too. She went as an international student [*yuhak-saeng*]. It wasn't that she was rich [i.e., as was the case with many *yuhaksaeng* in those days]. She was a senior at Dongguk University. That's a Buddhist university, so I just figured she was studying Buddhism. But she wasn't; she was studying political science. *That was the early 1960s! What sort of girl was studying political science at that time, when all those men were rushing into it?!* That was during the Park Chung Hee regime. I thought she was crazy. What? Did she have nothing else to do that she had to do *that*?

Clearly, Tony's mother was taken aback by this young woman, her faithful friendship on the one hand, her brazen aspirations on the other. As she put it, "*What sort of a girl?!*"

As it turned out, just as Tony's mother headed for Germany, the friend went off to Japan on a fellowship from a private foundation. It was when Tony's mother left Germany that the friend was making her way to study in Germany, where she eventually completed a doctorate. For Tony's mother, this friend had broken with gender norms, especially those that Tony's mother needed to abide by as a married woman: "In those days, I really couldn't understand why a girl would study that stuff. . . . It was because she was single that she could do it." In the meanwhile, Tony's mother had come to the United States and the friend was contemplating moving there too. She wrote to ask Tony's mother to sponsor her. And here the story mounts.

> At the time I had become the wife of a student, and you can imagine how poor we were. . . . But my friend didn't understand that. For her, that was a really critical moment in her life, but I couldn't even dare to think about it [i.e., sponsoring her]. Why? It wasn't only a question of economic leeway; it was also a time when our legal status was unstable. I couldn't even contact her. And it was a few years later that I had children, and then between this and that the years passed by. . . . It had been, well, over a decade that we had been out of touch, and about three years ago . . . I had been feeling guilty about it. . . . And it isn't as if I have many friends. *She is my only friend.* So three years ago I was looking at the newspaper and I saw her there. . . . I mentioned it to someone, telling him that this woman was *my best friend in the world.*

The man to whom Tony's mother mentioned this friend learned of her whereabouts, and Tony's mother promptly called her university office in South Korea. And now the climax of the story: "How could we have a long conversation when she didn't even recognize my name? She didn't remember me. So I told her to go off and think about it and slowly she remembered. So I called her a week or two later. . . . She had had so much potential and *if I could have only . . . I could have just brought her here . . .* She was single and she wouldn't have just been stuck in South Korea. In those days we just thought that somehow or other we had to leave South Korea." I originally took the climax to be this: that her "best friend in the world" had not even remembered her. As she ruminated on "what if" the friend could have emigrated to the United States, what if she could have sponsored her, I heard Tony's mother's sense of her friend's plight at being left in South Korea as a single woman.

When Tony's mother called a week later, the friend did muster some recall. Tony's mother related to me that as she thought about her own life, she found that there had been *some* returns on her efforts, and that she had indeed been able to transmit *some* things to her children. Her

friend, on the other hand, had remained single and had suffered deterio-
rating health in the aftermath of her own mother's death. "I told her that
even though I had been unable to host her years earlier, that I could now
host her comfortably for a night or two. . . . [In those earlier days] she
couldn't have possibly understood. She was a full-time Fulbright scholar
in Germany. *People can never understand the lives of others who have taken
different paths.* Even the people closest to you can't understand—how
could someone [understand] at a great distance?" Tony's mother struggled over her own part in her friend's fate and reflected on the lonely
condition of humanity—or of women?

Interpretation 1: *"I have never had the peace of mind, the room, for making
a friend"* As I mentioned, in that early talk I gave I expressed my
confusion. Why all this talk about a fleeting encounter from decades
ago? Drawing from our many hours of conversation that day, I offered
this interpretation: "I think she dwelled on this fleeting friendship because of her understanding that her own ambition, itself twisted in the
ravages of her familial and Korean past, had left her stranded, alone—
alone *with* all the kin who figure in the "family" stories and celebrations
of her son (Tony) and her brothers (Owen's father, Mr. Han, among
them). "When I think about it," she said, *"I have never had the peace of
mind [yoyu], the room, for making a friend."* Here I underscore that her
kin-work left no room for a friend. The friend in question—who as it
turns out did not even remember Tony's mother when decades later she
tracked her down by telephone (she even called back to try again)—was,
she told me, the *"only* friend" she ever had. For a talk on kin ties I
presented a gendered analysis of Tony's mother's loneliness, of this
lengthy story about her only friend who could not even remember her.
And I drew a contrast to Tony and Owen, ensconced in their web of kin
ties, reflecting on Tony's mother's sense that she had no room for a
friend (not unlike Owen's mother in this chapter). In a word, I took the
story to be foremost about a woman's loneliness: as a woman ensconced
in her own gendered duties as a wife and mother she had been unable to
sponsor her friend, and when that unique friend couldn't even recall
her, it only underscored that her whole life had not really allowed for
friends. Similarly, it was also gendered circumstances that led Tony's
mother to nursing and immigration. So, all told, I believed it was a story
about gender, immigration, and loneliness.

Interpretation 2: *"When I have time I want to study creative writing and reflect on my life"* I still think that my first interpretation is at least partly correct. The story is a meditation on loneliness generally and on the gendered workings of the Korean family. But I think I missed a central point. My reader can be the judge! A central theme in the story is the human incapacity to understand those in different situations. Her friend, she surmised, would have been entirely unable to understand why she was unable to sponsor her, and perhaps why she was unable even to reach her. But there is another chasm in the story that I had not reflected on: Tony's mother's complete inability to understand her friend's decision to study political science abroad, *as a woman*, in that day and age.

Today I take this story as one of both resolution and resignation. In telling the story, Tony's mother also reflected on the fruits of her own immigration and hard work. She had, she reckoned, achieved, "passed on," something. It seemed that with this comment she was playing devil's advocate to perhaps a more pessimistic perspective on the matter. But I also think that in the meanwhile she had come to understand the passion that drove her friend, her friend's dreams and ambition. I buttress this interpretation with evidence from the course of our conversation and from other interviews and correspondence since in which she reflected on her lifelong career as a nurse, a vocation to which she never felt well suited.

Tony's mother had regrets both about her career and about gaps in her learning. In a second interview she mused, "Where am I? Where am I now? I have not been able to learn very much. . . . *When I have time I want to study creative writing and reflect on my life.* . . . I want to resolve so many things." She continued that day with a reflection that brings together both of my interpretations: "It's all about my relation to my husband's family and to the Hans [her natal family]. *I am but a little speck there* [with her in-laws]. . . . The problems with my husband all come down to my not being a well-educated person. That is what pains me most." This comment referred to a much larger issue for her: her husband's disdain for her natal family, particularly his hubris about their lesser breeding, education, and refinement. She described herself as but a "speck" in both families, in her husband's for her limited education, and in her brothers' for her tenuous position: on the one hand, the immigrant sponsor of her brothers (a point that her un-immigrated

eldest brother made to me in no uncertain terms), but on the other hand
not quite a member of the patrilineage. It was *as a woman* in both
families that she found herself alone and unable to realize her own
dreams in the way that many of the men around her seemed to have, or
at least felt entitled to do so.

In a holiday card exchange years after we had met in person, Tony's
mother reiterated her desire to learn. In that card she described how
important learning is and she reported that she was learning how to type
Korean and that she was thinking about studying Chinese as well. Her
agonizing reflections on how she had been unable to contact, let alone
host or sponsor, her friend were, I think now, painful recollections of her
own earlier inability to even imagine a young woman with ambition to
study abroad, the very status that her husband held up constantly to
distinguish his own immigrant path from that of his wife and all of her
siblings. Tony's mother, I think, had come to understand "the sort of
girl" who studied political science and studied abroad *even* in the 1960s.
It was *this* gendered and education aspect of the story that I hadn't taken
stock of in my earlier interpretations. In my earlier analysis I focused
only on the gendered circumstances that prevented a lonely immigrant
woman from sustaining a friendship. Now I consider that with this story
Tony's mother meant also to reflect on her own achievements and plans.
Her story is in part another story of liberal dreams. She, like many Korean immigrant women (and for that matter many middle-aged women
in South Korea), registered the indignity of educational deprivation.[3]
She too, like the much younger Catherine, who is now making good on
her dreams, had dreams to develop herself, to assert (and to appreciate)
her own modernity and more global (in both senses) membership.

I end this chapter back in the intimate confines of family, with a story
that brings together Catherine and her paternal aunt through marriage,
the wife of Uncle Mark. Upon her family's arrival in the United States,
Catherine assumed the ritual responsibilities of the Han family, standing in for her sickly mother, who, as the eldest wife of the family in the
United States, was conventionally charged with these duties. The biggest ritual responsibility was the *chesa*, or ancestral services for the
Han grandparents. All hell broke loose when, after her mother's death,
Catherine announced that she would no longer host the entire extended

family for elaborate meals several times a year. Many, many things happened in the aftermath; there were many tears and profound disappointments. In the thick of it all, I was periodically meeting with Tony, who was himself deeply upset by the goings-on. Once he told me about a tear-drenched *chesa* evening in which he joined his mother and his eldest paternal aunt, who were celebrating alone, entirely against the grain of convention. *Chesa* "should" have been about the brothers with their wives doing the work, and in this case with Catherine staging the whole event.

It was from Uncle Mark's daughter, Emily, that I learned why her mother refused to join in on one of the visits to the farm. Emily's mother had been outraged that her husband and his brothers were heading to the farm the very same weekend as the first-year *chesa* commemoration of Catherine's departed mother. Here it is important to recall the kinship relations entailed: Catherine's mother (recently deceased) was the wife of Emily's father's elder (and eldest living) brother; she and Emily's mother were thus both Han family affines, married in. Emily's mother made the decision to stay home to join her niece Catherine as she commemorated her recently departed mother. For Emily's mother, this oversight of the Han brothers epitomized the maniacal focus of the Han men on themselves. By that point, Emily's mother was entirely fed up with her husband Mark's largesse to his extended (male?) family, and the marriage itself was in peril (a separation was imminent). As for the house at the farm, Emily's mother had long been adamant that not a brick be laid until her husband refurbished the *nuclear* family's home. (Today there is a house at the farm.) Emily's mother thus pitted her own nuclear family against the Hans. Emily, who was herself quite a spokeswoman for the Han family and the motor behind the second-generation cousins' trip to Hawai'i that Christmas, once said this about the farm: "The *boy* cousins love it." I end on this note to underscore that the meaning of "family" certainly worked differently for immigrant and second-generation men and women.

CONCLUSION

Throughout *The Intimate University* I have documented the ways Korean American undergraduates experience the contemporary American university, warts and all. I have not intended to portray their experience as singular, as Korean Americans, Asian Americans, or racialized students (all of which, of course, they are). The paradoxes of the American university today—for example, the tensions between its rhetorical embrace of diversity on the one hand, and its colorblindness on the other; its persistent liberal ideologies even as it grows ever more corporate in its structure and curricular focus—are paradoxes faced by all undergraduates. But I have argued that Korean American experiences are indeed distinctive on all three counts.

RACE (BUT WHO'S COUNTING?)

As racialized Americans, Korean Americans bear a particular burden with all of their student colleagues upon whom particular racial stereotypes are foisted, among them stereotypes that are relevant to these students' ability to realize the prevailing college ideals of our day. As Asian Americans they share with their colleagues, first, particular images of the model minority, both the idea of exemplary students and its odd bedfellow, the image of striving, instrumental college actors; and second, the contradiction between their obvious experience as minorities at a racialized university and the fact that Asian Americans most often do not officially count, for instance, as minorities in affirmative action measures. Indeed, at the U of I I have witnessed many times when Asian Americans were literally, numerically, that is, not counted as minority students. Finally, as Korean

Americans, they are again racialized as the children of America's most entrepreneurial ethnicity, well known and portrayed for its high rate of small entrepreneurs who have become icons in our urban landscape. Popular films and novels have convinced me of this. And at the U of I, we have observed that Korean Americans are racialized further for their particular social constellations, among them their highly visible ethnic church (even as it grows increasingly multicultural). It is not an exaggeration to say that at the U of I, Koreans and Korean Americans are the campus's most visible ethnicity, accentuated by the large presence of international undergraduate and graduate students and the growing population of Koreans who are neither international nor entirely Korean American, hailing as they do from precollege study abroad.

Why do these particular burdens matter to the college experience of the students I have introduced here? I have argued that as they try to realize their college ideals, these students take on particular challenges. I consider these racialized challenges because the work of these ideals— among them growing, exiting one's comfort zone, and receiving a liberal or universal education—are filtered through racialized images (e.g., of the instrumental striver) and experiences (e.g., of segregation) that appear to thwart their fulfillment. I hope my portraits have shown that race works subtly, less often with the blunt hand of racist incidence (although there are those too) and more often as the daily warp and woof of the fabric of college life and meaning making.

As William G. Bowen and Derek Bok argue in their important defense of the politics and positive outcomes of affirmative action, it is legitimate to hone in on race, even as it is "but one aspect of diversity . . . because it is the use of race, alone among dimensions of diversity, that has been under political and legal challenge. And we need to ask directly why people accept so readily the legitimacy of considering other dimensions of diversity but pause, and often feel uncomfortable, when race is used."[1] Like many other scholars, I have worked in this book to bring race to the fore precisely, as Bowen and Bok assert, because it is that dimension of diversity that can be so easily elided. Furthermore, in some ways this dimension has been elided for Asian Americans even more for having never been the focus of those political and legal challenges, for not figuring prominently in the country's watchful eye on segregation.

CONCLUSION

(SELF-)SEGREGATION

At the heart of this book is segregation, that palpable feature of college (and all school) landscapes that many observers note: the apparent
grouping by race or ethnicity.[2] It is not an exaggeration to say that
regardless of any Korean American's actual social life and interaction at
the U of I, at the millennial turn Korean Americans were necessarily
self-conscious about their *apparent* segregation on campus. Whether or
not they grappled with their own segregation—and many did, both in
and out of the then largely ethnic church—or worked hard to distinguish
themselves from this apparently segregated ethnic fold, they were compelled to face it as a problem. It posed a problem because it contradicted
both intimate or personal and institutional college ideals of growth and
the experience of diversity. As we have seen, one is simply supposed to
somehow exit the "comfort zone."

In large part I think that segregation troubled the students in this
book because it appeared to be self-segregation, namely the *choice* of
students who could have organized their lives differently. Certainly,
it would be untenable to assert that those Korean American students
whose social lives centered on Korean American social networks and
interactions exercised no choice; of course they did. But when we appreciate that the racialized burdens I described earlier are borne collectively,
it is no surprise that ethnically organized social groups or social lives
persist. Now, with the assertion that these groups or social constellations take on racial work (or reaction), I do not want to overstate the case.
Not all intraethnic camaraderie should be seen in this light; some of it
should be appreciated as just that, comfort zones, plain and simple. But
I think that the portraits in this book convince that some intraethnic
camaraderie does speak to these particular burdens and the work they
inspire or demand.

Matt Simmons, a columnist for the *Daily Illini*, the U of I student
newspaper, weighed in on self-segregation, writing that "it is not as big
of a problem as some perceive it to be" (20 October 2005). Interestingly,
Simmons joined many student newspaper columnists around the country who in recent years have grappled with self-segregation. His editorial
absolved the university of all culpability, urging his classmates instead,
"Go to [your] parents and ask them why they segregated themselves

based on race [i.e., in their neighborhoods]." While on the one hand, Simmons directed his readers to larger social inequities, such as residential segregation, on the other hand he chocked up what he described as "some self-segregation on campus . . . more to convenience and familiarity than racial animosity." The students in this book have shown that segregation often (but not always) is troubling and that they felt the need to answer to it. As I argued in the introduction, I refuse the handy distinction between segregation imposed by race and racism and self-segregation that has nothing to do with race or, in Simmons's words, "racial animosity." Neither does that distinction make sociological sense, nor does it do justice to the experience of Korean American students of color at the American university. *The Intimate University* is not willing to absolve the university of all responsibility for the segregation that, as we have seen here, so many Korean Americans feel the need to answer for. Recall the student voices in this book that do indeed challenge the university's indifference.

INTRAETHNIC OTHERING

Prominent throughout this book, and unsurprisingly the fieldwork that led to it, was the persistent urge (or need?) of many students to distinguish themselves from other Korean Americans, regardless of the shape of their ethnic life. Theirs offered collectively powerful instances of what some scholars have labeled "intraethnic othering." Both during and beyond the fieldwork phase, I wrestled with this: Why were the members of this community working so busily to be anything but "typically Korean," even in their most ethnic social circles, such as the Korean American church?

Here too I name race, buttressed by the many scholars who have helped us appreciate the often odd and seemingly illogical ways in which race and racism are named. The compunction to dissociate is this: the desire to run free of those racialized associations that impede one or another dream or ideal. It is quite simply, for example, the desire to fulfill college or American dreams that compels individuals to rid themselves of the stereotypical stuff of ethnic cloth. This too is a racial burden and one, I assert, that exerts an enormous toll. To draw lines and distinctions on the ethnic map, often even as the apparent contours of one's life are so very ethnically mainstream or normative, is labor intensive, and I hope that the reader has been able to glimpse some of that across these pages.

This work accompanies yet other labor that I have not taken up at great length here: the work of interethnic distinction making. Well documented, for example, are the ways Asian Americans often disidentify with other communities of color, effectively claiming their own model minority status (e.g., from other Asian American groups, among them refugee populations in particular, and blacks and Latinos).[3] Both of these sorts of labor exert a psychological toll on individuals (which we have seen in this book) and arguably a collective toll on ethnic (e.g., pan–Korean American) and coalitional (e.g., Asian American) politics.[4] Many scholars have made wonderful theoretical contributions by challenging us to consider how whiteness, as a veritable hegemonic norm, a constellation of a validated American life, configures this intraethnic and interethnic othering.[5] I am quite confident in asserting that the intraethnic othering that can be found in this book speaks to exactly this: faced with ethnic and racial stereotypes, students clamor for (subethnic) distinctiveness through which to claim full American belonging, be it at the university or in American society at large. Intraethnic othering is indeed a language in which the Korean Americans in this book spoke to, even as they were sometimes silent on, race and racism.

FAMILY

Further, I hope to have demonstrated in these pages that intraethnic othering is often expressed through reflections on the most intimate domain, the family. My exploration of the Han family looked at both the sociological differences within a single extended family (of occupation, immigration history, and gender) and the many lines of distinction that family members drew among themselves, distinctions that speak to diverse ways of claiming the university and, yes, America. The Han family reminds us that there is no single way to belong and that indeed there are powerful ways in which some people can turn membership on its head. In the case of this family we observed that some members literally paraded the stuff of ethnic stereotypes as a way to contest the university and to name race and racism outright. But the Han family exploration, in conjunction with some of the voices from part I, also reminds us of the powerful ways those claims are gendered and classed. It is through the Han family that we also witness the extent to which the liberal ideals of individual growth and belonging in the American fold constitute a transnational project, a constellation of ideas and efforts that run through the genealogies of families and the history of the transnational and postcolonial South Korea as it is embodied in immigration itself. As I have argued, immigrant and college dreams work as a powerful couplet, linking the generations in their sometimes elusive projects.

In spring 1999, in the middle of my research, Chancellor Michael Aiken addressed the parents of prospective U of I students in *postscript*, a university publication, with these words: "We look forward to welcoming your family into the University of Illinois family!" We need to ask what that college family really is and *who* (*which families*) are really welcomed into its intimate fold.

THE UNIVERSITY: WHAT IS TO BE DONE?

As undergraduates (in my classes, at least) inevitably ask after they have read some critical academic analysis (and rightly so), What is to be done? (And why didn't the scholar tell us?) I will take this on, but first let me recognize, fairly so, that there are some things that have already been done.[6]

When I began this book's research in 1997, over seven years of student and faculty activism at the U of I had led to the formation of the Asian American Studies Committee, charged with the task of making initial hires to support the development of an Asian American Studies Program. My own career at the university, beginning in 1990, paralleled this activism. In spring 1991 the Asian-American Student Alliance was formed, dedicated to "educate the campus community on issues related to human/civil rights violations against Asians and Asian Americans and to promote activities directed at alleviating these violations."[7] Having been involved in this activism since 1990, in 1997 I was appointed a faculty member of that committee, joining three colleagues, two ex-officio members, and three students. In 2000, just as I was nearing the end of my formal research for this book, the program was inaugurated. All the while a parallel, and in some ways more difficult struggle was being waged for an Asian American cultural center, a space for broad-based Asian American and coalitional programming and social activity including and beyond the curriculum. (This had been formally proposed as early as 1994.) The Asian American Cultural Center was finally promised in 2003 and realized in 2005, concretely as a new building that was added as an extension to the Asian American Studies Program building, a building that had been dramatically moved down the street on a truck in 2001.

Why am I reviewing these histories? Because these distinctive university spaces for Asian American studies curriculum and extracurricular life represent institutional acknowledgment of the racialized particularities of the Asian American experience.[8] Indeed, the Asian American studies curricular offerings, given today by the program's fifteen core and eight affiliated faculty members, are devoted to just this intellectual and arguably political project. As I put the finishing touches on this manuscript in fall 2008, there are eighteen Asian American studies courses a student can choose from, among them Asian American Youth, Asian American Chicago, and Asian American Education, all of which will certainly take up a number of the issues raised in this book, and as such are raised by the lives and voices of my research interlocutors. And the Asian American Cultural Center, in the words of its own mission statement, "provide[s] arenas for the exploration of personal and community identities and opportunities to increase understanding and valuing of differences." To my knowledge, none of the students I spoke with from 1997 to 2001 had taken an Asian American studies course, and indeed in those days the pickings were still slim. Of course, today while it is by no means only Asian American students who take these courses, it is still but a small number of non–Asian Americans who take them. But I know anecdotally, from both Asian American and non–Asian American students in my own Asian American studies offerings, how transforming the Asian American scholarly literature is for all students, and for non–Asian Americans how transforming the experience of a class with an Asian American plurality can be.

Revealingly, in my own recent teaching of Korean America in spring 2007, a cross-listed course between the Asian American Studies Program and the Department of Anthropology, the vast majority of the students elected to focus their required semester-long pilot research project on an aspect of intraethnic othering, each student struggling with both its nature and impact.[9] They queried why and how and with what effects Korean Americans on campus ("we" for some and "ethnic others" for others) spend so much time and effort distinguishing them-selves from one another. I would like to think that classes like these, allowed by the provision of new institutional spaces, change the equa-tion for some Asian Americans because of the way they together make Asian American a "color that does matter," a race that counts, even as affirmative action measures belie Asian American difference.

I would also like to point to another local change: the dramatic demo-graphic transformation of AAC, the Korean American church featured in this book, whose membership today is over 40 percent non–Korean American. While I have asserted elsewhere that the church nonetheless remains remarkably Korean and that many of its non-Korean adherents experience it as a Korean American church, this new demography does mark a real transition.[10] As I have indicated throughout this work, at the time of my ethnographic research AAC was iconic of U of I Korean America, standing metonymically for its mainstream and for its segre-gation. While I do not think that this configuration has been completely toppled, I am certain that research today would point us to realignments and new social formations. Of course, AAC is not an official university unit and can hardly speak to institutional change, but I think the church, intimately tied to the university by its congregation, speaks to a chang-ing university, with changing student needs, proclivities, and demands.

Let me now return to the matter of what is to be done. The students in this book speak to the enduring dreams of higher education; again and again they have registered their lofty goals and their high expectations. Collectively, I hear them asking this of the American university: that it meet them by respecting their racialized realities; that it foster spaces in and beyond the curriculum that really make good on the promise of diversity; and that it understand the particular vision they bring with them to college, one that is necessarily nurtured in the immigrant cru-cible. I listen to them asking that the university truly be a place for the forging of intimate ties beyond the comfort zone. I think that they echo the sentiment of Nancy Cantor, who served as the chancellor of the U of I in the aftermath of this research from 2001 to 2004, and who was closely involved during her preceding University of Michigan years with that university's defense of affirmative action in the *Grutter* and *Gratz* cases. Cantor wrote this about universities "at their best": "[They] can be safe havens for the development of [a truly integrated] community, based on intergroup dialogue, the civil airing of conflict among students who, as peers, perceive each other as equals."[11] Yes, theirs is a tall order and Cantor's a monumental goal.

But, in a very different vein, I also think that the Korean American students in this book challenge the university and its observers to imagine segregated spaces that nobody has to worry about or apologize for, or for that matter to label as self-segregated. Instead, these ethnic spaces can be understood as inevitable features of a country and a university still gripped by the realities of race, even as the university makes its own noteworthy efforts to forge new ties and spaces. As coincidence would have it, I was scheduled to talk about Korean American scholarship at an evening meeting of the Korean American Student Association (scheduled at the Asian American Culture Center) just days after the Virginia Tech massacre by an ethnic Korean on 16 April 2007. (Although I had been told to "keep it light" long before the massacre, this event was in fact the valiant effort of some students to foster a substantive conversation among the members.) I abandoned my notes and instead opened a conversation about Virginia Tech—how could I not have? A heated debate followed as to whether it made sense for Korean American groups and individuals and also for South Korean officials or groups to apologize for the incident, as many had already, namely, for the Korean ethnicity of the perpetrator of the hideous shooting that gripped the world. While some spoke out to say that it was indeed absurd for South Koreans or Korean Americans to take racial responsibility for the actions of a clearly very mentally ill coethnic, most students agreed that their hands were tied: regardless of whether they made any claims of responsibility as Korean Americans, the rest of American society would indeed make this ethnic or racial association. As such they considered the apologies preemptive of the sort of ethnic retaliation they feared and about which there had already been news through the media and the ethnic grapevine. (And of course in post-9/11 America, we all know of a recent chapter of ethnic, racial, or religious retaliation.) While there was a part of me—and I shared my thoughts candidly—that felt that these Korean or American efforts were counterproductive, creating ethnic news and association where in fact there had seemingly been little (the mainstream media had been very cautious in this vein), I was powerfully reminded of the persistence of race in the lives of these students who, while recognizing all of the problems, as I had, of this ethnic response, saw no other possibility.

Perhaps in the ideal university, or in the ideal America, the students in this book might have worried less about their own or other Korean Americans' apparent segregation, and perhaps some of them would have been able to more easily taste college life beyond the comfort zone, all the while being able to relish those features of the comfort zone that make sense and, yes, make for comfort while away at college.

Finally, and perhaps most prosaically, but most intimately for the likes of me, a professor of the humanistic social sciences, I would like to remind the reader of the call that my student interlocutors made to the professoriate: that we make our classes meaningful venues in which young people can indeed grow and prepare themselves for a transformed and transforming world.[12]

CONCLUSION

INTRODUCTION

1   Interesting accounts of the discrepancies between the real and the
imagined university include Bronner, *Piled Higher and Deeper*; Nathan,
My Freshman Year.

2   Stereotyped images of Asian Americans and Asian American cultures
widely circulate throughout America's cultural and media landscapes.
Comprehensive examinations of the portrayal of Asian Americans in
popular media include Feng, *Identities in Motion*; Hsing, *Asian America through the Lens*. On gendered aspects and masculinity in particular, see J. Chan, *Chinese American Masculinities*; Chen, "Feminization of Asian (American) Men in the U.S. Mass Media." For Korean American women, see H. Lee, "A Peculiar Sensation." More brief discussions on the relationships between Asian Americans, media, and stereotypes can be found in Suzuki, "Asian Americans as the Model Minority"; Taylor and Stern, "Asian-Americans"; Mok, "Getting the Message." See also Chang and Kiang, "New Challenges of Representing Asian American Students in U.S. Higher Education"; S. S. Lee, "Over-represented and De-minoritzed."

3   For a qualitative study of contradictions between the liberal tenets of
education and multiculturalism, see Martinez Alemán and Salkever, "Mission, Multiculturalism, and the Liberal Arts College." For a study on how liberalism shapes white college students' color-blind racism, see Bonilla Silva and Forman, "'I Am Not a Racist But. . . .'" Dipesh Chakrabarty proposes the term "interactive multiculturalism" as a politics of multiculturalism that goes beyond the usual liberal-pluralist stance in which the culture of public life is assumed to be singular and homogeneous. See Chakrabarty, "Reconstructing Liberalism?" In "Race and Ethnicity" Henry T. Trueba argues that American universities are usually caught between a desire to retain a rhetoric of liberalism and the practice of a neoconservative pedagogy which perpetuates existing racial and class differences in American society. For a reflec-

tion on concepts such as diversity and disciplinarity in the American university context, see Appadurai, "Diversity and Disciplinarity as Cultural Artifacts." For a study of Asian American student experience of diversity at the University of California at Berkeley, see Woo, "Asian Americans in Higher Education."

4   Marcia Baxter Magolda's research on college students is exemplary of a longitudinal approach. See *Making Their Own Way*, which focuses on self-authorship and higher education.

5   Broadly, there are two large bodies of literature on transnationalism. The first discusses the remittance economy and the political participation of the homeland; see Hsu, *Dreaming of Gold*. The second addresses modernity and transnationalism; see Appadurai, "Global Ethnoscapes."

6   For helpful analysis of the intersections of race and class, see Hartigan, *Racial Situations*; Ortner, "Reading America"; Roediger, *The Wages of Whiteness*. For the intersection of race and gender, see Foley, *The White Scourge*; hooks, *We Real Cool*.

7   See the website http://nsse.iub.edu/.

8   There is a vast literature on theories of student development that charts the roles of institutions of higher education in the cognitive and psychosocial developments of later adolescence. Evans, Forney, and Guido-DiBrito, *Student Development in College*, provides an excellent introduction to the most influential theories. See also Baxter Magolda, "Constructing Adult Identities"; Beyer, Gillmore, and Fisher, *Inside the Undergraduate Experience*; Boyer, *College*; Chickering and Reisser, *Education and Identity*; Kohlberg, "Stage and Sequence"; Pascarella and Terenzini, *How College Affects Students*.

9   On the liberal arts, see Keohane, "The Mission of the Research University"; Rhodes, "Undergraduate Education" in *The Creation of the Future*; Rosovsky, "The Purposes of Liberal Education."

10 On the land grant mission and service orientation of schools like the University of Illinois, see Rudolph, *The American College and University*; Thelin, *A History of American Higher Education*. For thoughtful contemporary perspectives on the mission of the research university, see Keohane, "The Mission of the Research University"; Rhodes, "The American Research University Today" in *The Creation of the Future*.

11 There is a growing literature on the corporatization of the university. For excellent examples, see Derek Bok's *Universities in the Marketplace*,

and the work of Shelia Slaughter, who is pessimistic about the fate of the so-called liberal arts: Slaughter and Leslie, *Academic Capitalism*; and Slaughter and Rhoades, *Academic Capitalism and the New Economy*.

12   On the identity crisis of the American public university, see Birnbaum and Shushok, "The 'Crisis' Crisis in Higher Education"; Gumport, "Built to Serve."

13   On higher education and the American dream, see Brint and Karabel, *The Diverted Dream*; Erisman and Looney, *Opening the Door to the American Dream*.

14   The term "model minority" was first used by William Petersen in 1966 in "Success Story, Japanese-American Style." Petersen praised Japanese Americans as the model minority in opposition to blacks because of their hardworking cultural values. For a critique of the model minority myth, see S. Lee, *Unraveling the "Model Minority" Stereotype*. Two works touching on the function of the model minority myth in contemporary American culture are Lowe's *Immigrant Acts* and Eng's *Racial Castration*. For comprehensive discussions on the effects of conceiving Asian Americans as a model minority within the realms of higher education, see S. Chan and Wang, "Racism and the Model Minority"; Ahn Toupin and Son, "Preliminary Findings on Asian Americans." Many scholars have appreciated the pernicious effects of this stereotype on other racialized groups singled out in contrast to Asian Americans; see, for example, Prashad, *Everybody Was Kung Fu Fighting*.

15   See Hyunhee Kim's dissertation, "Ethnic Intimacy: Race, Law and Citizenship in Korean America," for a remarkable discussion of small entrepreneurship as a particular feature of this stereotype in the case of Korean America. Kim explores what it means that Korean Americans represent the highest small entrepreneurial ethnicity as it intersects with Korean American racialization. She elaborates how it is that on the one hand Korean Americans are seen as particularly aggressive in the public sphere while on the other hand their own social mobility desires are tied up in their sense of themselves as hardworking and entrepreneurial. See also Abelmann and Lie, *Blue Dreams*; J. Lee, *Civility in the City*; C. J. Kim, *Bitter Fruit*; K. Park, *The Korean American Dream*.

16   In her critique of the multicultural curriculum of American universities, Hazel Carby argues that multiculturalism has become one of

the current code words for race; see "The Multicultural Wars." In her critique of the American anthropological notion of race as purely based on biology, Kamala Visweswaran warns against the danger of a current trend in American society to replace race with culture; see "Race and the Culture of Anthropology." For a critique of the American racial ideology of color blindness, see Prashad, *Everybody Was Kung Fu Fighting*.

17   On multiculturalism and its affiliated crises, see D'Souza, *Illiberal Education*; Graff, *Beyond the Culture Wars*; Levine, *The Opening of the American Mind*; Nussbaum, *Cultivating Humanity*; Wilson, "The Canon and the Curriculum."

18   Evidence of how Asian Americans suffer psychologically disproportionately in college can be found in Greenberger and Chen, "Perceived Family Relationships and Depressed Mood in Early and Late Adolescence." The two authors found comparatively high levels of symptoms of psychological distress (such as depression, low self-esteem, and negative affect) in later adolescence among Asian American youth. A cross-ethnic analysis of data from the National Longitudinal Study of Adolescent Health demonstrated that Asian American adolescents consistently reported the highest levels of angst and the lowest levels of self-esteem among the four major ethnic groups. See also Bankston and Zhou, "Being Well vs. Doing Well"; Cheryan and Bodenhausen, "When Positive Stereotypes Threaten Intellectual Performance"; B. S. K. Kim and Omizo, "Asian and European American Cultural Values."

19   Here, and throughout the book, I italicize words or phrases of my research interlocutors that are central to my interpretations and analyses.

20   For a critique of the empty promise of the commercialized university metaphor of kinship and its equally empty pursuit of diversity, see Prendergast and Abelmann, "Alma Mater." For a fine-grained ethnographic study of race and diversity in elementary schools, see Lewis, *Race in the Schoolyard*. Mica Pollock's book *Colormute* is another excellent ethnographic study of the dilemmas of everyday American race talk and silence in an American high school. For a case study of the University of California at Berkeley, see Duster, "The Diversity of California at Berkeley." For a critical reflection of affirmative action at the University of Michigan, see Gurin et al. *Defending Diversity*. See also Gurin, Dey, Hurtado, and Gurin, "Diversity and Higher Education";

Hurtado, Milem, Clayton-Pedersen, and Allen, "Enhancing Campus Climates for Racial/Ethnic Diversity"; Milem, "Increasing Diversity Benefits."

21   In "'FOB' and 'Whitewashed,'" Karen Pyke and Tran Dang offer a fascinating analysis of the popular use of subethnic identifications, in particular the way California Korean and Vietnamese Americans valorize a "bicultural" middle against their "whitewashed" peers who sustain false ideas about the possibility of full integration and their "FOB" coethnics who reinforce mainstream stereotypes of Asian Americans as perpetually foreign. They assert, as I do in this book, that this subethnic labeling, which points to differing "acculturative trajectories," is an adaptive response to racial oppression. In "Ethnic Intimacy," a study of intraethnic othering among New York City Korean American lawyers and clients, Hyunhee Kim makes a similar argument with wonderful ethnographic illustration. The same processes are at work, other scholars argue, in the way Asian American groups distinguish themselves from one another (e.g., Korean Americans from Vietnamese Americans), namely, how Asian Americans are racialized collectively leads groups to distance themselves from one another. See Kibria, "Race, Ethnic Options, and Ethnic Bonds"; S. S. Lee, "Over-represented and De-minoritized"; and Ong, *Buddha Is Hiding*.

22   For a larger look at the intersections of Korean immigration and class, see Hurh and Kim, *Korean Immigrants in America*. An insightful account of this trend within the context of the family and intergenerational issues can be found in Pyke, "'The Normal American Family' as an Interpretive Structure of Family Life among Grown Children of Korean and Vietnamese Immigrants."

CHAPTER 1: HERE AND THERE IN CHICAGOLAND KOREAN AMERICA

1   For an excellent analysis of popular ideas about a normative trajectory of Korean American small business families, see K. Park, *The Korean American Dream*. For a comparative study of the Chinese American experience, see Louie, *Compelled to Excel*.

2   For critical studies on Asian American communities that are less territory-bound and more fluid, see Bonus and Võ, *Contemporary Asian American Communities*. For the inscription of geographical places with unequal power relations, see Self, "Writing Landscapes of Class, Power, and Racial Division."

3   For a comprehensive study of immigration to the United States, see Portes and Rumbaut, *Immigrant America*. For Asian immigration patterns in Los Angeles, see Ong, Bonacich, and Cheng, *The New Asian Immigration in Los Angeles and Global Restructuring*. For a study of Korean American demographics and residential distribution in the Chicago area, see "Demographics and Residential Distribution" in Chun, Kim, and Kim, *Koreans in the Windy City*.

4   Although FOB can be used in a derogatory manner, Joe and many other students used it to simply describe these later immigrants. The image of FOBS has changed considerably over time; although it once was nearly synonymous with "nerd," Joe's use speaks to radically changed images. Recently its meaning has changed again to refer to a stylish, wealthy, and cosmopolitan person, reflecting South Korea's global presence in youth media industries, such as film and music. Also, FOB is increasingly used to describe ways of being, as in "fobby," that are elective rather than ascribed by immigration history. For an excellent linguistic discussion of new ways that identity can be manipulated, see Kang and Lo, "Two Ways of Articulating Heterogeneity in Korean American Narratives of Ethnic Identity."

5   See Korean Educational Development Institute, *Chogi Yuhak*. Before the 1990s studying abroad was confined to college graduates who pursued higher degrees in higher educational institutes. Beginning early in the 1990s Korean parents sent their children abroad as an escape from fierce competition for college entrance examinations or as an alternative means to prepare the children. South Korea's early study abroad has experienced steep increases since 2000, when the country began to recover from the IMF crisis. The number of Korean *chogi yuhak* students increased six times between 2000 and 2006, from 4,397 to 20,400 (the figure 45,431 includes students leaving for parents' emigration and temporary work relocation for Korean corporations abroad). Other data show that the upsurge is particularly prominent among younger students. In 2006, 13,814 elementary school students left for *chogi yuhak* (3,464 elementary school students left in 2002), while 9,246 middle school students and 6,451 high school students left for the same reason (3,301 and 3,367 left in 2002). See "Ch'anggan 19 Chunyon: Chogi Yuhak Pit kwa Kunul—'Ch'odung ttae Katta Ocha' Yonryong ch'ung Singgap'ol dung Tongnama Yuhak" (Nineteenth Anniversary Special Report: Light and Shade of Studying

Abroad Early—'Try It in Elementary School' Age Heading to Southeast Asia Such as Singapore), *Kukmin Ilbo*, 10 December 2007, 5.

6   See Chai, "Competing for the Second Generation"; Chong, "What It Means to Be Christian"; Alumkal, "Being Korean, Being Christian."

7   See Solberg, *The University of Illinois, 1867–1894*, for a comprehensive history of the U of I.

8   See, for example, Hossler, Braxton, and Coopersmith, "Understanding Student College Choice"; Hossler and Gallager, "Studying Student College Choice"; Stewart and Post, "Minority Students' Perceptions of Variables Affecting Their Selection of a Large University." See also Bouse and Hossler, "Studying College Choice: A Progress Report"; Cabrera and La Nasa, "Understanding the College-Choice Process"; Kinzie, *Fifty Years of College Choice*; Litten, "Different Strokes in the Applicant Pool"; Manski and Wise, *College Choice in America*; Teranishi, Ceja, Antonio, Allen, and McDonough, "The College-Choice Process for Asian Pacific Americans."

9   UIC is distinctive both for the racial diversity of its urban environs and for its undergraduate student composition, which is considerably more diverse and urban than that of the U of I. The Asian American numbers at the time of this book's research were not strikingly different: next to the U of I's 14 percent (undergraduates only) in 1997, the figure for UIC was 13 percent, although by 2007 it had risen to 19.5 percent. But the starkest contrast comes with the numbers of other minorities at UIC: 7 percent African Americans and 5 percent Latinos in 1997, and 9.3 and 13.6 percent, respectively, by 2007. Needless to say, the face of UIC is very different from that of the U of I. A June 2004 white paper prepared for the presidential search of the University of Illinois system (which includes the U of I, UIC, and the University of Illinois at Springfield) reported, "UIC's student body is one of the most diverse in the country," and "Many students are the first in their families to attend college." The Korean American estimation of and experience at UIC is necessarily colored by the ways Chicagoland Korean America is skewed toward the suburbs for residence and the U of I for college.

CHAPTER 2: THE EVANGELICAL CHALLENGE

1   This chapter draws on conversations about Christianity throughout my fieldwork and on the participant observation of Kate Wiegele with

two small groups. It is Cindy's small group that is featured most here. "ACC" is a pseudonym.

2   Some scholars have begun to document the multicultural transformation of formerly largely Korean American churches. See Abelmann and Lan, "Christian Universalism and U.S. Multiculturalism"; Dhingra, " 'We're Not a Korean American Church Any More.' "

3   Balmer, *Encyclopedia of Evangelicalism*.

4   On this atmosphere, see Bryant, "A Portrait of Evangelical Christian Students in College," 3.

5   Kwang Chung Kim and Shin Kim, for example, report that "between 60 and 65 percent self-identify with Protestantism." "Ethnic Roles of Korean Immigrant Churches in the United States," 72.

6   The information comes from an undated study cited in "Guidelines for Developing Korean Ministries," issued by the Office of Korean Congregational Enhancement. The same study found that in Los Angeles, weekly attendance for Korean American church affiliates was even higher, 83.5 percent. The study also notes that of Korean immigrants, 77 percent are affiliated with Christian churches. Alan Wolfe cites a Presbyterian Church USA study with similar weekly attendance statistics: Korean, 78 percent; white, 28 percent; Latino, 49 percent; and African American, 34 percent. *The Transformation of American Religion*.

7   Some of the students I spoke with were involved in other secular Korean or Asian American student groups, but these were most often singled out for their unserious ("purely social") nature. Several students took the time to comment on the frivolity of such groups, for which the focal activities were the likes of beauty pageants. As such, for their somewhat marginal place in students' lives (large member lists that hardly corresponded to a core group), they were never singled out as problematic in the way of AAC. Recall that Joe in chapter 1 described the high school church group as in fact *the* Korean group. While there were more politically involved Asian American activists at the time of this research (Korean Americans among them), they were not among my research interlocutors. This, though, is another story to be told. In the conclusion I discuss important U of I developments in Asian American studies that were just taking off at the time of this research.

8   My analysis here echoes that of Rebecca Y. Kim, who in "Second-Generation Korean American Evangelicals" argues that it is second-

generation shared immigrant experiences of intercultural and intergenerational conflict that draw these young people to ethnically organized churches rather than any Korean "cultural" features. These findings contradict scholarship that documents cultural maintenance through the church. See, for example, Kelly Chong's interesting argument about the sacralization of ethnic culture via Christianity in "What It Means to Be Christian." See also Cha, "Ethnic Identity Formation and Participation in Immigrant Churches." For a fascinating analysis of the ways Korean American Buddhists distinguish their own liberal (i.e., self-reliant, open-minded) religious practice from that of their Protestant coethnics, see Suh, "Being Buddhist in a Christian World."

9   Many scholars have treated the tension between ethnic particularism and Christian universalism in the Korean American church. See, for example, Alumkal, "Being Korean, Being Christian"; Busto, "The Gospel According to the Model Minority?" There is a growing literature on race and ethnic Christianity; see, for example, Leong, "Racial Spirits"; Jeung, *Faithful Generations*; Yang, "ABC and XYZ." Scholars have documented how ethnic religious participation works against Asian American activism. See Busto, "The Gospel According to the Model Minority?"; S. Lee, *Unraveling the "Model Minority" Stereotype*.

10 Other studies have made similar observations. A UCLA study of 3,700 students by the Spirituality in Higher Education Project, sponsored by the Higher Education Research Institute at UCLA, found that fully two-thirds of college student respondents felt their professors didn't provide ample opportunities to discuss big questions such as the meaning of life and other spiritual or religious matters, or questions such as "What am I going to do with my life?" See Connor, "The Right Time and Place for Big Questions." This discussion is echoed in Sommerville, *The Decline of the Secular University*. He writes, "The secular university is increasingly marginal to American society and . . . this is a *result* of its secularism. In effect, I mean that questions that might be central to the university's mission are too religious for it to deal with" (4).

11 A number of scholars have documented how second-generation Korean American Christians attempt to distinguish themselves from their parents' religious practice. See Chai, "Beyond 'Strictness' to Distinctiveness." Min and Kim, "Intergenerational Transmission of Reli-

gion and Culture," offer the interesting analysis that the stark religious differentiation between the generations mediates against the transmission of ethnic culture and identity. See also H. H. Kim and Pyle, "An Exception to the Exception"; Chai, "Competing for the Second Generation." For a gendered look at intergenerational religious differentiation, see S. Park, "The Intersection of Religion, Race, Gender, and Ethnicity in the Identity Formation of Korean American Evangelical Women." Rudy Busto offers an analysis of the intersections of the model minority myth and religion in "The Gospel According to the Model Minority?"

12 There is a large body of literature on the function of Christianity, both its secular and spiritual contributions, for the immigrant generation. See, for example, K. C. Kim and Kim, "Ethnic Roles of Korean Immigrant Churches in the United States."

13 Like other evangelical college students on other campuses, "they seek a faith that is not simply obligatory or handed down, but that is the consequence of conscious choice," "deliberately constructed and owned." Bryant, "A Portrait of Evangelical Christian Students in College," 7. These students also reflect a general charismatic or Pentecostal concern with spiritual authenticity.

14 Many scholars have documented gendered aspects of the Korean American Christian experience. See, for example, Abelmann and Lan, "Christian Universalism and U.S. Multiculturalism"; J. H. Kim, "The Labor of Compassion"; Chong, "What It Means to Be Christian." Conservatism in gender and sexuality is not uncommon among campus evangelicals in general. See Bryant, "A Portrait of Evangelical Christian Students in College"; Perry and Armstrong, "Evangelicals on Campus."

15 See Abelmann and Lan, "Christian Universalism and U.S. Multiculturalism."

CHAPTER 3: SHATTERED LIBERAL DREAMS

1 I was able to interview Mary's parents as well as the parents of nearly a dozen of my interlocutors.

2 See Hye-young Jo's " 'Heritage' Language Learning and Ethnic Identity" for a fascinating study of Korean-language instruction at an American university with a particular focus on cultural and linguistic authenticity.

3   A number of scholars have offered analyses of the particular ways race, gender, and ethnicity intersect for Asian America; they point to how various (and often contradictory) ideas about femininity and masculinity are imposed on Asian American female and male bodies, posing real challenges to gendered identity for all Asian Americans, and young people in particular. See, for example, Espiritu, "Beyond Dualisms"; Pyke and Johnson, "Asian American Women and Racialized Femininities."

CHAPTER 4: AN (ANTI–)ASIAN AMERICAN PRE-MED

1   The Sacrament of Reconciliation qualifies a person to go to confession, so Owen was most likely referring to confession.

CHAPTER 5: FAMILY VERSUS ALMA MATER

1   See Abelmann, *The Melodrama of Mobility*, for a discussion of sibling divergence in education.

2   For the Latino experience in this vein, see Garrod, Kilkenny, and Gómez, *Mi Voz, Mi Vida*; Valencia, *Chicano School Failure and Success*; Valencia, " 'Mexican Americans Don't Value Education!' "

3   See Janelli and Yim, *Ancestor Worship and Korean Society*, for an excellent discussion of gender, hierarchy, and kinship in South Korean families.

4   See Zhou, "Coming of Age at the Turn of the Twenty-first Century," for information on comparative language isolation among American immigrant groups.

5   For a general overview of rising higher education costs nationwide, see Trombley, "The Rising Price of Higher Education." See also Ehrenberg, *Tuition Rising*; Institute for Higher Education Policy, *The Tuition Puzzle*; Rhodes, "The Cost of Higher Education" in *The Creation of the Future*.

CHAPTER 6: INTIMATE TRACES

1   For discussions of South Korean colonialism and modernity, see Cumings, *Korea's Place in the Sun*; Robinson, *Korea's Twentieth Century Odyssey*; Lie, *Han Unbound*.

2   There is a sizable body of literature on campus architecture, campus planning, and the campus environment. See, for example, Chapman, *American Places*; Dober, *Campus Architecture*; Gaines, *The Cam-*

pus as a Work of Art; Kenney, Dumont, and Kenney, Mission and Place; Turner, Campus. In his study of the University of Chicago, The Uses of Gothic, Block suggests that "collegiate gothic" buildings organized around Oxbridge-like quadrangles came to be associated with the first real American universities and thus entered the imagination as quintessentially campuslike.

3   In "Unlikely Revolutionaries," Charles Kim makes the important argument that Mr. Han's generation wrestled with the considerable gap between post-Liberation ideals and promises, which were prominent in at least the formal rhetoric and curriculum of schooling, and the sobering realities of social hierarchy, autocracy, and patriarchy (both in and beyond schools).

4   See Seth, Education Fever.

5   For a discussion of cosmopolitan striving in South Korea today, see S. J. Park and Abelmann, "Mother's Management of English Education in South Korea."

6   In "The 'Cooling-out' Function in Higher Education," Clark describes this accommodation to reality as "cooling out." Brint and Karabel, in The Diverted Dream, similarly refer to the "management of ambition."

CHAPTER 7: IT'S A GIRL THING

1   For an excellent volume that insists on gender as a critical parameter in the study of immigration, see Hondagneau-Sotelo, Gender and U.S. Immigration.

2   Yen Le Espiritu offers a fascinating analysis of the working of gender, ethnicity, and the idea of close-knit family for Filipino America in Home Bound. See in particular chapter 7, "We Don't Sleep Around Like White Girls Do."

3   See Abelmann, The Melodrama of Mobility; S. J. Park, "The Retreat from Formal Schooling."

CONCLUSION

1   Bowen and Bok, The Shape of the River, xliii.

2   See, for example, Beverly Daniel Tatum's 1997 national bestseller (with a 2003 revised edition), Why Are All the Black Kids Sitting Together in the Cafeteria?

3   See Kibria, "Race, Ethnic Options, and Ethnic Bonds"; N. Kim, "A View

from Below"; Lipsitz, "The Possessive Investment in Whiteness"; Ong, *Buddha Is Hiding*; Prashad, *Everybody Was Kung Fu Fighting.*

4   For discussions of pan-ethnic Asian American identities and politics, see Espiritu, *Asian American Panethnicity*; Kibria, "Race, Ethnic Options, and Ethnic Bonds"; Chung, *Legacies of Struggle.*

5   Among excellent discussions of the working of whiteness in this manner, see Lipsitz, "The Possessive Investment in Whiteness"; Prashad, *Everybody Was Kung Fu Fighting*; Pyke and Dang, " 'FOB' and 'Whitewashed.' "

6   For a very revealing discussion of the ethnic and racial politics at the U of I that preceded the formation of ethnic studies programs, see Williamson, *Black Power on Campus.*

7   Cunningham and Llewellyn, "University of Illinois at Urbana-Champaign."

8   For the institutional history of Asian American Studies, see S. Chan, *In Defense of Asian American Studies*; Hu-DeHart, "The History, Development, and Future of Ethnic Studies (Multicultural Education)."

9   I taught this course through the U of I's Ethnography of the University Initiative (www.eui.uiuc.edu), a project that I cofounded and codirect, in which students conduct and have the opportunity to web-archive research on the U of I. Many of the projects from that class are web-archived in the U of I digital repository, IDEALS, www.ideals.uiuc.edu. See in particular two collections, Diversity on Campus / Equity, and Access and Student Communities and Cultures.

10   Abelmann and Lan, "Christian Universalism and U.S. Multiculturalism."

11   Cantor, introduction, 11.

12   For an interesting argument about the increasing meaninglessness of the American university, see Sommerville, *The Decline of the Secular University.*

BIBLIOGRAPHY

Abelmann, Nancy. *The Melodrama of Mobility: Women, Class, and Talk in Contemporary South Korea.* Honolulu: University of Hawai'i Press, 2003.

Abelmann, Nancy, and Shanshan Lan. "Christian Universalism and U.S. Multiculturalism: An Asian American Campus Church." *Amerasia* 34, no. 1 (2008), 65–84.

Abelmann, Nancy, and John Lie. *Blue Dreams: Korean Americans and the Los Angeles Riots.* Cambridge, Mass.: Harvard University Press, 1995.

Ahn Toupin, Elizabeth S. W., and Linda Son. "Preliminary Findings on Asian Americans: 'The Model Minority' in a Small Private East Coast College." *Journal of Cross-Cultural Psychology* 22, no. 3 (1991), 403–17.

Alumkal, Antony W. "Being Korean, Being Christian: Particularism and Universalism in a Second-Generation Congregation." *Korean Americans and Their Religions,* ed. Ho-Youn Kwon, Kwang Chung Kim, and R. Stephen Warner, 181–91. University Park: Pennsylvania State University Press, 2001.

Appadurai, Arjun. "Diversity and Disciplinarity as Cultural Artifacts." *Disciplinarity and Dissent in Cultural Studies,* ed. Cary Nelson and Dilip Parameshwar Gaonkar, 23–36. New York: Routledge, 1996.

——. "Global Ethnoscapes: Notes and Queries for a Transnational Anthropology." *Modernity at Large: Cultural Dimensions of Globalization,* 48–56. Minneapolis: University of Minnesota Press, 1996.

Balmer, Randall. *Encyclopedia of Evangelicalism.* Waco, Tex.: Baylor University Press, 2004.

Bankston, Carl L., III, and Min Zhou. "Being Well vs. Doing Well: Self-Esteem and School Performance among Immigrant and Nonimmigrant Racial and Ethnic Groups." *International Migration Review* 36, no. 2 (2002), 389–415.

Baxter Magolda, Marcia B. "Constructing Adult Identities." *Journal of College Student Development* 40 (1999), 629–44.

——. *Making Their Own Way: Narratives for Transforming Higher Education to Promote Self-Development.* Sterling, Va.: Stylus, 2001.

Beyer, Catharine Hoffman, Gerald M. Gillmore, and Andrew T. Fisher. *Inside* the Undergraduate Experience: The University of Washington's Study of Undergraduate Learning. Bolton, Mass.: Anker, 2007.

Birnbaum, Robert, and Frank Shushok Jr. "The 'Crisis' Crisis in Higher Education: Is That a Wolf or a Pussycat at the Academy's Door?" In Defense of American Higher Education, ed. Philip G. Altbach, Patricia J. Gumport, and D. Bruce Johnstone, 59–84. Baltimore, Md.: Johns Hopkins University Press, 2001.

Block, Jean F. The Uses of Gothic: Planning and Building the Campus of the University of Chicago, 1892–1932. Chicago: University of Chicago Library, 1983.

Bok, Derek. Universities in the Marketplace: The Commercialization of Higher Education. Princeton, N.J.: Princeton University Press, 2003.

Bonilla Silva, Eduardo, and Tyrone A. Forman. " 'I Am Not a Racist But . . .': Mapping White College Students' Racial Ideology in the USA." Discourse and Society 11, no. 1 (2000), 50–85.

Bonus, Rick, and Linda Trinh Võ, eds. Contemporary Asian American Communities: Intersections and Divergences. Philadelphia: Temple University Press, 2002.

Bouse, Gary A., and Don Hossler. "Studying College Choice: A Progress Report." Journal of College Admission 130 (1991), 11–16.

Bowen, William G., and Derek Bok. The Shape of the River: Long-term Consequences of Considering Race in College and University Admissions. Princeton, N.J.: Princeton University Press, 1998.

Boyer, Ernest L. College: The Undergraduate Experience in America. New York: Harper and Row, 1987.

Brint, Steven, and Jerome Karabel. The Diverted Dream: Community Colleges and the Promise of Educational Opportunity in America, 1900–1985. New York: Oxford University Press, 1989.

Bronner, Simon J. Piled Higher and Deeper: The Folklore of Student Life. Little Rock, Ark.: August House Publishers, September 1995.

Bryant, Alyssa N. "A Portrait of Evangelical Christian Students in College." Essay Forum on the Religious Engagements of American Undergraduates, SSRC Program on Religion and the Public Sphere. 2007. http://religion.ssrc.org.

Busto, Rudy. "The Gospel According to the Model Minority? Hazarding an Interpretation of Asian American Evangelical College Students." Amerasia Journal 22, no. 1 (1996), 133–47.

Cabrera, Alberto F., and Steven M. La Nasa. "Understanding the College-Choice Process." Understanding the College Choice of Disadvantaged Students:

New Directions for Institutional Research, No. 107. San Francisco: Jossey-Bass, 2000, 5–22.

Cantor, Nancy. Introduction to *Defending Diversity: Affirmative Action at the University of Michigan,* ed. Patricia Gurin, Jeffrey S. Lehman, and Earl Lewis, 11. Ann Arbor: University of Michigan Press, 2004.

Carby, Hazel. "The Multicultural Wars." *Black Popular Culture,* ed. Gina Dent, 187–99. Seattle: Bay Press, 1992.

Cha, Peter T. "Ethnic Identity Formation and Participation in Immigrant Churches: Second-Generation Korean American Experiences." *Korean Americans and Their Religions,* ed. Ho-Youn Kwon, Kwang Chung Kim, and R. Stephen Warner, 141–56. University Park: Pennsylvania State University Press, 2001.

Chai, Karen J. "Beyond 'Strictness' to Distinctiveness: Generational Transition in Korean Protestant Churches." *Korean Americans and Their Religions: Pilgrims and Missionaries from a Different Shore,* ed. Ho-Youn Kwon, Kwang Chung Kim, and R. Stephen Warner, 157–80. University Park: Pennsylvania State University Press, 2001.

——. "Competing for the Second Generation: English-Language Ministry at a Korean Protestant Church." *Gatherings in Diaspora: Religious Communities and the New Immigration,* ed. R. Stephen Warner and Judith G. Wittner, 295–331. Philadelphia: Temple University Press, 1998.

Chakrabarty, Dipesh. "Reconstructing Liberalism? Notes toward a Conversation between Area Studies and Diasporic Studies." *Public Culture* 10, no. 3 (1998), 457–81.

Chan, Jachinson. *Chinese American Masculinities: From Fu Manchu to Bruce Lee.* New York: Routledge, 2001.

Chan, Sucheng. *In Defense of Asian American Studies: The Politics of Teaching and Program Building.* Urbana: University of Illinois Press, 2005.

Chan, Sucheng, and Ling-chi Wang. "Racism and the Model Minority: Asian Americans in Higher Education." *The Racial Crisis in American Higher Education,* ed. Philip G. Altbach and Kofi Lomotey, 43–68. Albany: State University of New York Press, 1991.

Chang, Mitchell J., and Peter N. Kiang. "New Challenges of Representing Asian American Students in U.S. Higher Education." *The Racial Crisis in American Higher Education: Continuing Challenges for the Twenty-first Century,* ed. William A. Smith, Philip G. Altbach, and Kofi Lomotey, 137–58. Albany: State University of New York Press, 2002.

Chapman, M. Perry. *American Places: In Search of the Twenty-first Century Campus.* Westport, Conn.: Praeger, 2006.

Chen, Chiung Hwang. "Feminization of Asian (American) Men in the U.S. Mass Media: An Analysis of 'The Ballad of Little Jo.'" *Journal of Communication Inquiry* 20, no. 2 (1996), 57–71.

Cheryan, Sapna, and Galen V. Bodenhausen. "When Positive Stereotypes Threaten Intellectual Performance: The Psychological Hazards of 'Model Minority' Status." *Psychological Science* 11 (2000), 399–402.

Chickering, Arthur W., and Linda Reisser. *Education and Identity,* 2nd ed. San Francisco: Jossey-Bass, 1993.

Chong, Kelly H. "What It Means to Be Christian: The Role of Religion in the Construction of Ethnic Identity and Boundary among Second-Generation Korean Americans." *Sociology of Religion* 59, no. 3 (1998), 259–87.

Chun, Hyock, Kwang Chung Kim, and Shin Kim, eds. *Koreans in the Windy City.* Chicago: East Rock Institute for the Centennial Publication Committee of Chicago, 2005.

Chung, Angie Y. *Legacies of Struggle: Conflict and Cooperation in Korean American Politics.* Stanford, Calif.: Stanford University Press, 2007.

Clark, Burton R. "The 'Cooling-out' Function in Higher Education." *American Journal of Sociology* 65 (1960), 569–76.

Connor, Robert W. "The Right Time and Place for Big Questions." *Chronicle Review* 52, no. 40 (2007), B8.

Cumings, Bruce. *Korea's Place in the Sun: A Modern History.* New York: Norton, 1997.

Cunningham, Clark, and Yuki Llewellyn. "University of Illinois at Urbana-Champaign." *Privileging Positions: The Sites of Asian American Studies,* ed. Gary Okihiro, 85–89. Pullman: Washington State University Press, 1995.

Dhingra, Pawan. "'We're Not a Korean American Church Any More': Dilemmas in Constructing a Multi-racial Church Identity." *Social Compass* 51, no. 3 (2004), 367–79.

Dober, Richard P. *Campus Architecture: Building in the Groves of Academe.* New York: McGraw-Hill, 1996.

D'Souza, Dinesh. *Illiberal Education: The Politics of Race and Sex on Campus.* New York: Free Press, 1991.

Duster, Troy. "The Diversity of California at Berkeley: An Emerging Reformulation of 'Competence' in an Increasingly Multicultural World." *Beyond a Dream Deferred: Multicultural Education and the Politics of Excellence,* 231–55. Minneapolis: University of Minnesota Press, 1993.

Ehrenberg, Ronald G. *Tuition Rising: Why College Costs So Much*. Cambridge, Mass.: Harvard University Press, 2000.

Eng, David. *Racial Castration: Managing Masculinity in Asian America*. Durham, N.C.: Duke University Press, 2001.

Erisman, Wendy, and Shannon Looney. *Opening the Door to the American Dream: Increasing Higher Education Access and Success for Immigrants*. Washington, D.C.: Institute for Higher Education Policy, 2007, www.ihep.org.

Espiritu, Yen Le. *Asian American Panethnicity: Bridging Institutions and Identities*. Philadelphia: Temple University Press, 1992.

——. "Beyond Dualisms: Constructing an Imagined Community." *Asian American Women and Men*, 108–19. London: Sage, 1997.

——. *Home Bound: Filipino American Lives across Cultures, Communities, and Countries*. Berkeley: University of California Press, 2003.

Evans, Nancy J., Deanna S. Forney, and Florence Guido-DiBrito. *Student Development in College: Theory, Research, and Practice*. San Francisco: Jossey-Bass, 1998.

Feng, Peter X. *Identities in Motion: Asian American Film and Video*. Durham, N.C.: Duke University Press, 2002.

Flower, John A. *Downstairs, Upstairs: The Changed Spirit and Face of College Life in America*. Akron, Ohio: University of Akron Press, 2003.

Foley, Neil. *The White Scourge: Mexicans, Blacks, and Poor Whites in Texas Cotton Culture*. Berkeley: University of California Press, 1997.

Gaines, Thomas A. *The Campus as a Work of Art*. New York: Praeger, 1991.

Garrod, Andrew, Robert Kilkenny, and Christina Gómez, eds. *Mi Voz, Mi Vida: Latino College Students Tell Their Life Stories*. Ithaca, N.Y.: Cornell University Press, 2007.

Graff, Gerald. *Beyond the Culture Wars: How Teaching the Conflicts Can Revitalize American Education*. New York: Norton, 1992.

Greenberger, Ellen, and Chuansheng Chen. "Perceived Family Relationships and Depressed Mood in Early and Late Adolescence: A Comparison of European and Asian Americans." *Developmental Psychology* 32 (1996), 707–16.

Gumport, Patricia J. "Built to Serve: The Enduring Legacy of Public Higher Education." *In Defense of American Higher Education*, ed. Philip G. Altbach, Patricia J. Gumport, and D. Bruce Johnstone, 85–109. Baltimore, Md.: Johns Hopkins University Press, 2001.

Gurin, Patricia, Eric L. Dey, Sylvia Hurtado, and Gerald Gurin. "Diversity and Higher Education: Theory and Impact on Educational Outcomes." *Harvard Educational Review* 72 (2002), 330–66.

Gurin, Patricia, Jeffrey S. Lehman, Earl Lewis, Eric L. Dey, Sylvia Hurtado, and Gerald Gurin. *Defending Diversity: Affirmative Action at the University of Michigan.* Ann Arbor: University of Michigan Press, 2004.

Hartigan, John, Jr. *Racial Situations: Class Predicaments of Whiteness in Detroit.* Princeton, N.J.: Princeton University Press, 1999.

Hondagneu-Sotelo, Pierrette. *Gender and U.S. Immigration: Contemporary Trends.* Berkeley: University of California Press, 1999.

hooks, bell. *We Real Cool: Black Men and Masculinity.* New York: Routledge, 2004.

Hossler, Don, Tim Braxton, and Georgia Coopersmith. "Understanding Student College Choice." *Higher Education: Handbook of Theory and Research,* ed. J. C. Smart, 231–88. New York: Agathon Press, 1989.

Hossler, Don, and Karen S. Gallager. "Studying Student College Choice: A Three-Phase Model and the Implications for Policymakers." *College and University* 62, no. 3 (1987), 207–21.

Hsing, Chün. *Asian America through the Lens: History, Representations, and Identity.* Walnut Creek, Calif.: AltaMira Press, 1998.

Hsu, Madeline. *Dreaming of Gold, Dreaming of Home: Transnationalism and Migration between the United States and South China, 1882–1943.* Stanford, Calif.: Stanford University Press, 2000.

Hu-DeHart, Evelyn. "The History, Development, and Future of Ethnic Studies (Multicultural Education)." *Phi Delta Kappan* 75 (1993), 50–54.

Hurh, Won Moo, and Kwang Chung Kim. *Korean Immigrants in America: A Structural Analysis of Ethnic Confinement and Adhesive Adaptation.* Rutherford, N.J.: Fairleigh Dickinson University, 1984.

Hurtado, Sylvia, Jeffrey F. Milem, Alma R. Clayton-Pedersen, and Walter Recharde Allen. "Enhancing Campus Climates for Racial/Ethnic Diversity: Educational Policy and Practice." *Review of Higher Education* 21 (1998), 297–302.

Institute for Higher Education Policy. *The Tuition Puzzle: Putting the Pieces Together.* Washington, D.C.: Institute for Higher Education Policy, 1999.

Janelli, Roger L., and Dawnhee Yim. *Ancestor Worship and Korean Society.* Stanford, Calif.: Stanford University Press, 1982.

Jeung, Russell. *Faithful Generations: Race and New Asian American Churches.* New Brunswick, N.J.: Rutgers University Press, 2005.

Jo, Hye-young. "'Heritage' Language Learning and Ethnic Identity: Korean Americans' Struggle with Language Authorities." *Language, Culture and Curriculum* 14, no. 1 (2001), 26–41.

Kang, Agnes M., and Adrienne Lo. "Two Ways of Articulating Heterogeneity in

Korean American Narratives of Ethnic Identity." *Journal of Asian American Studies* 7, no. 2 (2004), 93–116.

Kenney, Daniel R., Ricardo Dumont, and Ginger Kenney. *Mission and Place: Strengthening Learning and Community through Campus Design*. Westport, Conn.: Praeger, 2005.

Keohane, Nannerl O. "The Mission of the Research University." *Higher Ground: Ethics and Leadership in the Modern University*, 59–83. Durham, N.C.: Duke University Press, 2006.

Kibria, Nazli. "Race, Ethnic Options, and Ethnic Bonds: Identity Negotiations of Second-Generation Chinese and Korean Americans." *Sociological Perspectives* 43, no. 1 (2000), 77–95.

Kim, Bryan S. K., and Michael M. Omizo. "Asian and European American Cultural Values, Collective Self-Esteem, Acculturative Stress, Cognitive Flexibility, and General Self-Efficacy among Asian American College Students." *Journal of Counseling Psychology* 52 (2005), 412–19.

Kim, Charles. "Unlikely Revolutionaries: South Korea's First Generation and the Student Protests of 1960." Ph.D. diss., Columbia University, 2007.

Kim, Claire Jean. *Bitter Fruit: The Politics of Black-Korean Conflict in New York City*. New Haven, Conn.: Yale University Press, 2000.

Kim, Henry H., and Ralph E. Pyle. "An Exception to the Exception: Second-Generation American Church Participation." *Social Compass* 51, no. 3 (2004), 321–33.

Kim, Hyunhee. "Ethnic Intimacy: Race, Law and Citizenship in Korean America." Ph.D. diss., University of Illinois, 2008.

Kim, Jung Ha. "The Labor of Compassion: Voices of 'Churched' Korean American Women." *Amerasia Journal* 22, no. 1 (1996), 93–105.

Kim, Kwang Chung, and Shin Kim. "Ethnic Roles of Korean Immigrant Churches in the United States." *Korean Americans and Their Religions*, ed. Philip G. Altbach, Patricia J. Gumport, and D. Bruce Johnstone, 71–94. University Park: Pennsylvania State University Press, 2001.

Kim, Nadia. "A View from Below: An Analysis of Korean Americans' Racial Attitudes." *Amerasia Journal* 30, no. 1 (2004), 1–24.

Kim, Rebecca Y. "Second-Generation Korean American Evangelicals: Ethnic, Multiethnic, or White Campus Ministries?" *Sociology of Religion* 65, no. 1 (2004), 19–34.

Kinzie, Jillian L. *Fifty Years of College Choice: Social, Political and Institutional Influences on the Decision-Making Process*. Indianapolis, Ind.: Lumina Foundation for Education, 2004.

Kohlberg, Lawrence. "Stage and Sequence: The Cognitive Developmental Approach to Socialization." *Handbook of Socialization Theory and Research*, ed. David A. Goslin, 347–480. Chicago: Rand McNally, 1969.

Korean Educational Development Institute, ed. *Chogi Yuhak: Kukmin Uisikkwa Silt'ae* (Studying Abroad Early: People's Perception and Status Quo). Korean Educational Development Institute, 2005.

Lee, Helen. "A Peculiar Sensation: A Personal Genealogy of Korean American Women's Cinema." *Screening Asian Americans*, ed. Peter X. Feng, 133–55. New Brunswick, N.J.: Rutgers University Press, 2002.

Lee, Jennifer. *Civility in the City: Blacks, Jews, and Koreans in Urban America*. Cambridge, Mass.: Harvard University Press, 2002.

Lee, Sharon S. "Over-represented and De-minoritzed: The Racialization of Asian Americans in Higher Education." *InterActions: UCLA Journal of Education and Information Studies* 2, no. 2 (2006), 1–16.

Lee, Stacey. *Unraveling the "Model Minority" Stereotype: Listening to Asian American Youth*. New York: Columbia University Press, 1996.

Leong, Russell. "Racial Spirits: Between Bullets, Barbed Wire and Belief." *Amerasia Journal* 22, no. 1 (1996), vii–xi.

Levine, Lawrence W. *The Opening of the American Mind: Canons, Culture, and History*. Boston: Beacon Press, 1996.

Lewis, Amanda. *Race in the Schoolyard: Negotiating the Color Line in Classrooms and Communities*. New Brunswick, N.J.: Rutgers University Press, 2003.

Lie, John. *Han Unbound: The Political Economy of South Korea*. Stanford, Calif.: Stanford University Press, 1998.

Lipsitz, George. "The Possessive Investment in Whiteness." *The Possessive Investment in Whiteness: How White People Profit from Identity Politics*. Philadelphia: Temple University Press, 1998.

Litten, Larry H. "Different Strokes in the Applicant Pool: Some Refinements in a Model of Student College Choice." *Journal of Higher Education* 53 (1982), 383–402.

Louie, Vivian S. *Compelled to Excel: Immigration, Education, and Opportunity among Chinese Americans*. Stanford, Calif.: Stanford University Press, 2004.

Lowe, Lisa. *Immigrant Acts: On Asian American Cultural Politics*. Durham, N.C.: Duke University Press, 1996.

Manski, Charles F., and David A. Wise. *College Choice in America*. Cambridge, Mass.: Harvard University Press, 1983.

Martinez Alemán, Ana M., and Katya Salkever. "Mission, Multiculturalism, and the Liberal Arts College: A Qualitative Investigation." *Journal of Higher Education* 74, no. 5 (2003), 563–96.

Milem, Jeffrey F. "Increasing Diversity Benefits: How Campus Climate and Teaching Methods Affect Student Outcomes." *Diversity Challenged: Evidence on the Impact of Affirmative Action*, ed. Gary Orfield and Michal Kurlaender, 233–49. Cambridge, Mass.: Harvard Education Publishing Group, 2001.

Min, Pyong Gap, and Dae Young Kim. "Intergenerational Transmission of Religion and Culture: Korean Protestants in the U.S." *Sociology of Religion* 66, no. 3 (2005), 263–82.

Mok, Teresa A. "Getting the Message: Media Images and Stereotypes and Their Effect on Asian Americans." *Culture, Diversity, and Mental Health* 4, no. 3 (1998), 185–202.

Nathan, Rebekah. *My Freshman Year: What a Professor Learned by Becoming a Student.* New York: Penguin, 2005.

Nussbaum, Martha. *Cultivating Humanity: A Classical Defense of Reform in Liberal Education.* Cambridge, Mass.: Harvard University Press, 1997.

Office of Korean Congregational Enhancement. "Guidelines for Developing Korean Ministries." National Mission Division, Presbyterian Church, USA. www.pcusa.org/korean/strategy.htm.

Ong, Aihwa. *Buddha Is Hiding: Refugees, Citizenship, the New America.* Berkeley: University of California Press, 2003.

Ong, Paul, Edna Bonacich, and Lucie Cheng, eds. *The New Asian Immigration in Los Angeles and Global Restructuring.* Philadelphia: Temple University Press, 1994.

Ortner, Sherry. "Reading America: Preliminary Notes on Class and Culture." *Recapturing Anthropology: Working in the Present*, ed. Richard G. Fox, 163–90. Santa Fe, N.M.: School of American Research Press, 1991.

Park, Kyeyoung. *The Korean American Dream: Immigrants and Small Business in New York City.* Ithaca, N.Y.: Cornell University Press, 1997.

Park, So Jin. "The Retreat from Formal Schooling: 'Educational Manager Mothers' in the Private After-school Market of South Korea." Ph.D. diss., University of Illinois at Urbana-Champaign, 2006.

Park, So Jin, and Nancy Abelmann. "Mother's Management of English Education in South Korea: Class and Cosmopolitan Striving." *Anthropological Quarterly* 77, no. 4 (2004), 645–72.

Park, Soyoung. "The Intersection of Religion, Race, Gender, and Ethnicity in the Identity Formation of Korean American Evangelical Women." *Korean*

Americans and Their Religions, ed. Ho-Youn Kwon, Kwang Chung Kim, and R. Stephen Warner, 193–207. University Park: Pennsylvania State University Press, 2001.

Pascarella, Ernest T., and Patrick T. Terenzini. *How College Affects Students: A Third Decade of Research.* San Francisco: Jossey-Bass, 2005.

Peck, Richard. *Fair Weather.* New York: Dial Books, 2001.

Perry, Evelyn M., and Elizabeth A. Armstrong. "Evangelicals on Campus." *Essay Forum on the Religious Engagements of American Undergraduates,* ssrc Program on Religion and the Public Sphere. 2007. http://religion.ssrc.org.

Petersen, William. "Success Story, Japanese-American Style." *New York Times Magazine,* 9 January 1966.

Pollock, Mica. *Colormute: Race Talk Dilemmas in an American School.* Princeton, N.J.: Princeton University Press, 2004.

Portes, Alejandro, and Rubén G. Rumbaut. *Immigrant America: A Portrait.* Berkeley: University of California Press, 1996.

Prashad, Vijay. *Everybody Was Kung Fu Fighting: Afro-Asian Connections and the Myth of Cultural Purity.* Boston: Beacon Press, 2001.

Prendergast, Catherine, and Nancy Abelmann. "Alma Mater: College, Kinship, and the Pursuit of Diversity." *Social Text* 24, no. 1 (2006), 37–53.

Pyke, Karen. " 'The Normal American Family' as an Interpretive Structure of Family Life among Grown Children of Korean and Vietnamese Immigrants." *Journal of Marriage and the Family* 62 (2000), 240–55.

Pyke, Karen, and Tran Dang. " 'fob' and 'Whitewashed': Identity and Internalized Racism among Second Generation Asian Americans." *Qualitative Sociology* 26, no. 2 (2003), 147–72.

Pyke, Karen D., and Denise L. Johnson. "Asian American Women and Racialized Femininities: 'Doing' Gender across Cultural Worlds." *Gender and Society* 17, no. 1 (2003), 33–53.

Rhodes, Frank H. T. *The Creation of the Future: The Role of the American University.* Ithaca, N.Y.: Cornell University Press, 2001.

Robinson, Michael E. *Korea's Twentieth Century Odyssey: A Short History.* Honolulu: University of Hawai'i Press, 2007.

Roediger, David R. *The Wages of Whiteness.* New York: Verso, 1991.

Rosovsky, Henry. "The Purposes of Liberal Education." *The University: An Owner's Manual,* 99–112. New York: Norton, 1990.

Rudolph, Frederick. *The American College and University: A History.* Athens: University of Georgia Press, 1990. (Originally published in 1962.)

Self, Robert. "Writing Landscapes of Class, Power, and Racial Division: The

Problem of (Sub)Urban Space and Place in Postwar America." *Journal of Urban History* 27, no. 2 (2001), 237–50.

Seth, Michael J. *Education Fever: Society, Politics, and the Pursuit of Schooling in South Korea*. Honolulu: University of Hawai'i Press, 2002.

Slaughter, Sheila, and Larry Leslie. *Academic Capitalism: Politics, Policies, and the Entrepreneurial University*. Baltimore, Md.: Johns Hopkins University Press, 1997.

Slaughter, Sheila, and Gary Rhoades. *Academic Capitalism and the New Economy: Markets, State, and Higher Education*. Baltimore, Md.: Johns Hopkins University Press, 2004.

Solberg, Winton U. *The University of Illinois, 1867–1894: An Intellectual and Cultural History*. Urbana: University of Illinois Press, 1968.

Sommerville, C. John. *The Decline of the Secular University*. Oxford: Oxford University Press, 2006.

Stewart, Mac A., and Phyllis Post. "Minority Students' Perceptions of Variables Affecting Their Selection of a Large University." *Journal of Multicultural Counseling and Development* 18, no. 4 (1990), 154–62.

Suh, Sharon A. "Being Buddhist in a Christian World." *Being Buddhist in a Christian World: Gender and Community in a Korean American Temple*, 165–203. Seattle: University of Washington Press, 2004.

Suzuki, Bob H. "Asian Americans as the Model Minority: Outdoing Whites? Or Media Hype?" *Change*, November/December 1989, 13–19.

Tatum, Beverly Daniel. *"Why Are All the Black Kids Sitting Together in the Cafeteria?" and Other Conversations about Race*. New York: Basic Books, 1997.

Taylor, Charles R., and Barbara B. Stern. "Asian-Americans: Television Advertising and the 'Model Minority' Stereotype." *Journal of Advertising* 26, no. 2 (1997), 57–62.

Teranishi, Robert T., Miguel Ceja, Anthony Lising Antonio, Walter R. Allen, and Patricia McDonough. "The College-Choice Process for Asian Pacific Americans: Ethnicity and Socioeconomic Class in Context." *Review of Higher Education* 27 (2004), 527–51.

Thelin, John R. *A History of American Higher Education*. Baltimore, Md.: Johns Hopkins University Press, 2004.

Trombley, William. "The Rising Price of Higher Education." *College Affordability in Jeopardy: A Special Supplement to National Crosstalk*, winter 2003, www.highereducation.org.

Trueba, Henry T. "Race and Ethnicity: The Role of Universities in Healing Multicultural America." *Educational Theory* 43, no. 1 (1993), 41–53.

Turner, Paul Venable. *Campus: An American Planning Tradition*. Cambridge, Mass.: MIT Press, 1984.

Valencia, Richard R. *Chicano School Failure and Success: Past, Present, and Future*. London: Routledge/Falmer, 2002.

——. " 'Mexican Americans Don't Value Education!' On the Basis of the Myth, Mythmaking, and Debunking." *Journal of Latinos and Education* 1, no. 2 (2002), 81–103.

Visweswaran, Kamala. "Race and the Culture of Anthropology." *American Anthropologist* 100, no. 1 (1998), 70–83.

Williamson, Joy Ann. *Black Power on Campus: The University of Illinois, 1965–75*. Urbana: University of Illinois Press, 2003.

Wilson, John K. "The Canon and the Curriculum: Multicultural Revolution and Traditionalist Revolt." *American Higher Education in the Twenty-first Century: Social, Political, and Economic Challenges*, ed. Philip G. Altbach, Robert O. Berdahl, and Patricia J. Gumport, 427–47. Baltimore, Md.: Johns Hopkins University Press, 1999.

Wolfe, Alan. *The Transformation of American Religion: How We Actually Live Our Faith*. New York: Free Press, 2003.

Woo, Deborah. "Asian Americans in Higher Education: Issues of Diversity and Engagement." *Race, Gender and Class* 4, no. 3 (1997), 122–43.

Yang, Fenggang. "ABC and XYZ: Religious, Ethnic and Racial Identities of the New Second Generation Chinese in Christian Churches." *Amerasia Journal* 25, no. 1 (1999), 89–114.

Zhou, Min. "Coming of Age at the Turn of the Twenty-first Century: the Demographic Profile of Asian American Youth." *Asian American Youth: Culture, Identity, Ethnicity*, ed. Jennifer Lee and Min Zhou, 33–50. New York: Routledge, 2004.

Nancy Abelmann is an Associate Vice Chancellor for Research and
the Harry E. Preble Professor of Anthropology, Asian American Studies,
and East Asian Languages and Cultures at the University of Illinois,
Urbana-Champaign.

Library of Congress Cataloging-in-Publication Data
Abelmann, Nancy.
The intimate university : Korean American students and the problems
of segregation / Nancy Abelmann.
p. cm.
Includes bibliographical references and index.
ISBN 978-0-8223-4597-9 (cloth : alk. paper)
ISBN 978-0-8223-4615-9 (pbk. : alk. paper)
1. Korean American college students. 2. Korean Americans—Education.
3. Model minority stereotype—Psychological aspects. 4. Racism—United States.
I. Title.
E184.K6A24 2009
378.1'9829957073—dc22   2009029301